HD
8005.2
.U53
N46
1987

Maier, Mark.

City unions

CITY UNIONS

MARK H. MAIER

CITY UNIONS

Managing Discontent in
New York City

RUTGERS UNIVERSITY PRESS

NEW BRUNSWICK AND LONDON

Library of Congress Cataloging-in-Publication Data

Maier, Mark.
    City unions.

    Bibliography: p.
    Includes index.
    1. Trade-unions—Municipal employees—
New York (N.Y.)   I. Title.
HD8005.2.U53N46   1987   331.88'113520747'1   86-26031
ISBN 0-8135-1228-X
ISBN 0-8135-1229-8 (pbk.)

British Cataloguing-in-Publication information available.

For Anne and my family

Contents

Acknowledgments   ix

List of Abbreviations   xi

1. Introduction   3

2. Prelude to Collective Bargaining:
    Unionizing Efforts Prior to 1954   11

3. Transit Labor Relations:
    Evolution of a City Strategy   30

4. The Wagner Years:
    Collective Bargaining for the Few   44

5. Social Service Workers:
    Challenge to the City   57

6. District Council 37 and OCB:
    Consolidation of Collective Bargaining   77

7. Police and Firefighters:
    First Organized, Last Recognized   92

8. United Federation of Teachers:
    The Making of a Bureaucracy   108

9. Managing Discontent:
    Changing City Strategy   137

10. Union Response:
    Shaped from Above and Below   151

11.   The Fiscal Crisis and Beyond   171

Notes   193

Index   215

Acknowledgments

This book reflects the collective wisdom of all those who assisted me in the project: friends, teachers, research librarians, union members, union leaders, and city officials, many of whom were generous with their time and knowledge. I want to especially acknowledge the assistance of two close friends, Tom Venanzi and Barbara Shollar, for providing many years of friendly support and for their extraordinary attentiveness to the ideas developed in this study. Tom and Barbara are proof that wisdom and insight are not limited to one's field of academic expertise.

Colleagues who provided guidance and support include Richard Betheil, Tom Michl, Andrea DiLorenzo, Richard McGahey, Roger Waldinger, Bill Tabb, Larry Sawers, Susan Shaw, Carrie Stern, Terri Suess, and especially Michael Swerdlow, who was faithful at difficult times during the manuscript's preparation. For several years Kristie Jayne also shared with me the satisfactions and problems of writing a book.

The project began as a Ph.D. dissertation at the New School for Social Research. I especially thank David M. Gordon, first for guiding me toward the study of political economy at the Graduate Faculty of the New School for Social Research, and then for strongly influencing my thinking. David's careful analysis of labor issues provided the basis for many of the ideas contained in this book; his unflagging efforts as a dissertation adviser helped bring that stage of the work to a successful end. Robert Heilbroner also assisted in the development of the thesis and shared some of the secrets of his powerful writing style in forceful yet gentle criticism during the manuscript's early stages. I thank Ross Thomson for his advice during the dissertation stage. And finally, Ken Fox maintained a continued interest in the project and gave me valuable advice about publishers.

I had the good fortune of getting to know the extremely helpful librarians at the College of New Rochelle—Fred Smith, Rosemary Lewis, Lillian Landman, Mimi Fitzgerald, and Gloria Greco. At Tamiment Library, home of Social Service Employee Union and United

Federation of Teacher archives, Debra Bernhardt and K. Sudheendran
were particularly helpful. The staffs of several unions assisted my
efforts: librarians at District Council 37 were both friendly and knowl-
edgable; Robert Wechsler at the Transport Workers Union answered
questions about his informative exhibit on the history of that union.
Similarly, I thank the staffs at the Brooklyn Public Library, the New
York City Municipal Reference Library, and the research facilities of
the Office of Collective Bargaining. At the New York Public Library,
David Beaseley provided information about the librarians' local itself.

Innumerable union members offered commentary, sometimes if
only to admit that they didn't know to which union they belonged (itself a revelation about a union's internal education); but more often
they provided rich reflection on the problems and prospects on unionization. Among those who were particularly helpful and willing to be
recognized are Susan Metz, Lew Friedman, Michael Padwee (all of
whom gave me access to their private files), Lous Heitner, and Mary
Bricker Jenkins. Other observers and participants in the union movement who shared their experiences and insights include: Bernie Bellush, Bert Cochran, Jim Garst, Margaret Levi, Sumner Rosen, Bill
Schleicher, David Selden, and the knowledgeable outside reviewers
engaged by Rutgers University Press. Some of these sources agreed
with my conclusions, others vehemently dissented; in any case, I assume full responsibility for the accuracy and consistency of the
analysis.

The College of New Rochelle Faculty Fund provided financial assistance, allowing me in pre–word processing days to employ the
phenomenal skills of Ann Garvey as typist and editor. Finally, I thank
Marlie Wasserman of Rutgers University Press for her sustained support during the manuscript's long gestation period.

List of Abbreviations

AFL	American Federation of Labor
AFSCME	American Federation of State, County, and Municipal Employees
AFT	American Federation of Teachers
ATU	Amalgamated Transit Union (formerly Amalgamated Association of Street, Electric Railway, and Motor Coach Employees of America)
BMT	Brooklyn-Manhattan Rapid Transit Company
BRT	Brooklyn Rapid Transit Company
CATU	Committee for Action through Unity
CIO	Congress of Industrial Organizations
COBA	Correction Officers Benevolent Association
DC 37	District Council 37 (of AFSMCE)
EFCB	Emergency Financial Control Board
FLM	Fur, Leather, and Machine Workers Union
HSTA	High School Teachers Association
IBT	International Brotherhood of Teamsters
IRT	Interborough Rapid Transit Company
ISS	Independent Subway System
MTA	Metropolitan Transportation Authority
MVO	Motor Vehicle Operators
MBA	Motormen's Benevolent Association
NEA	National Education Association
NLRA	National Labor Relations Act
NLRB	National Labor Relations Board
NYSUT	New York State United Teachers
OCB	Office of Collective Bargaining
PBA	Patrolmen's Benevolent Association
PERB	Public Employee Relations Board
SCMWA	State, County, and Municipal Workers of America
SSEU	Social Service Employees Union
SSTA	Secondary School Teachers Association
TA	Transit Authority

TBO	Teachers Bargaining Organization
TU	Teachers Union
TWU	Transport Workers Union
UFA	Uniformed Firefighters Association
UFOA	Uniformed Fire Officers Association
UFT	United Federation of Teachers
UPW	United Public Workers
USA	Uniformed Sanitationmen's Association

CITY UNIONS

1

Introduction

Public employees are very much in the news. During the last two decades they made headlines with first-ever strikes by schoolteachers, firefighters, and police. More recently, public workers are at the center of the storm surrounding municipal finances. They suffer layoffs and wage cuts, and in some accounts also bear the blame for public sector insolvency.

Despite the attention given to public workers, there is a curious lack of understanding in almost all descriptions of the changes affecting public employment. The misinformation is all the more surprising when we consider the sophistication with which labor issues are understood when they are far away. Few observers of Poland, for example, would be so foolish as to assume that a particular person represents the interests of working people just because that leader is currently recognized by government officials. Nor would we presume that the interests of Polish workers is inherently counter to that of the community at large, limited simply to higher pay and more benefits.

Yet, when it comes to understanding labor relations in our own cities, typically we make these mistakes. The language we use in describing labor relations belies just such a narrow focus. The "labor interest," for example, is often synonymous with the point of view of the labor leader currently involved in negotiations. The "resolution" of labor conflicts is identified as whatever percentage increase in wages can be agreed to during collective bargaining. Only rarely do we ask: how did that union leader come to be recognized as the offi-

cial representative of labor? Or: why are labor relations disputes reduced to relatively small differences in opinion about proposed increases in remuneration?

This book asks elementary questions. How did municipal unions
come into being? Why did labor laws in the public sector evolve as
they did? The method is historical, tracing the rise of unions and collective bargaining procedures in New York City from their origins in
the nineteenth century to their present form. We see that it was men
and women government employees, not only their more visible union
leaders, who struggled together, risked their jobs, and endured public
wrath in order to raise the issues of pay, staffing, and levels of service.
The result is an account that brings public workers into their own
history.

The historical perspective presented in this book also bears upon
matters of public policy. Currently attention has turned toward conservatives who blame liberal politicians of the 1960s for New York
City's fiscal crisis. With titles like *The Cost of Good Intentions, The
Streets Were Paved with Gold*, and *Lessons of the Lindsay-Wagner
Years*,[1] they argue that overgenerosity by zealous liberals created today's fiscal crisis. Defending past policies are liberals and radicals
who point out that public sector wages are not out of line with similar private sector jobs.[2] And newspaper headlines notwithstanding,
public sector strikes actually occur far less frequently than private
sector ones. Liberals and radicals therefore conclude that more general economic malaise, not specific liberal policies, is to blame for
New York City's fiscal crisis.

Both conservatives and liberals rely on New York City for evidence
about the source of urban problems. Yet nowhere is there an adequate
account of the history behind today's labor relations issues in New
York City—a gap that this book attempts to fill. The lack of attention
to labor history, which applies not just to New York City municipal
workers, but to public workers in general, is a consequence of the
theoretical perspective and used by most analysts. Liberals and conservatives alike set up models that deny the importance of the historical questions asked in this book.

Managing Discontent

Liberal policy prescriptions are based on what is known in labor
economics as the institutionalist school of thought, an outlook sum-

marized most comprehensively in Clark Kerr, John Dunlop, Charles Myers, and Frederick Harbison's *Industrialism and Industrial Man*.[3] Briefly, the book argues that the major problem facing both private enterprise and state-run economies is how to structure the relationship between managers and the managed. Successful resolution of this issue invariable involves a "web of rules" that accommodates tensions, while at the same time increases the economy's productivity.

Institutionalist analysis specifically of the public sector begins with Sterling Spero's 1948 *Government as Employer*.[4] During the twenty-five years that followed, institutionalists dominated the labor relations literature, repeatedly advocating changes in federal, state, and local laws, which until the 1960s gave little protection to public sector unions. Then, beginning with Wisconsin in 1962, forty states passed legislation—or a "web of rules"—to permit public sector collective bargaining. Institutionalists exhaustively catalogued these laws, correlating them with what they predicted would be a decline in strikes and an increase in productivity.

According to institutionalists, the proper course for labor relations is whatever lessens conflict and aids production. The role of the social scientist is to guide labor policy toward this happy middle ground, guarding against those from the Right or the Left who would upset the finely tuned manager-managed relationship. But by advocating what C. Wright Mills called the "management of discontent,"[5] institutionalists implicitly endorse the power of managers over the managed; they never question *why*—despite the best efforts of institutionalists—conflict continues to surface. As a result, institutionalist historical analysis overlooks whatever events created the necessity for the web of rules. In other words, institutionalist accounts pay little attention to the underlying social relations that lead to the discontent in need of being managed.

Suppressing Discontent

If the 1960s were the heyday of liberal institutionalists, then the 1970s and 1980s belong to conservatives, or neoclassicists, as they are known to labor economists. Neoclassical public sector labor analysis has its seminal work, *The Union and the Cities*, a Brookings Institution study by Harry H. Wellington and Ralph K. Winter.[6] In criticizing institutionalist policy, Wellington and Winter invoke the textbook neoclassical objection to unions: that they distort operation of the free market. Union wages are alleged to be higher than theoretically optimum market levels, while union-imposed rules about the pace or manner of work interfere with efficient production.

In the public sector, the impact of unions is intensified because consumers have little choice but to pay for government services. Consequently, governments are able to pass along high labor costs without losing many customers. Government employees help elect their employers, who are thus vulnerable to election-time pressure to raise wages in return for votes. All of these factors contribute to a labor-management environment with few checks on union demands. In the neoclassical-conservative view, the fiscal crisis experienced by many U.S. cities after 1975 is evidence that unions indeed used collective bargaining to win excessively high wages while stymieing management efforts to improve productivity.

Not surprisingly, much neoclassical economic analysis takes a detailed look at the remuneration of public workers, comparing wages and benefits between union and nonunion employers and between public and private workers. Neoclassical historical treatments, by contrast, are sketchy, focusing almost exclusively on political relationships between unions and elected officials. Almost never is there a description of the lengthy organizing drives that preceded collective bargaining, nor is there much discussion of current conflict between union leaders and their members. As in the case of institutionalist analysis, the neoclassical theoretical assumptions preclude a full consideration of union growth.

Understanding the 1930s

Problems with traditional approaches are best illustrated by their analyses of Depression-era U.S. labor relations, a critical period when industrial unionism was first established. In conventional accounts, scholars describe the 1935 National Labor Relations Act (NLRA) as labor's "Magna Carta": it fundamentally altered government policies in order to promote unionization and collective bargaining. The result, institutionalists claim, was a labor relations system fairer for workers and beneficial for the economy as a whole. Conservatives, while grudgingly accepting the fact that collective bargaining is here to stay, nonetheless complain that unions distort the allocation of resources, reduce productivity, and benefit some workers at the expense of others.

A number of social scientists, many of them working within a Marxist framework, now question both institutionalist and conservative readings of history.[7] What occurred during the 1930s was neither sudden beneficence on the part of President Roosevelt, nor miscalculation, as conservatives would have it; rather, it was part of a conscious shift in strategy that began even before the Roosevelt presidency. Collective bargaining itself dates back to the nineteenth century, although at that time the primary role of government was to undercut union organizing drives with conspiracy indictments or, when bargaining took place, to permit management domination of unions. In the years preceding the Roosevelt presidency, a series of court decisions and the Norris-La Guardia Act limited the use of injunctions against strikes and struck down yellow dog contracts (promises by employees not to join a union as a condition of employment). The revised analysis attributes this shift in policy to fears about the explosive character of class conflict that emerged even before the Depression. Then, following an unprecedented wave of strikes in 1934, President Roosevelt and Congress accepted even stronger pro-union legislation in the NLRA. Later, sit-down and general strikes forced U.S. corporations to bargain with the newly formed CIO unions.

In summary, the new analysis concludes that the continual escalation of class conflict made it necessary for government and major industrialists to introduce collective bargaining as an alternative preferable to left-wing or rank-and-file insurgency. Social scientists continue to debate details and matters of emphasis, in particular the role of the Communist party and the origin of seemingly spontaneous worker protests. In any case, what emerges is a perspective sufficiently consistent to identify three primary concepts that contrast it with neoclassical and institutionalist interpretations.[8]

1. An analysis of labor relations needs to examine relations of production as well as relations of exchange. While most orthodox economists concentrate on understanding relations of exchange, such as bargaining strategies, labor contracts, and remuneration levels, the new tradition has set itself the dual task of understanding relations of production as well as relations of exchange. Dissatisfaction about the workplace may concern workers as much as wages or benefits; cooperation on the job is as important to management as labor costs, since workplace conflict can be as disruptive as a traditional strike. Inspired by the work of Harry Braverman, Marxists in particular have produced a growing literature on changes at the workplace, which is helpful for understanding labor-management conflict, productivity levels, and even the cyclical growth of the U.S. economy.[9]

2. Institutions have the potential for tracking labor conflict into forms acceptable to management. This approach puts a new perspective on the liberal-conservative policy dispute: collective bargaining is neither a resolution of labor-management conflicts nor a giveaway program by liberal politicians. Instead, the institution of collective bargaining is another stage in the ongoing conflict between workers and management, which may be a step forward for workers, but also may result in management limiting future gains by labor. In general, even with the most management-dominated unions, workers are able to negotiate better terms of employment than with no union protection whatsoever. Consequently, management is never eager to recognize labor unions and does so only when union representation appears preferable to continued labor protest under militant leadership. Collective bargaining can then be designed so that the laws, organizations, and even the choice of union leaders help minimize worker protest and maximize acceptance of management initiatives.

3. The analysis should distinguish between levels of abstraction; the categories "labor," "unions," and "labor leaders" cannot be used interchangeably. Labor is not the same category as the labor union, a distinction rarely made in neoclassical or institutionalist accounts. In examining the labor movement it is important to look not only at what is said and done by labor leaders, but also at the activities of individual workers as well as interactions between union leaders and the rank and file. Although viewing history from the "bottom up" is difficult, doing so uncovers considerable evidence about the importance of the rank and file in the growth of unions and in current problems of collective bargaining. One trend appears repeatedly: labor union leaders tend to be more conservative than their members, trying to put off strikes and enforce previously negotiated contracts. Significantly, the conservative nature of union leaders, as well as the centralized and antidemocratic organization of many unions, can be attributed to management-written rules for collective bargaining, deliberately aimed at these results.

New York City's Municipal Unions

The recent growth of U.S. public sector unions is analogous to the expansion of private sector unions during the 1930s and consequently provides an opportunity to apply the alternative approach to a more recent example.[10] In a sudden and unexpected wave of organizing, public sector union membership jumped from slightly over 1 million in 1960 to over 3 million in 1976, accounting for over 80 percent of total union growth both public and private during that time period.[11] This study looks at New York City, where the rapid expansion of municipal unions was representative of the national trend. Public sector bargaining did not originate in New York City (union recognition occurred earlier in Philadelphia and Cincinnati), but New York City municipal labor relations laws and contracts served as models for other cities throughout the United States. Thus, in tracing the origins of New York City policies, we also account for a widely accepted collective bargaining structure.

Chapter 2 traces the roots of New York City labor protest back to the nineteenth century, when police, firefighters, and street sweepers organized underground unions at a time when union membership meant automatic loss of one's job. Beginning in 1896, New York City experimented with a new way to deal with unions: the city tried to preempt grass-roots organizing efforts by recognizing a union with an outlook acceptable to management. The strategy proved successful on two separate occasions for street sweepers and later for clerical and administrative workers.

By the 1950s, the city administration learned how to bring about favorable results without such blatant meddling in union affairs. Chapters 3 through 8 present case studies of unions for transit, general civil service, social workers, police, firefighters, and teachers. In each case, city officials tried to manipulate the rules under which unions were recognized so that only desirable unions would be chosen. Management could help favored unions by changing the size of bargaining units and controlling the timing of union representation elections. If all else failed, it was usually possible to oust an unfavorable union by accusing its leadership of Communist influence.

Contract negotiations also took place in a legal framework that carefully limited union activity. Those topics allowed at the bargaining table were so restrictive that unions had little say about the quality of service provided. As a result, New York City prevented the creation of potentially powerful coalitions between unions and users of city services. Also, city officials insisted that union leaders prevent strikes and help enforce management-directed work rule changes. Even when a worker protest had no sanction from the union, it was the responsibility of union leaders to have workers return to their jobs. Thus, official city policy strengthened divisions between union leadership and the rank and file, as well as between the union and the community at large.

The best evidence for the limitations on unions imposed by New

York City management is in the exceptions. On three occasions workers successfully cast unions outside the mold established by the city.
Social workers, firefighters, and police, remarkably different groups
of workers, in the recent past formed unions with a high degree of
rank-and-file participation in all important union decisions. Pressure
from city officials had little effect on leaders of these unions, who
were under constant threat of recall from a well-informed membership. Significantly, all three unions negotiated contracts with more
remuneration, more control over their workplaces, and more regard
for the quality of community service than other groups of New York
City employees.

The history of labor relations recounted in this book suggests trou-
bling trends that cut across liberal and conservative lines. While most
contemporary accounts ignore labor history, thus denying municipal
workers the lively background of their own unions, they also do something far worse: both liberals and conservatives miss the origins of
management's attempts to control the practice of unionism. Chapters
9 and 10 show how most analyses, including many sympathetic to the
unions, attribute the problems with unions today (lack of democracy
and lack of concern for the public) to unions themselves. In fact, as
chapter 11 describes for the 1975 fiscal crisis, management policies
consistently undercut rank-and-file participation in unions and sub-
verted cooperation between public workers and the communities
they served. It is testimony to the tenacity of union members and the
responsiveness of union leaders that there remains any sort of democratic tradition or any level of concern for the general welfare of the
city.

2

Prelude to Collective Bargaining

Unionizing Efforts Prior to 1954

Five case studies tracing the rise of collective bargaining for New York City transit workers, general civil service employees, social workers, teachers, and uniformed service workers (police and firefighters) form the core of this book. As a prelude to these detailed case studies, this chapter summarizes the pre-1950 history of New York City municipal labor relations. By looking at this seemingly less important period, it becomes evident that employee demands for union recognition, backed by militant protest, date to early in the century. Moreover, despite the absence of enabling legislation, New York City granted de facto collective bargaining rights to a few favored unions, setting important precedents for the conduct of labor relations when unionization was extended to all city employees.

The most common government attitude toward public sector unions during the pre–World War II period was summarized by a New York State Supreme Court justice: "to tolerate or recognize any combination of Civil Service employees of the government as a labor organization or union is not only incompatible with the spirit of democracy but inconsistent with every principle upon which our Government is founded."[1] Guided by such principles, prior to the 1950s, New York City had never signed a formal contract with any public union, and with the exception of the transit system, which had been unionized while still in private hands, there was no formal protection of the right of city employees to join unions.

Beginning at the turn of the century, however, a small but influential group of policy advisers, now known collectively as institutionalists, began to recommend a startlingly different approach. John R. Commons, a founder of this school of thought, observed while studying New York City street sweepers in 1911: "We cannot get away from organization. These employees will organize in one way or another. The real solution is not to try and destroy the organization of public servants, but to give them official recognition, to give them a part in the administration of the department and then to hold them to that responsibility."[2]

What excited Commons was an experiment conducted a decade earlier by Colonel G. E. Waring in New York City's Street Cleaning Department. According to Commons, Waring's policies confirmed the institutionalist principle that labor-management committees work to management's advantage: they increase productivity by resolving employee grievances in a manner that appears fair to workers, while at the same time supplanting worker-controlled labor unions with labor representatives accountable to the employer. Although short-lived in New York City, this early experiment with street cleaners presaged management strategy of later decades.[3]

Appointed commissioner of the Street Cleaning Department in 1894, Colonel Waring inherited a department beset by a stingy budget, complaints of the dirty streets, and antagonistic employer-employee relations. Several years earlier the department had attempted to enforce unpaid overtime, prompting angry employees to join the Knights of Labor and strike to win back a normal work week. By the time Waring took office, management had regained an upper hand over the Knights, who suffered nationwide decline in the antilabor climate that followed the 1886 Chicago Haymarket bombing.

But instead of using the opportunity to reject the street cleaners' demands for a union, Waring shocked contemporaries by introducing a new union for his employees. From each of the department's forty-one sections, employees were asked to elect one representative to the "Committee of 41," a group empowered to evaluate grievances brought by any individual street cleaner. The committee met in private, where it considered whether each grievance deserved the attention of a higher departmental tribunal consisting of five employee and five management representatives. The numbers-minded colonel (who had made his reputation by compiling the first U.S. Census on social conditions) published glowing reports about his experiment. He pointed out that only 25 percent of all grievances were considered reasonable, evidence that street cleaners were as harsh as management in weeding out unsubstantiated complaints. Moreover, almost every case referred to the joint labor-management tribunal resulted in a settlement acceptable to both sides, proof to Colonel Waring that employees and employers could cooperate in resolving workplace conflicts.

The new city administration elected in 1898 disbanded the Committee of 41 and adopted a more typical authoritarian attitude toward the street cleaners. But true to Commons's prediction that "employees will organize," street sweepers tried to maintain the existence of a labor organization, Teamster Local 658. Management, no longer following Commons's advice to "give them official recognition," forced the union underground. Between 1906 and 1911, the union led three strikes to protest twelve-hour workdays with mandatory nighttime duty and fines for minor infractions such as trotting one's horse too quickly or mixing ashes in with other garbage. Initially the strikes were successful, winning back a ten-hour day. But in 1911 the city warned, "not one of the strikers gets back into city employment again."[4] Replacements, hired in advance, took over strikers' jobs and the union was permanently ousted from the department.[5]

This swing in strategy—from institutionalist-backed preemptive recognition of "trustworthy" unions, to a more traditional vigorous opposition to all unions—typified labor relations of the early twentieth century. The National Civic Federation, a consortium of industrial and labor leaders, promoted such experiments as Waring's Committee of 41 on the grounds that management could avoid costly strikes by negotiating with reasonable labor leaders.[6] More often, as in the case of New York City street cleaners, management rejected the Civic Federation advice, deciding instead to eliminate unions with strikebreakers, and indeed by 1930 reduced U.S. unionization to under 10 percent.[7]

Union Busting on the Subways

Among those unions victim of the post–World War I anti-union campaign were those organized by New York City subway workers. Technically, the subway lines were privately owned between 1904 and 1940. But because of generous public subsidies to build the lines and subsequent government regulation of fares and operating conditions, they were in fact quasi-public corporations. As a result, city, state, and federal government officials had considerable influence over subway labor relations and actually managed one subway line when it declared bankruptcy. The Interborough Rapid Transit Company (IRT) opened service in 1904, followed by the Brooklyn Rapid Transit Company (BRT) in 1913. The BRT went bankrupt in 1918 and was reconstituted in 1923 as the Brooklyn-Manhattan Rapid Transit Company (BMT). The IRT and BMT were joined with city-owned lines (first opened in 1932) under public ownership in 1940.

During the first three decades of subway operation, all unionization efforts failed. Government support for the unions was lukewarm at best, allowing one union contract to be signed while the BRT was under court receivership. Otherwise the mood of the courts was to allow employers broad powers in their anti-union activity. Not until 1934 and the New Deal legislation did unions receive sufficient protection to mount a successful campaign on the subways. The Transport Workers of America (TWU) then gained union representation for subway workers on both privately owned lines, only to lose their exclusive collective bargaining rights in 1940. At that time the entire subway system came under public control, thus exempting employees from National Labor Relations Act protection, which applied only to private sector workers.

Despite the frequent setbacks in their organizing campaigns, subway workers supported unions continuously from the day in 1904 when the first line rumbled up Broadway from Wall Street. The tradition of joining unions came from workers' experiences in New York's existing rapid transit lines, the electric railways, which ran along major streets in all five boroughs and connected to streetcar service in the surrounding suburbs. By far the largest union of city transit workers was the Amalgamated Association of Street, Electric Railway, and Motor Coach Employees of America, an unwieldy name reflecting the fast-changing nature of urban rapid transit. Known to its members simply as the Amalgamated, the union was formed as an American Federation of Labor (AFL) affiliate in 1892. Today it is the largest organization of transit workers in the United States, accounting for 60 percent of total membership in transit unions and 80 percent of all contracts signed by transit workers.[8] In New York City, however, the Amalgamated never gained more than token short-term contracts for any group of subway workers. By 1934, after three decades of incessant organizing drives by the Amalgamated, there was no union representation whatsoever for subway workers in the city with the largest subway system in the world.

The Amalgamated's failure in New York City can be traced to fierce opposition to unions from subway companies, led by the IRT. In 1916 the Amalgamated, having won union contracts for surface transit workers, signed up large numbers of IRT employees and approached the company for contract talks. But IRT management responded with a whirlwind campaign, convincing 8,000 employees to sign "working agreements," which in return for wage increases allowed the company to argue that it was now impossible to negotiate with the union. As IRT president Theodore Shonts explained in a full-page *New York Times* advertisement, why should the company be "compelled to cancel and annul contracts" or "to impair any of the fundamental rights belonging to any man to work"?[9] Subway workers, unaware that the working agreements were intended to replace union contracts, voted to strike and were joined by surface trolley line workers who feared the IRT might rescind their already-signed contracts.

The IRT was fully prepared for a walkout, having hired 3,000 strikebreakers in advance, many from out of town and others recruited from Columbia University. Practically the entire New York City police force was on duty, with two men assigned to each trolly and subway car. The company suffered a temporary setback when the strikebreakers, who had not yet been paid, themselves went out on strike and tried to seize IRT headquarters. Later a march led by Mother Jones attempted to rally public support for the strike. But subway service soon returned to normal and Shonts waited out the strike on surface transportation. In the end, the IRT canceled all previous labor contracts—except, of course, the individual working agreements—and permitted strikers to return to work only if they resigned from the Amalgamated. As management explained, "The world owes no man a living unless he earns it, and the man who grumbles while gaining a livelihood is not legitimately entitled to such."[10]

The now-defeated Amalgamated was replaced by a company-sponsored organization, the "Brotherhood of the IRT," in which membership was mandatory. In 1926, a secret society within the Brotherhood called for a strike and gained enough support to shut down IRT subway service for two weeks. But in a repeat of the 1916 strike, strikebreakers were able to reestablish service, once again defeating the nascent independent union.[11]

Brooklyn Rapid Transit lines also faced two major union organizing drives, neither more successful than those by IRT employees. In 1918, BRT motormen used a National War Labor Board ruling to demand union recognition. The company refused and hired strikebreakers to keep the lines running, including one motorman, Anthony Lewis, a signal towerman who received two days of training. After fourteen hours on the job in one day, Lewis ran his train at 50 miles per hour off a particularly tricky curve near Brooklyn's Prospect Park, killing 102 people, by far the worst disaster in New York City transit history. Subsequent lawsuits contributed to an already unsteady BRT financial situation, leading finally to bankruptcy and handling of company affairs by former secretary of war Lindley M. Garrison.

Negotiating with court-appointed management, the Amalgamated was now able to sign a contract, but one year later, when they went out on strike, the union was barred by the court from further negotiations. A $1.25 million spy campaign kept the company informed of union activity, an "operating" expense conveniently deducted from payments made by the company to the city for bonds used to build the subways. With little incentive to settle the strike, management took the same stance as the IRT, requiring all subsequently hired employees to sign a yellow dog contract, promising that they were not a member of the Amalgamated and would not join the union. A company union was set up, with membership not mandatory but advisable, because company union members were more likely to receive favorable reports in medical examinations administered by company physicians.[12]

Rise of the TWU

These kind of anti-union tactics are now illegal in the private sector. In 1928, the U.S. Supreme Court voided the IRT anti-union individual labor contracts, and in 1932 the Norris-La Guardia Act banned yellow dog contracts of the sort enforced by the BRT. Both these measures anticipated support by the national government for union recognition, culminating in the 1935 National Labor Relations Act. This pro-union shift gave a dramatic boost to union organizing efforts in the New York City transit system. In contrast to the failures of the Amalgamated, a new union, the Transport Workers Union of America (TWU), was able in only three years to sign up a majority of workers in the privately owned subway lines. Subsequent contracts with the IRT and BMT included the principle of the closed shop, which meant all subway workers in each company needed to join the TWU and that the TWU was the only union permitted to negotiate with the subway operator.[13]

Only the TWU made effective use of the newly established government protection for union organizing. Even though the Amalgamated and a number of other unions stepped up their organizing campaigns, none could sign up workers as quickly as the TWU. Within the first few months of its existence, the TWU claimed 600 members; after four years, membership topped 40,000. Three characteristics of the TWU contributed most significantly to its success. First, several key TWU organizers were members of the Communist party, an affiliation that provided them with funds, dedication to the cause of unions, and taught them the skills necessary for successful organizing.[14] Communist party backing also meant that the union was red-baited, as for example by the Amalgamated, which reported, "The TWU is headed by four leading members of the Communist Party who are working under the orders of the Reds to Sovietize the American transit industry."[15]

Second, in part because of the Communist party connections of union organizers, the TWU was committed to building an industrial union that did not discriminate against workers because of their skill level. The union declared itself open to all workers, including blacks, for whom the union said it would fight the discriminatory company policies that kept blacks limited to the job of porter. During a brief affiliation with an AFL union, the International Association of Machinists, the TWU openly rejected its parent union's whites-only charter.

Third, the TWU appealed to the Irish heritage of subway workers, many of them political exiles from Irish rebellions earlier in the century. Michael Quill, union president from 1936 until 1966, was typical. After emigrating from County Kerry and unable to find better work elsewhere, Quill unwillingly accepted a noisy, dark subway job, for which he and other Irishmen qualified over non-English-speaking immigrants. TWU organizers formed secret societies, communicating in Gaelic code, consciously recreating the underground groups formed during the Irish war for independence.[16]

During the Depression, pay cuts had been unilaterally imposed on all subway workers. Pay for the unskilled was about 50 cents per hour for a seven-day week, consisting of eight hours of work per day, broken by hours of unpaid "swing time" (between the morning and evening rush hours).[17] Subway workers could legitimately complain that they never saw their children during daylight hours. Given these circumstances, interest by workers in the TWU was not surprising. IRT management officials noted the groundswell of protest and, although they rejected the TWU's call for recognition, made some efforts to remedy the most irksome conditions. The plan backfired; immediately the TWU printed up pamphlets claiming credit for the company's new stance.[18]

By July 1935, the union was ready for its first direct confrontation. The issue chosen, the replacement of 10-inch squeegies by marginally more unwieldy 14-inch ones, was in itself trivial, but symbolized to transit workers the arbitrary imposition of managerial authority and so prompted the first strike by subway employees since 1926 and successfully changed the company's squeegie size. The TWU's reputation flourished and membership grew, enabling the union to escalate protest to more significant issues. In January 1937 the TWU sponsored a sit-down at a BMT powerhouse to protest the suspension of union members. Other TWU members passed meals into the protesters by means of a rope and pulley, a sign of newfound solidarity among subway workers. When the BMT reinstated the suspended workers, the TWU's image was fixed as a militant union.[19]

Soon after the powerhouse sit-in, the TWU gained a National Labor Relations Board-sponsored representation election, which the union swept with 10,638 out of 11,585 votes on the IRT lines and 6,269 of 8,401 on the BMT. Both the preference for the TWU (over 80 percent) and the voting turnout (over 90 percent) indicated overwhelming support for the TWU, numbers never again even closely approximated in subsequent elections.[20]

The TWU organizing drive was not an entirely unblemished success. One branch of the subway system, the Independent Subway System (ISS), the city-operated line, remained without a TWU contract throughout the 1930s. The union signed up large numbers of ISS workers, but did so without protection from the NLRA, which did not cover public sector workers. In a series of rulings in 1937 and 1938, the New York State Labor Relations Board also exempted public workers from state law jurisdiction, thus leaving the union without legal recourse to force the ISS to enter into negotiations with the union.[21]

The union's victory on the IRT and BMT lines was further overshadowed by the bankruptcy of both private lines. As had been the case in 1919, the union negotiated with court-appointed receivers rather than company management. This time, however, in place of reconstituted private subway operation, the city prepared to buy the IRT and BMT lines for $326 million. City takeover of the entire subway system appeared so imminent in 1939 that the TWU agreed to continue the 1938 contract on the assumption that they would be able to obtain better contracts from city negotiators. The TWU based their optimism on efforts in the New York State Legislature to have the Board of Transportation, the ISS operator, assume contracts the union already had with the IRT and BMT. The TWU hoped that contract provisions, including the closed shop, would then be extended to ISS workers.

In practice, however, the city buy-out of the IRT and BMT, or "unification" of the subways, was a disaster for the union. The state legislature passed a bill protecting union members from discriminatory treatment and guaranteeing seniority for those with one-year tenure. But then Mayor La Guardia, the union's expected ally, announced he would not accept a closed-shop contract for transit workers. In 1941, the state legislature passed the Wicks Anti-Sabotage Bill, mandating criminal penalties for any work stoppage, whether organized by the union or individually by malcontent workers. In this anti-union climate, the union was forced to compromise, abandoning its campaign for a closed shop as well as the right to strike. In return for such concessions, the Board of Transportation agreed to consult with the union about pay schedules.[22]

The wartime settlements demonstrated the decline in the TWU's bargaining strength. The Board of Transportation told the TWU, "Separate agreements covering employment of Civil Service employees cannot be made with any one group of employees."[23] The TWU was "invited" to participate in conferences, but without the financial security afforded by the closed shop and dues checkoff (the ability to have union dues collected directly out of an employee's paycheck, rather than through individual solicitation). Union membership fell dramatically. Practically the only note of optimism for the TWU was the fact that competing unions weathered unification in an even worse manner. The Civil Service Forum, once popular among ISS subway employees, collapsed when the organization was shut out of War Labor Board hearings on the grounds that it was not a labor union.[24]

TWU leaders had hoped that public control would institutionalize union rights won from the private companies; instead, at the end of World War II the union enjoyed only an informal tradition of consultation. Chapter 4 describes how transit worker militancy after the war caused another shift in city strategy, this time granting union recognition to a less militant segment of the TWU.

Benevolent Associations

Like transit worker organizations, police and firefighter labor organizations have a long tradition in New York City. The Patrolmen's Benevolent Association (PBA) has been the dominant police organization ever since it was founded in 1894, while the Uniformed Firemen's Association (UFA)—at that time there were no women in either force—officially founded in 1917, was a direct outgrowth of the Firemen's Mutual Benevolent Association (FMBA), first organized in 1893.

Such continuity enabled these groups to lay the groundwork for what would become the most democratically run and effective unions in the city.[25]

Initially the PBA and FMBA called themselves "protective societies" rather than trade unions because they provided decent burial for police and firefighters stricken during the influenza epidemics of the 1890s. However, within a matter of months of their formation both groups extended their activity to other issues, although keeping the label "benevolent association" in order to avoid city strictures against unions. Whether unions or not, both the PBA and FMBA lobbied hard for new work hours, the most onerous aspect of their jobs. Since the Civil War, firefighters had worked a twenty-four-hour day with a total of four and a half days of leave per month. Police worked a two-platoon system, requiring a twelve-hour day and frequent all-night duty. The FMBA wanted a two-platoon work schedule that would give firefighters a twelve-hour day, while police argued for a three-platoon system with eight-hour days. Neither group succeeded through appeals to the city. But in 1911 the PBA won a state legislature law mandating the three-platoon rotation for the city police force. Firefighters finally won their demand after World War I.

Mayor John P. Mitchell's reform administration, elected in 1914, attempted to impose employee representation for police and firefighters along the lines of the street sweepers' Committee of 41. Under the prodding of reform-minded Municipal Civil Service Commission president Henry Moskowitz, Mayor Mitchell approved the formation of a new group, the Employees Conference Committee, to represent city police and firefighters in grievance proceedings. According to Moskowitz, "The democratic way of doing things . . . is to consult and confer with your [city employees]."[26] City administrators knew it was an auspicious time for an attack on the PBA and FMBA because both groups were wracked by internal disputes: several PBA officers were accused of misallocating pension funds and the FMBA president had just lost his city job. But even at this low point in the reputation of the associations, the administration could not gain support for the Conference Committee. When police voted overwhelmingly not to join, the city dropped its plans for an election among firefighters.[27]

Union or Professional Association?

The crisis created by the pension fund scandal and the Employees Conference Committee election pushed the PBA to meet and adopt a new constitution in 1914. It concentrated power in the hands of association president Joseph Moran, who occupied the office for the following twenty-four years. Moran was reelected without opposition every year until 1935, in part because of an election system that favored incumbents. As in many U.S. unions, instead of one-member, one-vote plebiscites, PBA officers were elected by a delegate assembly. And even though delegates nominally were accountable to stationhouses and thus to individual members, President Moran was able to pressure delegates into supporting him. Any delegate who expressed a dissenting opinion was likely to find himself transferred to a new post, thus not only losing his base of support at the precinct, but also with an undesirable job in a distant borough. Moran could threaten delegates with transfers because he enjoyed good relations with the Police Department, connections also requiring Moran not to engage the PBA in any activity that might embarrass city officials.

After Moran's retirement in 1938, four presidents led the PBA in a four-year period, reflecting conflict within the organization about its function. Young police hirees felt the PBA had become the exclusive preserve of older, superior officers who were afraid to rock the boat by openly questioning department policies. When these younger police threatened to walk out of the organization, a compromise was reached whereby members were allowed to vote directly for union officers. When the police force returned to its full complement after World War II, the stage was set for a more democratically run PBA and a less friendly relationship between PBA leaders and department administrators.[28]

Although the relationship between the fire commissioners and the firefighters association was never as close as that between the PBA and the police commissioner, the UFA also went through a shift in tactics between 1920 and 1945. During World War I the UFA thought it gained endorsement of the two-platoon schedule from mayoral candidates of both the Democratic party and the Fusion party (an independent anti-Tammany Hall group). When it turned out that neither would follow up on his promise, the UFA turned to the labor movement, joining the 1918 Labor Day parade. The action led to the reassignment of the UFA president to a job on distant City Island. UFA lobbying at the state capital finally won firefighters the two-platoon system in 1920, but even then the Fire Department insisted on mandatory overtime, thus making it possible periodically to reinstate the twenty-four-hour duty chart. In a comical but not unrepresentative confrontation, fire chief Kenlon suspended the two-platoon system in 1926, requiring overtime so that firefighters could parade for a commercial film, *The Fire Brigade*. When it was discovered that firefighting officers earned proceeds from the film, the UFA threatened to go public with the information; the two-platoon system was quickly reinstated.[29]

As in the PBA, two UFA presidents dominated the union for long periods: Alfred Guiness was president from the founding of the UFA in 1917 until 1927; Vincent J. Kane remained in office from 1931 until 1945. But in contrast to the PBA, there is evidence of significant rank-and-file participation in UFA policy making and general support for leadership decisions. A 1932 roster indicated 99 percent membership by eligible firefighters.[30] Moreover, the president was elected directly by members in what were often hotly contested elections. During World War II, Kane had to defend himself against charges that he was too friendly with Fire Department management. Firefighters were particularly upset that Kane had supported antimoonlighting legislation, leading to a 1945 censure vote and Kane's withdrawal from that year's election. His departure opened up the UFA to new, younger leadership that renewed the organization's commitment to collective protest.[31]

Following World War II, the PBA and UFA stood at turning points. Strategies would shift from seeking favors from city officials to a period of increasingly conflictive relations with their respective commissioners, culminating (as will be described in Chapter 7), in full-scale strikes. Yet, at this early stage, differences between these two organizations and other municipal unions are already evident. Foremost, both the PBA and UFA have a long tradition of active rank-and-file participation, signified by membership rates nearing 100 percent and by their democratic decision-making procedures. Even the long terms in office of presidents Moran and Kane were exceptions proving the rule: unlike almost every other city union, dissidents were able to mount campaigns to unseat incumbents. Case studies of other city unions show how union presidents' access to union publications and control over favors dispensed by the city enabled these incumbents to stay in office as long as they wished. Such was not the case in the UFA or the PBA.

AFSCME and Its Offspring

The circumstances of the PBA and UFA were exceptional. Far more representative of New York City labor relations during this early period was the history of the American Federation of State, County, and Municipal Employees (AFSCME). Several important New York City public sector unions began as AFSCME affiliates, most notably the United Public Workers, Local 237 of the Teamsters, and the Uniformed Sanitationmen's Association, also a Teamster local. The largest New York City union today, District Council 37 (DC 37), remains an AFSCME affiliate, but even it is a stepchild: for many years DC 37 was part of a dissident caucus within AFSCME, opposing the policies of national leadership until 1964 when DC 37 executive director Jerry Wurf won election as AFSCME national president.

AFSCME's curious role as parent, but not leader, of New York City unions stems from its history as a Midwest-based organization of civil servants. The union was founded in 1932 in Wisconsin by the state's Civil Service director, Colonel A. E. Garvey, who believed that an organization of employees could prevent encroachment on the service system by politically motivated appointments. Protecting jobs proved popular during the Depression; within a year almost one-half of eligible state employees had joined the union. Its first president, senior personnel examiner Arnold Zander, dreamed of building the organization nationwide. Armed with an AFL stipend and charter, he created AFSCME chapters in several states, mostly by enrolling already existing employee groups.[32]

Zander's appropriation method of building a national union succeeded in patching together a union in New York City, but proved unstable when groups began to secede just as quickly as they had joined. Only one year after AFSCME began organizing in New York, a large group followed vice-president Abram Flaxner into a new CIO affiliate, the State, County, and Municipal Workers of America (SCMWA). With a base of about 5,000 members, including many Welfare Department workers, SCMWA launched an organizing drive on a scale never contemplated by Zander. Assisted by funds from a new CIO affiliate, the Transport Workers Union, SCMWA targeted the Sanitation Department, where since the demise of the old street sweeper unions there had continued a sub rosa interest in unionism, and where workers still chafed under a forty-eight-hour work week and arbitrary management rules. In three years the organization claimed support from over 25 percent of the department and demanded recognition as a bargaining agent.[33]

The Preemptive Strategy

The success of SCMWA threatened Mayor Fiorello La Guardia, not only because it would bring a militant union into the Sanitation Department, but also because it would extend the growing power base of the TWU, which had supported the SCMWA organizing drive. Consequently Mayor La Guardia and his sanitation commissioner, William Carey, devised a plan to preempt bargaining with the CIO union by giving recognition to a more moderate union affiliated with the AFL. There was no city or state law regulating the recognition of unions, so La Guardia and Carey were free to support one union without taking a representation vote, thus likely disregarding the wishes of city employees. The result of their tilt toward the AFL prevented the CIO from representing Sanitation Department employees and set a precedent of favoritism for future New York City labor relations.

Open city opposition to the CIO union began when SCMWA asked commissioner of investigation William Herlands to look into kickbacks allegedly taken by AFL union leaders. Instead of investigating the AFL leaders, who had regained their jobs with the support of Mayor La Guardia, Herlands turned the tribunal on the CIO, asking about their political affiliation. Such queries were a serious threat to union members' city jobs; only a few months earlier several teachers had been dismissed by the New York City Board of Educaton for alleged Communist party membership.[34]

With SCMWA under siege by Herlands, La Guardia and Commissioner Carey arranged a complicated deal in which an AFL-affiliated union would be recognized as the only union in the Sanitation Department. In order to give the new union some respectability, the old Joint Council of Drivers and Sweepers was resurrected, breaking its ties with the discredited Civil Service Forum and joined to a growing national union, AFSCME. The new union, technically five separate locals, was called the Joint Board of Sanitation Locals and became the only union recognized by the department.

CIO leaders protested vigorously, pointing out that earlier the same year the city had argued CIO unions could not bargain for transit workers or welfare workers even though they represented a clear majority of employees in those departments. The city claimed civil service rules precluded any sort of union recognition. Now, complained the CIO, the city had contradicted this stand by recognizing the new AFL sanitation union. CIO leaders called for an election supervised by the State Labor Board to allow sanitation workers themselves to choose between AFSCME and SCMWA. But city officials refused to respond to the demand; instead of meeting with SCMWA, the sanitation commissioner pointedly drove upstate to Pawling, New York, to supervise construction of a vacation lodge the department was building for its employees. The AFSCME victory was final; CIO-organized unions never gained a foothold in the department.[35]

For AFSCME the deal backfired in 1951, when the entire Joint Board left to join the Teamsters, taking with it the bulk of AFSCME's New York City membership. The split occurred because of differing organizing strategies. On one side, John DeLury, head of the Joint Board of Sanitation Department Locals, advocated immediate gain for those he represented by currying favor from former members in "important positions,"[36] whom he could contact from his office in the Municipal Building. Indeed, after having assisted Vincent Impellitteri in his upset mayoral victory in 1950, DeLury succeeded in doubling Joint Board membership.[37]

AFSCME supporters claim that DeLury won a few small favors for his members at the expense of the long-term economic interests of the majority. Chief advocate of a more direct trade union strategy was AFSCME organizer Jerry Wurf. Son of immigrant Jewish textile workers living in Brooklyn, a Socialist and an idealist, Wurf was quite the opposite of pragmatic DeLury. Greatly influenced by Norman Thomas's Young People's Socialist League, Wurf worked as an organizer for the Hotel and Restaurant Employees Union before being recruited to AFSCME in 1947. His original task was to lure subway workers away from the TWU, a job he likened to trying to "melt an iceberg with a match."[38]

After a frustrating two years, Wurf reported to AFSCME president Zander that the future of the district council lay outside the transit system. However, Wurf claimed expansion was blocked by Henry Feinstein, the council's first president and leader of a group of city engineers lured away from the Civil Service Forum a decade earlier during one of Zander's drives to build AFSCME from preexisting locals. Now, Wurf argued, Feinstein compromised himself with a sweet deal, involving a city chauffeur for Feinstein and no new members for AFSCME. Zander gave Wurf the go-ahead to bypass Feinstein and revive the New York City AFSCME locals with the ultimate goal of replacing political patronage with full collective bargaining rights.[39]

Wurf's success during his first years was not auspicious. In 1952, Feinstein joined DeLury in the Teamsters, bringing with him about half the remaining district council membership. Feinstein called his new Teamster organization Local 237, a deliberate snub and play on the number of Zander and Wurf's District Council 37. The departure of DeLury and Feinstein from AFSCME left New York City public sector unions split into three major groups: DeLury and Feinstein's Teamster locals; the remaining locals in DC 37; and the remnants of what had been a large CIO union in the Welfare Department, now reduced in numbers by an anti-Communist drive (see Chapter 4). During the 1930s, disgruntled public workers joined unions in large numbers;

by the 1950s, there remained only tiny unions with dwindling membership, fighting each other as often as they confronted City Hall. Few would have predicted that Jerry Wurf's DC 37, with barely a thousand members, would be built in only fifteen years into a 100,000-member union.[40]

Early Teacher Unions

As with most other New York City public workers, only a small minority of teachers belonged to a union in 1950. These unions had been stronger during the 1930s, but none ever succeeded in winning a collective bargaining agreement. Still, the early teacher union experiences influenced later, more successful campaigns. Affiliation with the national labor movement, virulent anticommunism, and political factionalism were all traits of pre–World War II teacher unionism, which persisted until the 1960s, when teachers finally won collective bargaining rights.

For many years teachers had lamented their low pay. Turn-of-the-century teachers had particular cause for complaint: nationally salaries averaged just above $500, lower than the average factory wage. New York City teachers fared somewhat better, beginning at $720 per year, but much less than the pay of police or firefighters. Moreover, working conditions in New York City were demoralizing: class size averaged almost forty; buildings were in disrepair; supplies were difficult to order; and school authorities displayed a patronizing attitude toward teachers, especially women. As late as 1904 teachers were inspected visually by the superintendent to see if they were pregnant and could be suspended for "gross misconduct" if they married.[41]

In 1911 the 14,000-member International Association of Women Teachers successfully lobbied the state legislature for equal pay for women teachers. This first organizing drive differed from later efforts in that it was politically conservative. After its 1911 victory the association collapsed, in part because of its single-issue focus, but also because the organization's leader, Grace Strachan, shunned alliances with either the labor movement or feminists.[42]

A contrasting and far more successful strategy was pursued at the same time by Chicago women teachers, who under the leadership of Margaret Haley, civic reformer and suffragist, had organized Chicago's women teachers into the Federation of Teachers. This AFL affiliate won large pay increases and defeated efforts by the school board to introduce scientific management into the schools.[43] Haley's success inspired Henry Linville, a New York City Socialist and ardent trade unionist, to call a meeting in 1913 to form a New York teachers union. Invited speakers John Dewey and Charlotte Perkins Gilman squared off against Strachan on Linville's proposal that teachers be given a voice in school policy. Strachan led a significant portion of the audience out of the meeting, leaving a group of mostly male, Jewish, Socialist party members to form a new group, the Teachers League, with Linville as president. Three years later the league obtained an AFL charter, changed its name to the Teachers Union, and became Local 5 of Haley's American Federation of Teachers (AFT).[44]

Thus began a tradition in New York City of a teachers union that was Socialist, union-affiliated, and predominantly male. The first two characteristics are readily understandable. Most New York City unions of the period were tied to a left-wing party. These political views oriented teachers toward affiliation with the labor movement, rather than with professional organizations such as the independent National Education Association. More problematic is the absence of women in leadership of the Teachers Union and, as will be discussed in Chapter 8, also in its successor organizations. The early campaigns by women's groups in both New York City and Chicago indicate that the potential once existed for women to spearhead the teachers union movement. Why it was lost, or as least not manifested in later organizing drives, needs to be investigated further.

Teachers Union, Teachers Guild

Linville's Local 5, representing only 3 percent of New York City teachers, nonetheless ended up with disproportionate control over the national AFT. In 1917 a court ruled that Chicago teachers could not belong to an organization with wider union affiliation, forcing Haley's chapter, which had signed up 50 percent of Chicago teachers, to withdraw from the AFT. Other city school boards copied Chicago's example, decimating AFT membership and leaving the New York chapter as the bulwark of a much weaker national group.[45]

Linville's pet project, the *American Teacher*, became the union's link with the outside world. In the newspaper he promoted opposition to the militarization of schools during World War I and supported the right of free speech for teachers. However brave such civil libertarian stands, they gained the union few new members. Bread-and-butter issues were the responsibility of Abraham Lefkowitz, who, like Linville, was a long-time Socialist and union activist, but who now concentrated his efforts on making friends in the state capital, where he was Local 5's lobbyist. When Depression-era austerity caused the city to cut pay and even enforce a "payless furlough," Linville and Lefkowitz came under attack from Communist-leaning members, who pointed out the ineffectiveness of lobbying efforts and called for more activist approaches. The ensuing debate embroiled the union in a three-decade-long factional dispute. Even by the standards of inter-necine wars on the Left during the 1930s, the splits within Local 5 were extreme. And in an ironic reversal of roles, Linville, who cele-brated the Russian Revolution on the *American Teacher's* front page, and Lefkowitz, who had been condemned by the Board of Education for sharing a platform with radical labor leader William Z. Foster, now accused others in the Teachers Union of excessive left-wing influence.[46]

In 1933 a fact-finding committee chaired by John Dewey called for suspension of Communist-leaning groups from the union. When this recommendation failed to win the necessary two-thirds membership vote, Linville appealed to the national union for assistance, asking for a new local charter that would allow easier expulsion of the grow-ing radical minority, now estimated at 40 percent of the union's mem-bership. Pressured by AFL president William Green, AFT officers voted to help Linville maintain control over Local 5. But the wider member-ship of the AFT balked at such an antidemocratic move. In a conten-tious national meeting, delegates overturned their leaders' decisions, arguing, "The whole truth of the matter is that Dr. Lefkowitz, failing to dominate Local Five, asked us to wreck it and give him a union which he could control."[47]

Realizing their days as officers in Local 5 were numbered, Linville and Lefkowitz led 800 followers out of the union to create a new group, the Teachers Guild, rival of the Teachers Union for the follow-ing twenty-five years. Initially, the Teachers Union had the advantage of labor affiliation, an embarrassment to the committed trade union-ist Linville. Under the new Teachers Union leadership, the local now sponsored mass rallies and all-night picket lines, in particular pro-moting the cause of so-called permanent substitutes, who were in-creasingly taking the place of regular teachers, but with lower pay and benefits. As a result, Teacher Union membership rose to over 7,000, far more than under Linville's leadership.[48]

In 1939 the Local 5 militants squared off once more against Lin-ville and AFL president Green, this time on the issue of the AFT affiliation with the CIO. A large number of non-Communists and non–New Yorkers in the AFT supported Local 5's effort to bring the AFT into the more militant, fast-growing industrial-based CIO. They might have succeeded but for the Soviet-Nazi Pact and the assassination of Leon Trotsky, both of which occurred just before key AFT votes and gave credence to charges of Communist perfidy. The 1941 convention formally ousted Local 5 from the AFT and later replaced it with Linville's Teachers Guild, chartered as Local 2. Later the old Local 5, now called simply the Teachers Union, joined the CIO as part of the United Public Workers.[49]

Following World War II, teacher strikes swept the country. But in New York City the major conflict was still between the two locals. The guild repeatedly raised the charge of Communist influence in the Teachers Union. The state legislature joined in, passing the Feinberg Loyalty Law to eliminate "subversive persons from the public school system."[50] Over 300 New York City teachers were fired or resigned as a result of the law. And in 1950 the Teachers Union was barred from meeting with school officials because of its alleged Communist affiliation. Except for the occasional testimony by the union's legislative representative, Rose Russell, who was forced to report as an individual, not a union member, the Teachers Union never again had a significant influence on city labor relations. With only the much smaller and more conservative Teachers Guild remaining, union organizing faltered throughout the 1950s.[51]

Teachers, like general civil service workers, entered the 1950s with little union protection. Police and firefighters were somewhat better positioned because membership continued at a high level. But none of these city employees, including the uniformed service workers, enjoyed collective bargaining rights. Instead, labor relations policies in New York City ranged from harassment of union supporters, as in the case of left-leaning Teachers Union members, to preemptive recognition of a weak union, as in the case of John DeLury's Teamster local. Only labor relations with transit workers came close to the private sector model of regular contract negotiations, a process that became institutionalized during the 1950s. The circumstances of this change will be described in Chapter 3.

3

Transit Labor Relations
Evolution of a City Strategy

New York City's twelve-day transit strike of April 1980 was not supposed to happen. At least that was the plan of the chief negotiators for the union and for management. In March, one month before the expiration of the contract for 30,000 bus and subway workers, John Lawe, president of the Transport Workers Union Local 100, met with Richard Ravitch, head of New York's Metropolitan Transportation Authority (MTA). Over dinner at the boardroom club they agreed on a contract that would be relatively cheap for the MTA, but could make John Lawe look like a militant union leader winning pay increases for his members.[1]

How could the contract contain these seemingly contradictory goals—an inexpensive settlement for management, yet with sizable pay increases for workers? Even after the secret meeting between Lawe and Ravitch, the union and the MTA appeared to have irreconcilable goals in public. The union called for pay increases topping 30 percent annually, while Mayor Koch argued that the MTA could not finance pay hikes of more than 4 percent per year. The answer, of course, was compromise. But instead of simply splitting the difference, the boardroom meeting specified a scenario for the upcoming negotiations. It was a carefully scripted charade that assured the appearance of victory to both sides.

"Get the Restlessness Out of Their Systems"

Serious meetings between the MTA and the union were postponed until March 31, the final day of the old transit contract. Then, according to the boardroom plan, Ravitch would increase the MTA proposal to a "final offer" of 6 percent. Lawe would bring this offer to his Executive Board, which could be expected to reject it. As the midnight expiration of the old contract approached, Lawe would suggest a 7.5 percent contract to the MTA, which would accept the offer with mock dismay, providing that the union agreed to compensate productivity changes such as shorter coffee breaks. Lawe could then bring an apparent victory to his Executive Board for approval and the strike would be called off.

But what worked well in rehearsal failed onstage. As scheduled, Ravitch made his final offer of 6 percent late in the evening of March 31. And Lawe's Executive Board rejected the settlement as expected. However, when the union president returned to the board soon afterward to announce the "breakthrough" to 7.5 percent, the union representatives were not impressed and voted down this contract proposal as well. Lawe now had no choice; despite careful planning, the strike was on. For the following twelve days, New York City buses and subways stood in their storage yards, while millions of daily passengers found other means of transportation.

Lawe told a reporter after the strike that "every ten to fifteen years the members get restless and have to have a strike to get the restlessness out of their system."[2] After twelve days the restlessness of union members indeed seemed to subside. Under New York State's Taylor Law, for every day on strike transit workers faced a penalty of two days' pay. On April 11, when losses totaled over twenty days' pay, Lawe brought a new management offer to his executive board, a 20 percent pay hike spread over two years. On this contract the board vote split evenly, twenty-two to twenty-two, which Lawe interpreted as approval for the contract. The strike was over. The settlement terms were next submitted to the entire TWU New York City membership in a mail ballot. Included with each ballot was a statement from the union leadership warning members that rejection of the contract would mean an MTA-imposed contract with lower wages and benefit levels. Transit workers voted overwhelmingly to accept the contract.[3]

Most descriptions of labor conflict emphasize the opposition between management and unions. With little common ground between them, management and labor compromise their differences, usually in negotiations and, occasionally, after a strike. But events leading up to the 1980 transit strike suggest a more complex relationship, in which union leaders appeared as eager as management to avoid a strike. Management, too, stepped out of its adversary role to make sure that leaders of the transit union gained the support of union members. This symbiotic relationship between management and the union did not arise suddenly at the March boardroom meeting. It is a delicate affair, best understood in its historical context, beginning with the first contracts signed by the TWU during the 1950s.

An Emerging Relationship

As described in Chapter 2, by 1945 public ownership all but elimi-nated union recognition for subway workers. However, it did nothing about the underlying issues of worker dissatisfaction. At the end of World War II, pent-up worker unrest erupted across the country. The subways were no exception, as angry rank-and-filers refused to carry out management directives and rumors of an impending strike began to circulate. Allegiance to the TWU was still strong, a union allied now more closely than ever with the left-wing political movement in the city.

Given these potentially explosive circumstances, labor relations specialists counseled the Board of Transportation to reinstate collec-tive bargaining. According to these experts, the experiences of U.S. Steel and General Motors in 1937 showed that early union recogni-tion was preferable to confrontations in which workers showed sym-pathy for communist-led unions and were prepared to take such ex-treme action as occupying the workplace. By negotiating with unions, both U.S. Steel and General Motors were able to undercut militant union demands while guaranteeing strike-free production for the du-ration of the signed union contract.[4]

Mayor William O'Dwyer agreed that collective bargaining was needed on the subway system, but he did not like the current politi-cal makeup of the TWU, the only seriously contending union. In 1948, he set out to change the situation by advocating the ouster of what he called "communist-directed" union leaders, most especially Austin Hogan, then president of Local 100, second in command to TWU inter-national president Michael Quill.[5] Hogan claimed that O'Dwyer and Quill had arranged a deal in which Quill would receive city help in gaining exclusive control over the union in return for the expulsion of leftists and militants from the union. Subsequent events followed

Hogan's predicted scenario. He and three fellow militants were expelled from the union, and Quill announced he would not lead a strike, whatever the results of the upcoming negotiations. Mayor O'Dwyer granted subway workers a relatively hefty 24-cents-per-hour pay raise, making it clear that Quill was responsible. Then, for the first time ever, the fare was increased from 5 to 10 cents. Despite a past practice of opposing fare hikes, the union did not raise its voice in protest.[6]

Of course, behind-the-scene deals are typical of many types of negotiations. Nonetheless, the 1948 transit settlement left city transit labor policies with two new traditions. First, the city showed that it was not averse to direct interference in internal union affairs. The ostensible purpose of the O'Dwyer-inspired purge was to weed out Communists, an explanation likely to generate public support in the cold war climate. But this rationale does not ring totally true. Quill, who liked to be called "Red Mike," gave the public impression of association with the party, although veteran party members claim that he never actually joined. The city's campaign was against union militants, not simply communists.[7]

A second feature of the new labor policy was the limiting of union concern over price and quality of subway service. The TWU did not openly endorse fare hikes or cutbacks in service (Quill once advocated television sets, hostesses, and slot machines for the subways).[8] Ever since O'Dwyer had insisted that the union not oppose the 10 cent fare, the union never seriously linked the interests of subway workers to those of subway riders. Just such cooperation had been advocated by those union leaders purged in 1948.

Although the mayor's office believed that properly orchestrated union recognition would help management's position in transit labor relations, the Board of Transportation, an autonomous body, still balked at dealing with a union. Between 1946 and 1954 three commissions were established to convince the board and its 1953 successor, the Transit Authority, that collective bargaining should be allowed. The Cole Commission of 1950 argued that the most serious threat to the subway system came not from citywide strikes; after all, the TWU had never called one. Instead, the subway lines were disrupted most often when individuals or small groups of workers protested management policies by slowing down their work or refusing to do certain tasks. Such workplace actions had effectively thwarted efforts by the board to speed up duties performed by transit workers, in particular motormen and train inspectors. The commission pointed out that a formal union contract would require the union to help enforce work changes and limit wildcat activity.[9]

The Cole report only half convinced the Board of Transportation.

They signed a "Memorandum of Understanding" with the TWU in 1950, but still refused to allow an election to determine official union recognition.[10] Between 1950 and 1954, work stoppages occurred on the bus and subway lines at the rate of four per year,[11] so when the Transit Authority took over operation of the lines in 1953, and Robert Wagner, Jr., was elected mayor in 1954, both agreed that exclusive representation rights for a single, trustworthy union was the best way to prevent strikes and enforce new work rules.

Michael Quill understood the situation well; he told the Transit Authority, "The elimination of splinter groups in the representation election and the new contract [both under consideration in 1954] promise greater stability in dealings between transit labor and management than has been known for years."[12] Such words were a remarkable revision of the principle of industrial unionism under which the TWU and other CIO unions were founded. During the 1930s, it had been argued that distinction between workers on the basis of craft diluted union bargaining power: in unity there was supposed to be strength. However, in 1954 Quill was arguing that a single union was preferable not because of its ability to curtail production, but rather because a union like TWU could be used by management to suppress protest originating among small groups of workers.

The Transit Authority liked the idea of stability as proposed by Quill and called for the first union election ever on publicly run transit in New York City. As expected, TWU won handily with 75 percent of the vote and was granted exclusive bargaining rights for all public bus and subway lines, except for two small units in Queens and Staten Island. Because of their geographic isolation, these workers were permitted separate representation; they chose the Amalgamated Transit Union as their union and negotiated contracts that technically were separate, but in actual practice followed those negotiated by the much larger TWU.[13]

First Contracts

Soon after the 1954 election the TWU signed its first written contract with the Transit Authority, a contract including the no-strike promise and productivity pledges suggested by the Cole Commission several years earlier. The Transit Authority expected the union to uphold both of these provisions by preventing wildcat strikes and helping to enforce changes in work rules. But instead of guaranteeing labor peace, the outcome was the most stormy period ever in transit labor relations. Between 1954 and 1958 there were more strikes and other forms of labor protest than ever before—or since—on the New York bus and subway lines.

Of all the productivity changes demanded by the Transit Authority, the most controversial involved new sick leave rules. Noting that 60 percent of all sick leave applications were for a single day of absence, the TA claimed many workers took sick leave simply to have a day off. Unless the sick leave rules were changed, the TA told the TWU that a new contract could not be negotiated in 1955. In March of that year the TA and TWU announced a settlement: workers would be paid for the first day of sick leave only after nine consecutive days of sick leave had already accumulated, a plan the TA said would save $3 million every year.[14]

Contract talks got under way during the summer, following a pattern repeated in years thereafter. The TA opened with the declaration that a 5.3-cents-per-hour wage increase was all it could afford, a raise flatly rejected by the union. To signify its scorn at the offer and at TA inflexibility, the TWU called a membership meeting for the apparent purpose of taking a strike vote. However, once members were gathered in Madison Square Garden, TWU leaders reported a breakthrough in negotiations: the TA agreed to a three-year contract with raises totaling 17 cents per hour. Quill hailed the offer as a tremendous victory over management and obtained membership ratification on the spot against only fragmentary opposition.

Observers of the negotiations, both newspaper reporters and anti-Quill forces within the union, told a different story. According to them, the TA never intended to sign a 5.3 cents contract and had told the union so long before September. In return, the union never planned to strike and called the showdown meeting only when union leadership was certain that a settlement was close at hand. In the end, the union got 17 cents, apparently a dramatic improvement over 5.3 cents, and transit management received a three-year contract, containing union guarantees to enforce the no-strike provision.

Quill had promised stability in the transit system for three years. But in 1955, when the TA tried to eliminate some bus runs and cut the lead time between subway runs, workers again took things into their own hands and initiated wildcat work stoppages. Suspending suspected leaders of these protests failed to get workers back on the job, so the TA sent a telegram to the TWU reminding the union of its obligation under the 1955 contract.[15] Quill denounced the protests, ordered everyone back to work, and told the press that the protests were an effort by "some splinter groups in the subway systems to upset the exclusive bargaining rights that had been won by the TWU."[16]

Not surprisingly, Quill's popularity began to slip among union members. Quill was greeted with uncustomary catcalls when he went to bus yards and maintenance shops. More damaging to the union, one-third of the dues-paying members dropped out of the union during the the the first eight months of 1955 alone. Competing organizations surfaced, most notably the Subway Guild (later renamed the American Transit Union) and the Motormen's Benevolent Association (MBA). Both groups complained of discrimination by the TA against their members, who, they claimed, received disciplinary suspensions far more often than did TWU members. However, the real crackdown against these organizations occurred when their members took part in a series of work stoppages in 1956 and 1957.[17]

Turbulent Years

Ironically, it was the precautions taken by the TA against the threat of a subway strike that provoked the 1956 strike. In violation of the Transit Authority's own rules, motormen on passenger-carrying subways were ordered to instruct dispatchers in subway-operating skills so that the dispatchers could replace motormen in case of a strike. Two motormen refused to carry out the order and were suspended. In response, almost all BMT motormen and half of those on the IND walked off their jobs. On the hottest day of the summer of 1956, in the middle of the workday, traffic snarled to a halt and the city faced its first widespread subway shutdown in over thirty years.

Even though motormen reported back to work later in the evening, the TA meted out harsh penalties. All identifiable MBA leaders were suspended, 500 motormen were put on probation, and a court injunction was obtained against future MBA work stoppages. After lengthy hearings, five MBA leaders were suspended permanently and twenty-one others lost over $1,000 in wages. In handing out these penalties, the TA was concerned not so much with the specific incident that began the protest, but in holding the MBA accountable for the strike. Because of the spontaneous manner in which the strike started, it was difficult to prove that the MBA leadership was responsible. Moreover, their power in the MBA was not the traditional sort the TA had come to expect from the TWU. The *New York Times* described MBA president

Theodore Loos as an "amateur in the spotlight," who had been elected president simply because he spoke up at meetings. Court hearings against him had to be held during the free hours of his split shift because the TA would not grant him leave time to attend the proceedings. Of course the MBA had no way to compensate its leaders for financial losses.

TA hearings were a serious threat to MBA leaders. Lost wages or loss of one's job were more intimidating to MBA leaders than they would have been to the financially secure and professionally staffed TWU. As a result, MBA leaders tried to gain control over union membership, authority the TA mistakenly assumed the MBA leaders had during the June strike. Thus, when rumors spread in November that another strike was coming, MBA leaders opposed the plan and refused to call a membership meeting for fear the motormen might vote for a walkout. As leadership retreated from their earlier militant positions, interest in the MBA began to wane, so that by late fall only 500 motormen attended meetings, in contrast to the several thousand who had come to meetings the previous summer. In December, a New York State judge reversed the ongoing suspensions against MBA leaders. But he did so only on the condition that MBA leaders enforce a court injunction against another strike.[18]

With the MBA in decline, leadership of the dissident movement shifted to the American Transit Union and its membership in the maintenance yards. For several years the TA had been cutting back on subway maintenance. As repair jobs were eliminated, workers were demoted to positions as clerks and conductors. Relations between management and maintenance workers consequently were extremely tense and it took only a relatively trivial incident to spark a major protest. On November 13, 1956, four workers were penalized for returning late from lunch at the 207th Street repair yard. In response, over 500 men stopped work and refused to leave the shop until they were granted a meeting with the supervisor to discuss not only the penalties against the four tardy workers, but also the forced transfers that threatened all workers. The "stand-up" strike, as it was called, lasted for several hours, until 150 police came in to clear the workplace. The Transit Authority obtained a court injunction against future work stoppages and suspended those identified as protest leaders. Subsequent hearings resulted in four-day suspensions for forty-nine workers and almost year-long expulsion for the four suspected leaders, all members of the American Transit Union.[19]

The TWU response to the wildcat strikes by motormen and maintenance workers was not to try to remedy worker complaints. After all, it was TWU-led negotiations that brought about the productivity programs of such concern to workers. Instead of fighting the cutbacks and speedup, the union suggested to the city a simple mechanism for ending wildcat protests. TWU leaders claimed that if the union had the right to a union shop, in which all workers would necessarily belong to the TWU, then militant splinter groups would not exist. As Quill explained, "This reckless act [the MBA strike] would not have happened had there been the responsible safeguards of a union shop."[20] TWU Local 100 president Matthew Guinan added, "It is not possible for a union to demonstrate stability under an open shop contract."[21] The city did not give the TWU a chance to "demonstrate stability," because the possibility of a union shop for other city employees was more threatening than continued transit wildcat strikes. If a union shop was granted to the transit union, how could the city ignore similar requests for teachers, clericals, and other workers, who were just beginning to organize unions at the time?

Although the TWU did not convince the Transit Authority to grant them a union shop, the TA did reaffirm its commitment to single-unit bargaining. In 1957 another election was held, not on a title-by-title basis, which would have resulted in defeat for the TWU in several job titles, but for all subway workers in one giant transit system local. As a result the TWU won the election with about 60 percent of the vote, a victory tempered by a turnout of 16,622, about half the number of participants in the 1954 election.[22] And this pallid endorsement of the TWU was overshadowed by the most disruptive protest yet on the subways on December 9, 1957, when the motormen again shut down a large part of the subway system.

As in the case of the June 1956 strike, the motormen walked off their jobs without sanction from MBA leadership. By the time the MBA met to decide whether or not to call a strike, half of all motormen had already left their trains and the three top MBA leaders were on their way to jail for not having prevented the strike. Within a week the TA had service back to 75 percent of normal by having supervisors and new hirees run the trains. But just when it appeared that the MBA might be down for good, an event occurred that turned public sympathy in favor of the MBA and ruptured the alliance between the Transit Authority, Mayor Wagner, and the TWU. An electronic eavesdropping device was found at the MBA's Union Square headquarters.

Although company spies had always been part of management's strategy for keeping unions in check, in those pre-Watergate days electronic surveillance was an almost unheard-of intrusion into private affairs. An MBA official had heard two detectives discussing a supposedly private conversation he had just completed. A search of MBA offices turned up a hidden microphone, one of the several the TA admitted it had planted in MBA headquarters, social halls, and hotel rooms. The TA claimed it was trying to stop sabotage of the subways lines, alleging that bombs, chains, and tinfoil had appeared with increasing frequency on subway tracks. The newspapers ridiculed the TA story, since other unions, in particular the TWU, were not placed under similar scrutiny. Reporters suggested that the real reason for TA spying was not to catch saboteurs, but to anticipate MBA job actions so as to have strikebreakers ready for duty.

Mayor Wagner expressed shock at the TA's admission and promised a full investigation. At the same time he was trying to help the TA renegotiate the 1955 contract with the TWU, due to expire December 31, 1957. For Michael Quill, these negotiations also became unexpectedly important because he needed a generous-looking contract in order to quell dissent within the union. Motormen in particular were upset with Quill's leadership, as were many of the almost 20,000 transit workers who did not bother to vote in the December representation election and the several thousand members who had stopped paying their dues in recent years.[23]

As was now standard practice, the TWU threatened a strike. However, the TA was so certain the TWU would not strike that the city made no preparations for a strike even though the contract was not signed until late New Year's Eve, the last day of the old contract. The New York State CIO president told Mayor Wagner during the negotiations, "The TWU has often threatened strikes, but never called one . . . [this] is proof of responsibility."[24] On a national TV show several years later, Quill himself underscored the TWU record: "We haven't struck in the last thirty years; we haven't struck in the last fifteen years; we haven't struck in the last ten years; we have never struck the New York City subways."[25]

Nonetheless, as TA negotiators were well aware, the TWU needed significant contract concessions if the union was to regain lost support from transit workers. Consequently, the TA agreed to restore a pay for the first day of sick leave for some workers and to set up a $2.5 million fund for "skilled workers," an impressive-sounding sum, but one that eventually raised wages only between 1.5 cents and 10 cents per hour. In return, the union agreed to a new policy for sick leave, one not announced to union members, that allowed TA representatives to make surprise home visits to workers who had called in sick. (The practice was curtailed by a 1958 Supreme Court ruling.)

Furthermore, there was a plan to end the MBA-TWU feud. Harry Van Arsdale, New York City Central Labor Council president and a close associate of Michael Quill, assured Mayor Wagner that the AFL-CIO could arrange for the MBA to be incorporated into the structure of the

TWU. Negotiating this part of the arrangement proved difficult and succeeded only after months of intense bargaining. Finally, the MBA agreed to drop the outstanding lawsuits they had against officials involved in the bugging incident. In return the prison sentences facing MBA leaders were changed to suspended sentences—on the condition that they not be involved in any more work stoppages. The MBA then joined the TWU as a separate division without using its original name.[26]

Quill Needs a Strike

The 1958 contract assured the TWU of dominance among New York City transit workers and provided the Transit Authority with a seven-year period free from strikes. However, the issues critical to transit workers—low pay, limits on sick leave, and cutbacks in certain positions—remained unresolved. And a new, volatile element was now mixed with these concerns: the changing racial composition of the transit work force. In part, this shift represented the city's changing population; but it also resulted from less discriminatory Transit Authority hiring patterns. Prior to 1930 blacks were hired only as porters, and as late as 1938 there were no black motormen on any subway line. By the mid-1960s about half of all nonsupervisory subway positions were held by nonwhites.[27]

In many regards the TWU had an honorable record on the issue of race. The original union bylaws, written in 1934, called for membership regardless of race (see Chapter 2). Support by the union for the civil rights movement won the union numerous testimonials from black leaders, including Dr. Martin Luther King, Jr.[28] Nonetheless, TWU leadership in 1960 continued to reflect the time when a majority of the work force was of Irish background. As late as the 1970s, half of TWU Local 100 leadership had names indicative of an Irish background, while only two of the eleven officers were blacks. Not surprisingly, internal union dissent centered on the issue of race.[29]

Initially, this opposition to Quill's leadership was not formally organized. Yet it was widely rumored that Quill's control was tenuous, and given a strong opposition leader, his hegemony was open to challenge. Under these conditions Quill needed a new strategy for maintaining control over the union. Ten times in twenty-five years he had asked members for strike authorization without actually calling a strike. Always at the last moment Quill would bring a "miracle" contract offer to a mass membership meeting, where, as dissidents pointed out, Quill could gain acceptance of the contract because only the union leadership knew the settlement's precise terms. New Yorkers had become accustomed to the last-minute dramatics, which somehow never resulted in an actual strike.

Then, on January 1, 1966, New Yorkers woke up to find that the buses and subways really were stopped by a strike. The 1966 strike is often blamed on the inept leadership of neophyte mayor John V. Lindsay, who took office the same day the strike began. However, A. H. Raskin, veteran *New York Times* labor reporter, later concluded, "Most observers were convinced that Quill needed so big a wage increase in 1966, that no mayor could have given it without a strike." [30] What Quill needed to prove was that the union was not in cahoots with the TA. That charge was especially credible to black and Hispanic transit workers, who resented representation by a predominantly white leadership. Union membership meetings had become tumultuous, forcing Quill to protect himself at the speakers' podium with a phalanx of hefty supporters, while members chanted, "Strike now, now." [31]

Tragically, the 1966 strike and subsequent jailing of Quill contributed to the fatal heart attack he suffered on January 28, 1966. Nonetheless, the strike fulfilled its purpose and helped enhance the image of Quill's handpicked successor, Matthew Guinan, as TWU president. Ten years after the 1966 strike the TWU membership handbook still featured pictures of the jailed union leaders accompanied by the caption "The TWU was willing and able to shut down the town if it was necessary to accomplish the goals of its membership." [32]

Although the strike bolstered the position of Guinan, it left the union divided along the lines of race. Within the structure of the union, black dissidents claimed it was impossible to mount a challenge to union incumbents because those out of office had little access to union communication channels. Only after a court order in 1978, for example, did dissidents gain access to crew rooms and union bulletin boards to distribute information. [33] Twice black-led organizations tried without success to have the TWU decertified as the transit bargaining agent. In 1972, following that year's contract negotiations, pickets surrounded TWU headquarters denouncing the agreement, and rumors spread about a sickout on the bus lines. The union countered with television ads and personal appearances by union leaders to gain acceptance of the contract. The result, however, was only 56 percent approval, an extremely narrow margin for a contract vote and clear indication that the union leadership was in trouble. [34] For a brief time the New York City fiscal crisis (described in detail in

Chapter 11) deflected attention from intra-union conflict. In 1976 the Emergency Financial Control Board overturned an already negotiated contract, demanding lower cost-of-living increases, forcing the union to accept new contract terms. Even so, TWU leaders refused to call for a membership vote on the grounds that the Control Board had not canceled the previous contract, but just deferred pay raises to a later date. With inflation running at 6 percent, such postponement really meant reduced wages.[35]

By 1978, TWU leaders found themselves in a situation similar to that faced by Quill in 1966: members were likely to vote down almost any contract offer. When negotiations produced only 6 percent wage increases over two years and a cost-of-living clause conditional on productivity improvements, the leadership openly feared membership rejection. Already one Amalgamated Transit Union local, the Queens bus workers, had rejected the contract. Consequently, TWU leaders attempted to gain approval of the contract by counting ballots in a new manner: the votes of city bus and subway workers were to be comingled with those of employees of private bus line companies, who were negotiating a contract at the same time and who were expected to approve the contract. This maneuver so enraged union dissidents that they obtained a court injunction restraining the vote, forcing an embarrassed union leadership to withdraw the vote and mail out a second ballot. The second time around, the contract vote was extremely close. It passed for city bus and subway workers as a whole by only 318 out of 23,000 total votes. Among subway workers alone, a group more predominantly black and Hispanic, the contract was defeated by 2,000 votes. The margin of victory, therefore, was an overwhelming "yes" vote from white bus workers, who remained loyal to TWU leadership.[36]

Even though the contract passed, the traditional union leadership was in jeopardy. When Matthew Guinan resigned May 1, 1979, for health reasons, the TWU international presidency went for the first time to a non–New Yorker, former union executive vice-president William Lindner. John Lawe, an Irish-American, took over as Local 100 president, fully expecting a serious challenge in the upcoming 1979 election. But the opposition split between three candidates (two black and one white), thus allowing Lawe to slip in with just 43 percent of the vote. Controlling only 22 of the union's 45 Executive Board seats Lawe had a tenuous hold on the local; the stage was set for the events leading up to the 1980 strike.

This chapter suggests an untraditional picture of labor relations. Usually unions and employers are thought to have opposing goals with little common ground between them. However, in the New York City transit system, the main conflict was not so much between management and the union as between union leaders and union members. What emerges from this history is a pattern in which transit management, with active encouragement from New York City elected officials, tried to control the practice of unionism to such an extent that today bus and subway workers are distrustful not only of management, but of their own union as well.

Is such alienation inevitable? The history of another union in New York City's public sector suggests otherwise. The Social Service Employees Union (SSEU) stands in sharp contrast to the Transport Workers Union. Between 1961 and 1968 SSEU enjoyed widespread membership participation and, despite management efforts to curtail its power, successfully negotiated contracts not previously allowed for city employees (see Chapter 5). But before looking at SSEU Chapter 4 will chart the rise of other New York City unions between 1954 and 1964.

4

The Wagner Years

Collective Bargaining for the Few

In 1954 New York City municipal unionism was at a twenty-year low: with the exception of the Transport Workers Union and the police and firefighter associations, no union represented more than a small percentage of city employees. Immediately after taking office in 1954, Mayor Robert Wagner, Jr., instituted a series of policies seemingly aimed at changing city labor relations. A July 1954 Interim Order, for example, invoked the language of Senator Robert Wagner, Sr.'s National Labor Relations Act, declaring that New York City employees "had full freedom of association . . . to negotiate the terms and conditions of employment." [1] Previously city workers had no legal right either to join unions or negotiate their salaries, so in theory Mayor Wagner extended the rights of his father's "Wagner Act," the NLRA, to public workers.

In actual practice, however, the high-sounding Interim Order had little effect on the real conduct of city labor relations. During Mayor Wagner's first term, collective bargaining took place only in the transit system, where the TWU, backed by a militant rank and file, had already established union recognition during pre-1940 private sector operation of the subways. But outside the transit system, no other city employees were permitted to engage in collective bargaining; in fact, some of the mayor's appointees refused even to grant "freedom of association" and did not tolerate unions in their departments. Observers of Wagner's early years as mayor concur that the Interim Order fulfilled a campaign promise, but did not signify a major change in the orientation of city labor policies.[2]

Opening Moves

Mayor Wagner took only one deliberate step toward implementing the 1954 Interim Order: he appointed Ida Klaus, a National Labor Relations Board lawyer, to study the state of labor relations in the public sector. Wagner must have anticipated that Klaus would be favorably disposed toward encouraging collective bargaining for public sector workers since in her previous work for the NLRB she had distinguished herself by organizing the NLRB lawyers themselves into a union. But Klaus was given no specific directions about the desired outcome of her research—nor what would be done with it upon completion. The following year Klaus handed a 200-page study to Wagner's aides, who were stunned at its length and detailed coverage. The study maintained that collective bargaining for public employees was possible and could be instituted with procedures similar to those already in place for private sector workers. It was two years before Wagner called Klaus to discuss any possible use for her study.[3]

It is tempting to note similarities between Wagner's 1954 Interim Order and legislation affecting private sector workers during the 1930s. But during the earlier period the labor movement was able to use federal legislation immediately as a rallying cry for unionization. "The president wants you to join the union,"[4] proclaimed United Mine Worker placards, exaggerating grandly on Roosevelt's penchant for unionism, especially the left-leaning militant sort advocated by many CIO unions. Whatever the actual intent of New Deal labor policy (there is evidence that Roosevelt and some corporate supporters saw union recognition as a means to preempt more radical change), government support for union organizing gave the CIO both an impetus as well as legal protection for an unprecedented membership drive.[5] In the short span of two years, the CIO rallied almost 4 million previously unorganized coal, automobile, steel, rubber, and other industrial workers into its unions.

Nothing similar followed Mayor Wagner's 1954 proclamation. However, with hindsight, we can see that Wagner's changing labor relations policies provided an opening, albeit a slight one, for the tiny locals affiliated in Jerry Wurf's District Council 37 to begin what would eventually be an immensely successful organizing drive. Wurf's early

efforts were aimed primarily at a single group of city workers, the so-
called "laborers," unskilled workers mostly in the Parks Department
who, according to a 1921 state law, were supposed to be paid the prevailing rate for similar work in the private sector. In order to claim
such pay, relatively complicated complaints had to be filed with the
city controller (before 1954) and with the Salary Appeals Board
(after 1954). "Prevailing rate" lawyers, many well connected to the
Democratic party, capitalized on the situation by representing laborers in the appeals process for a fee based on how long the appeal
procedure took. As a result the lawyers had an incentive to delay proceedings, and even when pay hikes finally were won, the lawyers
kept a steep 10 percent of the increase.[6]

AFSCME offered to represent its members before the board for the
price of membership dues, a program so popular with the laborers
that by 1954 over half of DC 37's membership was in the laborers'
Local 924, almost all recruited after 1952. Then, buoyed by Mayor
Wagner's announced endorsement of collective bargaining in the Interim Order, DC 37 began to expand its representation strategy. Wurf
initiated a campaign to build a base large enough to call for direct
negotiations with city officials. His first target was the department
head for Local 924 workers, Commissioner of Parks Robert Moses.
The most independent of all department heads, Moses was well
known for his quasi-military rules, including strictly enforced dress
code (no mismatched socks), mandatory overtime (including six-day,
seventy-two-hour weeks), and no formal grievance procedures. Moreover, in clear disregard of the 1954 Interim Order, Moses blocked the
right to join labor organizations and forbade negotiations between labor unions and the department. Moses was then at the zenith of his
power, simultaneously running not only the City Parks Department,
but also the New York State Parks, Long Island Parks, the State Power
Authority, the Triborough Bridge and Tunnel Authority, and the Slum
Clearance Program.[7]

As is well documented by Robert Caro's The Power Broker, the
Robert Moses of the 1950s, while powerful, was nonetheless vulnerable. No longer did he carry the "white knight" image that he had
maintained throughout the 1930s. Local 924 used clever publicity
tactics, including a "Bob Moses Zoo," in which uniformed park workers sat behind bars, to point out how Moses flouted Wagner's 1954
Order. Embarrassed by newspaper coverage suggesting that Commissioner Moses could act independently of mayoral directives ("Which
Bob is boss?" they asked), Mayor Wagner forced Moses to reverse his
stand on unionism and hold representation elections in the department. AFSCME won easily, 4,097 to 173, and used publicity of the vic-

tory to sign up new members, so that within two years Local 924 claimed 80 percent membership among eligible workers.[8]

Accounts of Local 924 meetings indicate a vigorous organization; attendance levels were high for union meetings, about 30 percent. During a 1956 pay dispute the local threatened the city with its first strike by Career and Salary Plan employees. The action was called off by Jerry Wurf, who argued that Wagner had enough troubles at the time with a tugboat strike. Instead, the local packed a Board of Estimate meeting, where they threatened to filibuster the proceedings. The scenario was repeated in 1957, when the local voted to strike over a new classification scheme. Once again the protest was limited by union leaders to picketing City Hall; a meeting between Wagner and Wurf then resulted in a city promise that the reclassification plan would result in no loss of pay.[9]

All these successes helped Wurf step up his campaign to organize other city employees, particularly those in the welfare and hospital departments, where there was a longtime interest in unions dating back to the 1930s, but little current union activity. No union had occupied the void after the United Public Workers (UPW) was red-baited out of existence. Many of the most knowledgeable union organizers with a track record of success in the public sector, once affiliated with the UPW, found a new home with the Teamsters, which unlike DC 37 did not bar employment based on past political background. With their assistance, Teamster locals became DC 37's chief rival in trying to attract a large number of unorganized city workers.[10]

A Structure Emerges

Mayor Wagner also took note of this upsurge in union activity and proceeded to institute a new approach to labor relations. Between 1956 and 1965, Wagner moved the city toward full recognition of unions for its employees. Each of the steps taken by Mayor Wagner assisted unions in gaining representation rights, but also guaranteed that certain unions would be recognized and that these unions would be limited in bargaining power.

In 1956 New York City unions were granted the right to dues checkoff. Prior to checkoff, a good portion of the union organizer's workday was spent making rounds of workplaces trying to collect dues. During city-sponsored hearings on the matter almost all labor organizations testified in favor of checkoff, but disagreed on how it should be introduced. Relatively large unions—DC 37, Teamster Local 237, the sanitation union, and the police union—all argued that the checkoff should be limited to groups with majority representation in a department or agency. Smaller unions contended that workers should be able to direct dues to any organization of their choice. Wagner chose the second option, a nonexclusive checkoff policy, open to any labor organization certified by the city. The result was that numerous unions competed for membership within any single city department or within any classification of city workers. Certification itself was simply a matter of a request to the commissioner of labor, an advertisement in the *City Record*, and subsequent granting of the request by the city as long as the union could demonstrate interest in their union by 10 percent of the group under consideration. In 1957, Wagner further helped struggling unions by granting labor leaders time off with pay to conduct union business; small unions, which could not afford professional staff, particularly benefited from the time-release order.[11]

Mayor Wagner's major response to the incipient organizing drives came on March 31, 1958, when he promulgated Executive Order 49, the most far-reaching attempt to legitimate collective bargaining in New York City up to that date. EO 49 had its origins in Ida Klaus's 1955 study, long gathering dust in the mayor's office, but recalled in 1957 when the mayor, seeking advice on the growing union movement, consulted the labor lawyer. According to Klaus, who thought her advice had been ignored, Wagner asked, "What will this do for me, you know I'm running for reelection [for Mayor in 1957]?" Klaus remembers answering him, "We could call it the Little Wagner Act."[12] Actually, the *New York Times* had already labeled the 1954 Interim Order the Little Wagner Act, but Wagner followed Klaus's suggestion, made it a campaign issue, although not a decisive one in an election he won by almost 1 million votes.

In addition to possibly garnering a few more votes, EO 49 was aimed at a problem Wagner knew would not go away during his second term: increasing militancy by public sector unions. Ida Klaus counseled that the recognition of public unions was necessary to eliminate the threat of strikes because, as she later explained, "In 1958 there was as much need for eliminating chaos, conflict and strife in the City's relations with its own employees as there was for the elimination of the causes of strikes and industrial unrest in private industry in 1935."[13] Klaus stretches the analogy between New York City of 1958 and U.S. industry in 1935; only subway motormen had actually conducted a strike in the city, while private sector workers occupied factories and organized general strikes during the Depression. In any case, Wagner was convinced by institutionalists like Klaus that recognition of unions could bring stability to municipal agencies. Or as the introduction to the Executive Order stated, "Experience has indicated that labor disputes will be minimized . . . by permitting employees to participate . . . through their freely chosen representatives in the determination of the terms and conditions of their employment."[14] The hope was that with union recognition, city employees could resolve their disputes without resorting to the kind of protests embarrassing to Mayor Wagner.

A second reason institutionalists urged the preemptive recognition of public sector unions was that it would give employers greater influence over which organization would represent employees than if the employer waited until workers forced recognition on a recalcitrant management. In the case of Colonel Waring's Committee of 41 (see Chapter 2), he simply dictated the formation of an employee representative group as preferable to the Knights of Labor. Mayor Wagner permitted independent unions to represent city employees, but did not in fact allow the freedom of choice among unions as implied in the Executive Order. Unlike the NLRA, which established an independent board to interpret the act and rule in contested cases, EO 49 allowed the commissioner of labor (a mayoral appointee) and the mayor himself considerable discretion in determining union recognition. One former official describes Mayor Wagner's role bluntly: "Wagner would receive certain requests for certification himself and would just pick up the phone and call the people over at the Department of Labor and tell them who to certify and who not to certify."[15]

The vaguely worded Executive Order also gave Wagner and his commissioner of labor the latitude to set the rules of recognition as they liked. The proper size and inclusiveness of bargaining units, for example, were defined in the order only as "appropriate," thus enabling the commissioner to include or exclude groups of workers in ways that could help or hinder a specific union. If a favored union was strong among employees in one city department, then the bargaining unit would include that department only, whereas a union less strongly supported by Wagner might be forced to sign up workers in similar job categories in several city departments. Also, it was possible to hold elections at a time when a favored union was strong— or delay the election when the rival union was temporarily the most popular. Finally, elections were not always models of fair play; for example, city officials turned a blind eye to enterprising unions offering voters free lunches at the polling place.[16]

In addition to such selective certifications, the mayor's office also introduced a structural barrier to effective collective bargaining. Representation rights often were granted for small groups of employees, for example, all those in a department with a particular title. But negotiations were then limited to only those items that applied exclusively to that group of employees. In other words, for a job title like clerical worker it was necessary to organize workers in almost every city department before any meaningful negotiations could take place. On issues such as time and leave rules and many fringe benefits like pensions covered by the city's Career and Salary Plan, negotiations would be possible only when one union represented a majority of the more than 100,000 workers covered by that plan.[17]

Some job titles were exclusive to single city departments and thus far easier to organize. Firefighters, for example, gained the first certification in 1956. Sanitation workers followed soon afterward, gaining not only certification, but also the first written contract for city employees outside of the transit system. In this case, even though the city had no choice but to permit one union to represent all employees in the department, the mayor was careful to help favored union leaders gain control of the union, even when doing so meant overriding the wishes of union members.

The Price of Recognition

John DeLury's Teamster local, the Uniformed Sanitationmen's Association (USA), was certified as the bargaining agent for sanitation workers in August 1958. President DeLury attempted to portray subsequent negotiations with the city as a victory; thirty union members carried him in apparent triumph from a Board of Estimate meeting on pensions. In actual fact, however, the city concessions were minimal; members rejected a November offer on pensions in a 8,365 to 8 vote. The following day 4,000 sanitation workers clocked in one hour late, drawing the outrage of sanitation commissioner Paul Screvane and loss of pay for those involved. Negotiations reopened the following week and a settlement was reached including pay increases, but not the sought-after pension changes. This time USA membership approved the contract.[18]

Negotiations for the 1960 contract caught DeLury in a similar bind between union members and the city. At the end of July the union sponsored a one-day work stoppage that Wagner refused to call a strike so that he would not need to enforce the Condon-Wadlin Act. That evening union leadership convened a membership meeting, intending to call off the strike. Over 6,000 members attended the meeting, many standing outside the overcrowded hall. DeLury asked for a voice vote to end the strike. Even though "nays" clearly outnumbered "yeas" (according to a *New York Times* account), DeLury ruled the strike over and left the hall amid shouting and a few fistfights.[19] The following day, when the department threatened disciplinary action against anyone not working, about 60 percent of the work force returned. One week later the union agreed on a contract and ratified it at another well-attended meeting. In contrast to the contract of two years earlier, the 1960 pact included both a wage increase and an improvement in the pension plan for a total increase of $450 per worker.[20]

Those sanitationmen disenchanted with DeLury's policies met with organizers from Teamster rival DC 37 to consider a challenge to USA certification. According to DC 37, the city intervened to help the Teamsters by transferring dissident sanitation workers to outer borough jobs, an unattractive assignment with a long commute, and one in which the employee would have little contact with co-workers, making solicitation of support for DC 37 difficult. As a result, the DC 37 raid failed and DeLury continued his decades-long domination of the sanitationmen's union.[21]

Growth of DC 37

Despite the initial success of Teamster locals like the USA, it was AFSCME's DC 37 that came to dominate New York City labor relations by 1966. During most of the 1950s, DC 37 appeared a poor candidate to become the leader of all municipal unions. Even by 1959 membership was estimated at less than 20,000 by outside observers and only 30,000 by DC 37's probably inflated count.[22] Nonetheless, when DC 37 failed to win signed contracts for its certified locals, the union called a series of strikes, a willingness to take militant action that resulted in extraordinary 10 percent per year membership growth between 1960 and 1965.

In 1959, for example, negotiations ostensibly were under way between DC 37 locals and the city when Mayor Wagner announced unilaterally that the city budget for that year would include no pay raises. Since further bargaining was now meaningless, DC 37 head Jerry Wurf called a mass meeting at which 3,000 members voted for a one-day walkout by all union members. Wurf changed the plan to mass picketing outside City Hall, for which workers obtained leaves of

absence. The result amounted to a work stoppage "by permission";
attendance at the demonstration was large, 2,600 by newspaper accounts, 8,000 by union tally, forcing some city offices to close. Union
leaders pointed out to the press that Wagner, whom they called "Ber-
muda Bob," was vacationing when he could have been negotiating
with city employees.[23]

Zookeepers undertook the first full-scale strike by DC 37 members,
staying off the job for two months before winning a signed contract.
The strike began in April 1961 with much favorable newspaper publicity: monkeys, pythons, and goats appeared on the picket line to appeal for better care for their custodians. With small grants from other
DC 37 locals, the zookeepers sustained their strike till the end of May,
when they finally won a contract providing for overtime pay, Blue
Cross coverage, dues checkoff, and the right to bargain over working
conditions.[24]

Motor vehicle operators' (MVO) Local 983, among the largest of DC
37 locals, also needed a long strike to win a contract. They walked off
the job for ten days in November 1962. For the first time city services
were seriously impaired by a DC 37 strike: missing deliveries caused
cancellation of school hot lunches; sewer repair fell behind schedule;
city officials were without drivers; and at times ambulance service
was disrupted. As a result Mayor Wagner invoked the Condon-Wadlin
Act and dismissed sixteen MVO's from their jobs in the Police Department. Suddenly, Wagner, the erstwhile "friend of labor," faced united
opposition of the city's labor movement, including public sector labor
unions TWU, PBA, UFA, the Teamster locals, and even from Central Labor Council head Harry Van Arsdale.[25]

After a rally of well over 10,000 protesters, the largest demonstration to date by public sector workers, Wagner rescinded the dismiss-
als and ordered the workers "temporarily discharged" pending hearings. The strike then ended on terms favorable to Local 983. DC 37
heralded the contract's 37 cent per hour pay increase as a "victory for
all City employees and the end of Civil Service special pleading before the Salary Appeals Board." New members flocked to the local,
100 joining immediately after the strike, eventually doubling Local
983 membership and guaranteeing DC 37 popularity among drivers, a
job category traditionally dominated by the Teamsters.[26]

Most DC 37 locals still lacked certification as bargaining agents and
thus were forced to limit their efforts to appearances before the salary
boards. The union could claim credit for winning occasional concessions, including a 1961 promise to pay the federal minimum wage
(which applied only to the private sector). However, collective bargaining was a more powerful tool; one DC 37 study showed that work-

ers were twice as likely to win substantial civil service increases (of two grades) through collective bargaining, compared with salary board appeals. However, citywide bargaining would not be allowed until one union represented a majority of employees citywide. Two of the largest employee classifications still lacking union representation, clerical and hospital workers, were the key to that citywide majority. DC 37 membership had now caught up with and surpassed membership of Teamster Local 237. But whichever union could gain representation rights for the missing classifications would likely dominate collective bargaining for Career and Salary Plan employees as a whole.

The drive to organize hospital workers dated back to 1956, when DC 37 and Local 237 first went head to head. Jean Conturier, later director of the National Civil Service League, and James Farmer, later director of the Congress of Racial Equality, built up the tiny DC 37 Local 420 into an equal rival with the Teamsters.[27] By mocking the Teamsters as a union that tried to cozy up to city officials and accusing the Teamsters of using language such as "we would be grateful" or "we have received a number of favors," Local 420 tried to establish itself with the image of a militant union aiming at the goal of full-fledged collective bargaining.[28]

In early 1965 the gauntlet was thrown down: elections would be held granting one union, DC 37 or Local 237, bargaining rights for hospital workers. Rivalry between the two groups intensified. Several DC 37 organizers defected to the Teamsters, leading to accusations that they had been bribed. There were scuffles at each union's rallies; in one altercation a DC 37 organizer was stabbed. The election was held in December 1965 and the results were extremely close: DC 37 won among hospital aides 5,903 to 5,071 and among clericals 1,350 to 371, but lost among hospital cooks.[29]

Civil Rights, Union Rights

When asked what was the key to DC 37 success in the hospital elections, several union leaders involved in the victory answer without hesitation: Lillian Roberts. She was a hospital union organizer brought to New York from Chicago by then field staff coordinator Victor Gotbaum. Later, Roberts became DC 37's associate director and in 1981 she was appointed industrial commissioner for New York State. But she began her work life as a $23-per-week aide, the first black hired at the Chicago Lying-in Hospital. Roberts's career symbolized DC 37's ties to the civil rights movement. The union not only supported the protest movement of the time, but also linked the concerns of blacks directly to union goals. The same women who wanted to break down segregation laws also wanted to overcome institutionalized occupational barriers that kept black workers in low-skill, low-paying jobs with disagreeable hours and little respect from administrators. DC 37 demands began with dignity on the job such as the use of "Mr." and "Mrs." in addressing employees. Hospital workers were overwhelmingly black and female; as late as 1975, over half had not completed high school. The union obtained a U.S. Department of Labor grant to begin an upgrading program under which a nurse's aide, for example, could train to qualify as a licensed practical nurse. Interest in the program overwhelmed its sponsors; 3,000 applied when it was first offered.[30]

The upgrading program was not formally instituted until just after the hospital election; thus the election itself hinged on other issues. The Teamsters enjoyed an early lead, in part because of the popularity of Local 237's new president, Bill Lewis. In fact, he was so confident of victory that he turned down a compromise plan under which representation would be shared with DC 37. Lewis might indeed have carried the day had it not been for inadvertent assistance given to DC 37 by Mayor Wagner, who actually favored the Teamsters. As noted above, one of the mayor's means for influencing union recognition was to manipulate the date of representation elections. In this case the hospital election had been set for early 1965, a date DC 37 leaders realized left them hopelessly behind the Teamsters. They appealed to AFL-CIO president George Meany to intervene with Wagner and have the elections postponed. On the assumption that the non-AFL-CIO Teamsters would win the election in any case, and eager to do a favor for Meany, Wagner asked the Department of Labor to put off the election until December. Barry Feinstein, son of former Local 237 president Henry Feinstein, an inexperienced union organizer who was nonetheless coordinating the hospital campaign, mistakenly accepted the postponement as routine.[31]

Feinstein's error proved costly to Local 237; during the reprieve DC 37 redoubled its efforts, launching an exceptionally spirited campaign. Hospital aides and clericals received letters from George Meany and civil rights and union leader, A. Phillip Randolph, and individual home visits from DC 37 members. Civil rights leaders testified to the union's commitment to the cause, while Hudson River boat rides publicized the social side of union life. The theme of DC 37's campaign was labor militancy, counterposed to alleged Teamster failure to stage demonstrations or call strikes for city workers. The eventual mandate for DC 37 ended Teamster dominance as the single most powerful public union. Bill Lewis died shortly thereafter, leaving control of the now much weaker union to Barry Feinstein.[32]

The hospital election left clerical workers as the largest group of city workers still unclaimed by any union. Dispersed among numerous city departments, they had been largely ignored by union organizers, who found it far easier to reach those who worked in reasonably close proximity to one another. Even if a union succeeded in organizing clericals in one city department, city rules required majority representation before bargaining could take place on issues applicable to that classification. But for the same reason the clerical classification was an important prize for DC 37. If the union could win representation rights for this group, DC 37 would win the race to gain a majority of *all* Career and Salary Plan employees.

DC 37 began its campaign for the clericals in 1962. Starting with departments such as Welfare and Parks, in which the union already won large pay increases for other workers, the union distributed free copies of its newspaper, *Public Employee Press*, boasting that the union would be just as aggressive for the interests of clericals. Pay board appeals had been notably unsuccessful for clerical workers; in July 1962 the board postponed consideration of a wage increase and in 1963 granted a paltry one-grade increase. DC 37 pointed out that clericals were losing ground not only to other public employees, but that New York City clerical pay had increased only half as rapidly as it had in the private sector during the previous decade.[33]

Aided by dedicated and competent organizers, DC 37's campaign showed immediate results. Among clericals in the Transit Authority, DC 37 won 90 percent of the vote in July 1962 and five months later was a three-to-one victor in the Department of Hospitals. The hospital election brought in 3,500 new members in 1965, followed soon afterward by Board of Education clericals. Combined with 6,500 school aides also won by DC 37, it was clear to city administrators that the union would soon represent a majority in Career and Salary Plan employees.

As the union and the city prepared to tackle the first "citywide" contract, changes were about to take place in both groups' leadership. Robert Wagner was stepping down as mayor, to be replaced on January 1, 1966, by John Lindsay. And within DC 37, Jerry Wurf moved up to become national president of AFSCME. For a brief period Wurf attempted to manage the affairs of both AFSCME and DC 37. By early

1965, however, he realized the need to reduce his day-to-day involvement in New York and replaced his stand-in, Calogero Taibi, with another handpicked but far more independent leader, Victor Gotbaum.

Gotbaum had been brought to New York City initially as a field staff coordinator. Like Wurf, Gotbaum was Brooklyn-born, Jewish, and influenced by internecine socialist conflicts during his youth. But Gotbaum had received more formal education than Wurf, completing a masters in international affairs and working for the U.S. State and Labor departments before joining Chicago's AFSCME in 1957. Compared to the anti-union patronage system of Mayor Daley's Chicago, where AFSCME had a long history of failure and Gotbaum himself had lost a bitter hospital strike, New York City's AFSCME was on the verge of spectacular success. Not only was a citywide contract on the horizon, but only days after Gotbaum took on the New York assignment welfare workers began one of the longest New York City strikes. As will be described in the next Chapter, this strike prompted an entirely new structure under which DC 37 ultimately would negotiate its first citywide contract.

5

Social Service Workers
Challenge to the City

By all accounts, the Social Service Employees Union was an unusual union. Without formal affiliation to either the AFL-CIO or the Teamsters, this small, independent union represented 5,000 social investigators, home-care aides, and counselors in New York City's Department of Welfare between 1964 and 1969. SSEU made up for what it lacked in numbers with a dedicated membership who participated in the day-to-day affairs of the union to an extent found in few organizations and certainly not in any other New York City union. Even critics of the union admit that SSEU's influence in New York was far out of proportion to its size.[1] Present-day city rules for union recognition and contract bargaining are rooted in SSEU's precedent-setting contract signed in 1965. While SSEU now is only a semiautonomous unit of a much larger union, District Council 37 of AFSCME, the high standards set by SSEU during its heyday stand as a model for participatory union democracy.

As with almost all New York City public unions, the roots of SSEU go back to the 1930s, in particular to the State, County, and Municipal Workers of America, not to be confused with AFSCME, its AFL rival. SCMWA merged with the United Federal Workers in 1946 to form the United Public Workers, one of the largest public unions of the time, with 5,000 members in New York City.[2] The political sophistication of UPW members contributed to the union's success, as union activity was part of their deep commitment to social activism, most notably through the Communist party. After 1948, however, such affiliations became a handicap. As part of that year's nationwide anti-Communist witch-hunt, Mayor William O'Dwyer appointed a new welfare commissioner, Raymond Hilliard, a man who had built his reputation by removing alleged Communists from Chicago employment.[3]

Initially unconcerned by Hilliard's appointment, UPW leaders reassured their members with the union slogan "Commissioners come and go, but UPW lives on."[4] Indeed, everyone assumed Hilliard would soon resign after ineffective leadership, as had eight other welfare commissioners during the previous five years. But soon it became apparent that Hilliard's attack went to the heart of UPW power, the unusual alliance of Welfare Department administrators, union members, and welfare recipients.[5] Hilliard brought in his own staff from Chicago, thus blocking UPWs former tactic of appeals to sympathetic ears at welfare's central headquarters. All union meetings were forbidden on city property, as was the distribution of leaflets—practices tolerated previously by friendly welfare center supervisors. Hired informers reported union activities to Hilliard's staff, who then dismissed union leaders for minor violations of welfare rules. The national union movement itself joined in the red-baiting fever by expelling the UPW from the CIO on the grounds that UPW policies were "directed toward the achievement of the program of the Communist Party."[6] Hilliard then used the CIO decision to withdraw city recognition of the UPW's right to represent welfare workers.

The UPW had a tradition of allying with welfare recipients to press for welfare reforms through its Worker's Alliance, an action Hilliard argued was proof that the union wanted to make relief a "political weapon."[7] In order to counter the alliance's claim that relief payments were too low, he and his family lived on the welfare food allotment for one month—in their Riverside Drive apartment—which, he alleged, resulted in a most satisfactory diet, with money to spare at the end of the month. To make sure the poor paid their rent, Hilliard introduced bimonthly, two-party rent allotment checks. Along with surprise nighttime visits to look for a "man under the bed," such policing roles alienated welfare workers from their clients.[8]

By 1951 Hilliard could boast in *Colliers*, "How I cleaned up the Welfare Department."[9] With the UPW out of the way, the city recognized two small anti-Communist UPW rivals as the legitimate representatives for welfare workers: Local 371 of the Government and Civil Service Employees Organizing Committee, a CIO affiliate; and Local 1193 of AFSCME, an AFL group. When the CIO and AFL combined forces in 1955, the unions merged to become Local 371 of AFSCME.

Compared with the UPW, the new union was small, with about 1,000 members. Its relationship with the new welfare commissioner, James Dumpson, was extremely friendly; the union relied on favors from department officials as the main service it could offer members. But as critics later pointed out, the prime beneficiaries of the close cooperation between the union and the department were Local 371 presidents Raymond Diana, Anthony Russo, and Frank Petrocelli, all of whom stepped from union office to important city government positions—assistant to the mayor for labor relations, commissioner of labor relations, and executive officer in the Welfare Department, respectively.[10]

Out of the Ashes

UPW traditions were revitalized by a handful of former members who survived Hilliard's purges by being banished to what were then outpost welfare centers in Brooklyn. By the late 1950s, changing city demographics brought these once-isolated welfare workers into contact with large numbers of newly recruited welfare workers assigned to service the growing number of poor who also had been pushed to Brooklyn's outer reaches. One such former UPW member, Sam Podell, of the East New York Welfare Center, decided in 1959 to launch a campaign for what he called a "more militant and representative union."[11]

Opposing incumbent Local 371 leaders was no easy task. Means of communication within the union, bulletin boards and newsletters, were available only to those already in power. Thus it was difficult for dissidents to become known outside of their own welfare center. Elections favored incumbents or their nominees, who were placed on the ballot by committees controlled by union leadership, while challengers had to circulate petitions in order to be nominated. Incumbents knew the election rules best and could use technicalities to keep dissidents off the ballot altogether. In one much-contested case in 1963, Albert Coury was ruled ineligible for union office because his records showed him one day short of the full year of union membership required.[12]

Even though Local 371 leaders were well entrenched in office, they were increasingly out of touch with the majority of welfare workers, many of whom were new to the job. Between 1961 and 1963 there was an increase of 55 percent in potential union members, but a decrease in the number bothering to vote in union elections.[13] Fed up with union leaders too well connected to City Hall, yet unable to challenge them within the structure of Local 371, a group of activists, including Podell, decided in 1961 that it was time to create an entirely new union, the Social Service Employees Union.

In order to recruit members to the new union, it was first necessary to gain representation rights from the city's Department of Labor by being certified as a recognized labor organization. Since many SSEU leaders were once UPW supporters, opposition might have been expected from city officials. However, by the early 1960s old alliances had shifted. No longer did all public sector unions rely on favors from Mayor Wagner to gain benefits for members. In particular, Local 371's affiliates in District Council 37, park workers and motor vehicle operators, had taken a confrontational stance in labor relations, including strikes to win their demands. So, when ex-UPW members appeared at the Labor Department wanting to form a new union in opposition to a DC 37 affiliate, even one as moderate as Local 371, Mayor Wagner readily gave his approval. The ghost of Communist influence was now less menacing than the live militancy of DC 37's laborers.[14]

Recognition as a legitimate labor organization was a major symbolic step for these once-ostracized UPW members. Yet it did not signify real power under Mayor Wagner's system of bargaining. Dozens of labor organizations had been "recognized" as bargaining agents for literally hundreds of bargaining units, many of them overlapping, as they did in the welfare department. Unions did not sign contracts in the traditional sense, but presented evidence that their workers were underpaid and then waited for a time-consuming study to be conducted by the city about whether or not wages in New York differed from those nationwide. Local 371 leaders defended their advisory role on the grounds that friendly ties to Welfare Department officials had won union members such benefits as social security, a uniform allowance, elimination of Saturday work, and partial payment into a Blue Cross plan. SSEU supporters countered that benefits had actually deteriorated under Local 371's representation, allowing the city to take away nine leave days between 1956 and 1961 and to lower the starting salary for new workers.[15]

Whatever the merits of their past record, Local 371 leaders were now under pressure to produce results in the upcoming negotiations for the 1962 memorandum of agreement. For the first time ever, Local 371 leaders asked for a strike authorization vote and trumpeted the subsequent agreement as a victory for welfare workers. SSEU responded with leaflets showing the new agreement to be simply another in a long line of deals between Local 371 leaders and Commissioner Dumpson. As evidence they produced a letter signed by

Dumpson that seemed to indicate he knew in advance the union would not carry through with its strike threat. Moreover, SSEU argued the terms of the agreement had nothing to do with the newfound Local 371 militancy, but resulted from federal legislation of the previous year, mandating pay increases for welfare workers. Finally, and most damaging to Local 371's reputation, several months later SSEU was able to point out that pay hikes and workload reductions promised in the 1962 memorandum were not in fact forthcoming.[16]

To protest the city's failure to live up to the agreement, the most militant SSEU members, concentrated at the Brooklyn Borough Hall welfare center, walked off their jobs. The strike failed to win pay increases and caused a two-month suspension of several workers. (In typical paternalistic fashion, the department allowed them to return only after signing a statement: "I regret this incident.") But this first-ever walkout in the Welfare Department indicated to workers city-wide that unlike Local 371, which disavowed any support for the protest, SSEU was prepared to take militant action to protect member interests.[17]

The 1962 agreement also promised—but did not enforce—a cut-back in welfare worker caseloads. According to federal guidelines, the maximum caseload was supposed to be sixty; in New York City the *average* for all caseworkers was sixty-two. It was not uncommon for workers to serve as many as ninety clients at one time. With such large caseloads, any welfare worker who was committed to serve clients adequately was caught on a treadmill of work: every recommendation for additional assistance—such as school clothing, an allowance for a hot plate, or a rent supplement to prevent eviction—required that caseworkers check to make sure clients were honest in their representation of need. Workers either provided less than adequate service or, as was the case for many, put in unpaid overtime during evenings and weekends. Not surprisingly, turnover was high, which, coupled with slow Welfare Department hiring procedures, further exacerbated caseload problems for those still on the job.[18]

Since 75 percent of the city's multimillion-dollar welfare budget was reimbursed by the federal government, compliance with federal guidelines, including the maximum caseload of sixty, technically was a prerequisite for federal funds. SSEU leaders saw in this provision a source of pressure on the department and wrote to Washington authorities to complain about New York City violations. When Commissioner Dumpson learned of this letter he immediately suspended the four co-signers, including SSEU president Joe Tepedino and vice-president Judy Mage. Dumpson also tried to withdraw city recognition of SSEU because the union was "disrupting the morale of the staff and attempting to discredit the department," a result of their "suspicious" political leanings. Dumpson added he would be pleased to recognize a "responsible union."[19] However once again intimidation of SSEU backfired. The four workers were permitted to stay on the job while their case was before the courts, an appeal they won six years later. The union received much favorable publicity and gained members rapidly, growing five-fold between 1963 and 1964.[20]

A New Union

The new members flooding into SSEU came from two distinct backgrounds. One group consisted of relatively older, experienced caseworkers, many of them blacks or Jews who had taken a Welfare Department job during the Depression, when the civil service meant a secure job in a discriminatory labor market. For the most part they were longtime New York City residents and some of them had once been UPW members. The second group joining SSEU were recent transplants to New York City, younger workers who had attended college and were looking for a socially relevant career outside the business world.[21]

Although they came from different backgrounds, the two groups in SSEU shared a number of ideals. Both were committed to the concept of unions for so-called white-collar professionals. And both groups tended to support liberal or left-wing political positions, including the notion that the welfare system was degrading to welfare worker and recipient alike. What distinguished these two types of welfare workers was their concept of the union's purpose. Older workers saw the union primarily as an organization to fight for higher wages and better working conditions. They saw the effort as part of a more general political struggle for social justice, but it was one within which the union could play only a limited role. As the 1960s unfolded, many younger SSEU members saw the union itself as the basis for a movement toward broadly based social change. Veterans of the civil rights movement, in particular, believed as a member put it, "One *can* do something." To them it was quite conceivable that the union could be the catalyst, or perhaps even the nucleus, of a combined worker-welfare recipient movement that could radically alter social and economic conditions in the United States.

Despite such differences of opinion about the ultimate role of the union, both young and old workers agreed that the union would be

strong only if it was based on a high degree of rank-and-file participation. They shared the belief that SSEU should be a union in which
democracy meant not simply voting for a few union officers at infre-
quent intervals, but participation by all members in the union's functioning and decision making. In this regard, the SSEU was an un-
qualified success. Rank-and-file activity took place to as great an
extent as in any union of its size in the United States.

Union democracy did not come about simply by declaring it to be
the union's guiding principle. SSEU succeeded in gaining participation from large numbers of members because involvement in the
union was fostered from the first day welfare workers appeared on
the job. Whereas Local 371 greeted new recruits by leaving membership cards on their desks, SSEU organizers were trained by a Saul Alin-
sky–style manual to engage new workers in discussion about their
jobs, to counsel those new to the city about where to live, and above
all to explain how new members could help the union change the Department of Welfare. Literature handed out at Brooklyn's Wyckoff
Center was typical: "The union is not something distant or remote,
run by far off leaders in some office. It is here in the center and its
actions have the potential for dramatically changing the way in which
we spend about one half of our waking hours. Its potential and its
democracy, however, depend entirely on support from the individual
rank and file member." [22]

Each welfare center organized its own chapter with frequent meetings, a newsletter, and a limited right to pursue job protests independent of the union as a whole. Representation to the union's delegate
assembly, the main decision-making body, was based on work location with each elected representative directly accountable to his or
her workmates. The flow of information was further enhanced through
a taped telephone message changed daily to keep members abreast of
decisions made by the headquarters staff. Debate on important issues within the union was intense, with discussion in the delegate
assembly supplemented by a large number of ad-hoc leaflets and
commentaries in chapter newsletters. In an attempt to minimize empire building at the top, union officials were not allowed to succeed
themselves in office—although given the hotly contested nature of
union elections, it is doubtful that anyone would have remained in
office for many terms. [23]

The final measure of SSEU's success was its ability to win votes in a
head-to-head election against Local 371. The contest took place on
October 1964, preceded by a spirited debate between the two unions.
SSEU emphasized Local 371 leaders' connections to the Welfare Department's downtown headquarters and the local's unwillingness to

take militant action. Local 371 responded by charging SSEU with violating a sacred trust of the labor movement: never raid another union's jurisdiction. SSEU won the election among caseworkers, home economists, and children's counselors, leaving Local 371 with representation rights for supervisors and clericals (the latter group not contested in the election, and later separated into their own local within DC 37).[24]

Formal recognition for SSEU meant the union could negotiate a contract with the city instead of merely initiating memoranda of agreement. Based on Mayor Wagner's 1958 Executive Order 49, the city had already signed contracts with sanitation workers and small groups of laborers, each time granting a wage increase but not altering the standard benefit package provided under the civil service system.

SSEU had higher ambitions: in addition to significant wage increases, the union wanted new work rules as well. City officials studiously ignored SSEU's unusual demands, sending a low-level clerk to the first negotiating session with instructions to discuss nothing but incremental wage increases. Later the city raised its offer to a total $310 wage package, provided that the union accept a two-and-a-half year contract, longer than those usually negotiated. When the union still refused to budge, Mayor Wagner made a final gesture, agreeing to send the negotiations to a mediation panel, consisting of three city representatives and two representatives named by the union. Even with such obvious management domination, Wagner still insisted that working conditions were not a proper topic for consideration by the mediating group. Workload was ruled out of bounds because it did not pertain directly to wages and benefits; sick leave and vacation time, on the other hand, could not be discussed because such benefits needed to be kept uniform for all civil service employees.[25]

Mayor Wagner's intransigent position was based on advice from his Labor Department that SSEU was weak. Should the union call a strike, it was assumed the cold January weather would quickly chill any enthusiasm by union members for the picket line. Critics of SSEU argued that recent college graduates, who comprised a large percentage of the union's membership, would have only superficial commitment to the union's goals. Allegedly their demand for social justice was the passing fervor of youth, and their concern about benefits shallow since they had no family responsibilities; for them welfare work was only a temporary situation. Those with roots in the old UPW could possibly sustain a strike, but they were fewer in number. Conflict between the two groups was thought likely to tear the union apart. Finally, SSEU was thought to be isolated from the rest of the city's labor movement. Just because a small group of welfare workers appeared ready to strike, the city was not about to change its traditional pattern of labor relations.[26]

No one was surprised when SSEU walked out on January 4, 1965. What no one predicted was that they would win. Despite the bitter January cold, a practically empty union treasury, and no formal connections to any other union, SSEU shut down city welfare services for the entire month and later signed a contract that included substantial wage increases; work-rule changes and workload reductions; and a promise from the city to study inequities in the conduct of labor relations for *all* city employees. Obviously SSEU's power had been underestimated.

SSEU detractors were correct in observing the union's unusual makeup of young, college-educated members. What they missed was the truly remarkable characteristic of the union: widespread democratic decision making and a commitment to participation by members, be they young or old. Not only had members voted to go on strike, a process required in most union constitutions, but SSEU members had been involved in the bargaining process from the beginning, writing the union's demands, voting on the union's response to Mayor Wagner's "concession," and finally, planning the strike itself. So, even though union leaders got most of the publicity during the negotiations, they were, in the true sense of the word, representatives of several thousand Welfare Department employees.

A second reason for the SSEU victory was that, despite the union's apparent autonomy, and thus isolation from other groups, support was quickly garnered from other organizations, most notably spokespersons for welfare recipients and from the union's rival in the Welfare Department, Local 371. The department tried to paint SSEU members as callous about their responsibility to clients and told newspapers that welfare leaders were angry with middle-class welfare workers whose strike cut off funds to far needier welfare clients. Most city newspapers, themselves opposed to the strike, picked up this line of reasoning in their initial editorializing. Soon, however, it became apparent that civil rights leaders, including James Farmer and A. Phillip Randolph, as well as thirteen New York City NAACP chapters, all supported SSEU on the grounds that welfare workers and clients alike suffered from high caseloads and an inadequately paid welfare staff.[27]

Ironically, SSEU's most important ally during the strike was their traditional opponent, Local 371, which agreed to strike side by side with them. Support from Local 371 came not out of respect for SSEU— the two unions exchanged angry letters in the weeks prior to the strike—but out of a fear on the part of Local 371 leaders that their union might be viewed as less militant than SSEU.[28] Only two months

before, Local 371 had been stung by the loss of most of its members to
SSEU, just at the time when other DC 37 locals were in the middle of
their campaign to win representation rights for clericals, school aides,
and hospital workers (see Chapter 4).

The city offered Local 371 "special inducements" and promised
that the mayor "would take care of you" if they disavowed the strike.[29]
Nonetheless, DC 37 leaders were aware that failure to participate in
the welfare strike would brand DC 37 as a meek union and cause
workers to join SSEU, which now talked about organizing the welfare
clericals. DC 37's reputation also was important for former district
council executive director Jerry Wurf, who was recently elected
president of his national union, AFSCME. Since his campaign had
been based on the activism and successful growth of DC 37, losing
members from his home district to SSEU was embarrassment enough
and probably the result of inattention to local matters during his
drive for the national union presidency. Not to support a highly publicized strike by fellow city employees would have seriously undercut Wurf's growing nationwide prestige.[30]

"Never Before Has the City Agreed to . . ."

Once AFSCME Local 371, an AFL-CIO affiliate, joined the strike, support came from the labor movement throughout the city. Firefighter,
police, transit worker, hospital worker unions, and top labor leaders,
including Central Labor Council chief Harry Van Arsdale and International Ladies Garment Workers Union president David Dubinsky,
provided encouragement and financial assistance. Moreover, with
Local 371 members also off the job, the Welfare Department was forced
to shut down. The city had thought nonstriking personnel could continue to mail out welfare checks, even though it would be impossible
to check up on clients or process new ones. However, with only headquarters personnel trying to keep the system going, even the routine
processing of claims proved infeasible. Almost all welfare offices
closed their doors completely.

Mayor Wagner now found himself aligned against the combined
forces of the civil rights movement and most New York City unions,
an unaccustomed situation for the liberal mayor, "friend of labor,"
and son of the architect of the National Labor Relations Act. Concessions to the union came immediately: a mediation panel consisting of
two union representatives, two city negotiators, and one "respected

and knowledgeable" public representative would be empowered to settle the strike. Unlike Wagner's December mediation plan, this group was "tripartite" in structure, the principle that would come to dominate New York City dispute resolution. As a further concession to the unions, the mediation panel was allowed to discuss any topic, including those previously declared off limits, such as caseload, although the city still contended that many of these issues could not appear in the final contract. On this difference, the city's willingness to "discuss" but not "negotiate" key union demands, SSEU rejected Wagner's offer. Local 371 followed, again not wanting to appear any less militant than SSEU, even though leaders of the local favored the mayor's plan.[31]

SSEU called for a wider strike of other city employees, in particular those represented by DC 37. Local 371 spokesman Jerry Wurf refused, working instead behind the scenes to reach a compromise with Wagner, finally engaging AFL-CIO national president George Meany to wield his influence with the mayor to gain sufficient concessions to allow the unions to end the strike with a victory. Wagner yielded and agreed to give the mediation panel full latitude in its recommendations. Moreover, SSEU and Local 371 leaders, who had been jailed under the New York State's Condon-Wadlin Act, were released on the grounds that violation of the act did not occur within the "view and presence" of the court. Other provisions of the Condon-Wadlin law still threatened welfare workers with termination or three years without pay increases. But the city agreed not to oppose union efforts to challenge the law's constitutionality. (One year later a special state legislature vote rescinded Condon-Wadlin penalties against welfare workers, and the act itself was replaced in 1967 by the Taylor Law.) The final city concession was the appointment of the fifth mediation panel member: Brandeis University School of Social Work dean Charles I. Schottland, a man known to be sympathetic to the workload problems of social workers.[32]

On February 1, 1965, the strike ended and conflict moved to the Schottland panel, where for four months SSEU, Local 371, and the city debated the now familiar issues. SSEU continued to demand significant changes in the workplace, as well as revisions in the city's labor relations structure. AFSCME president Jerry Wurf and Seafarer's Union head Paul Hall, a longtime DC 37 supporter, represented Local 371. They made public pronouncements just as militant-sounding as SSEU's, but in private they chastised SSEU president Joe Tepedino for his uncompromising stance. In March an agreement was reached based on a three-to-two vote, in which Schottland voted with the two city representatives and the two unions opposed the settlement.

The final vote belied the actual terms of the report, which were quite favorable to the unions:

- 9 percent salary increases;
- caseload maximum of sixty;
- reserve pool of caseworkers equal to 10 percent of the work force to handle excess caseload;
- an automatic clothing grant fund for welfare recipients (that is, not requiring individual approval for each check);
- a new tripartite committee to study New York City's labor relations system.[33]

In many regards the contract was a complete union victory. Schottland himself underscored the unique quality of the agreement: "The Committee was fully cognizant of the impact of its recommendations on overall City policy and, perhaps, on public welfare throughout the U.S. Never before has the city agreed to arbitrate so many issues presently held to be 'not bargainable' because of the nature of New York City government; and never before has there been a strike of public welfare employees of such proportion."[34] The contract was in fact unique. The clothing grant clause clearly affected what the city termed "levels of service." The workload limit similarly committed the city to particular policies to guarantee sufficient staffing. And most significant of all, the committee empowered to study city labor relations could make recommendations to radically alter policies for all city workers—as indeed it did.

Why then did SSEU vote against such a seemingly favorable contract? SSEU negotiators wanted one additional concession: a timetable for implementing the contract, a concern that proved to be well founded. The Schottland Commission report only set guidelines; it took four more months of negotiations and several SSEU-sponsored lunchtime sit-down strikes to force the city to sign the agreed-upon contract. And even then the city balked at enforcing its terms, in particular the new workload limits. Once again, SSEU protested, this time with a work slowdown in which welfare workers provided only emergency service, such as protecting clients against pending evictions, but not conducting routine recertification visits. Wagner called the protest an act of "insubordination" and threatened to void the contract if the slowdown was not ended. The union argued the city was also in violation of the contract by not reducing caseloads to promised levels, but nonetheless called off the protest after a city concession not to penalize those involved.[35]

Confronting Liberalism

If 1965 was a year of success for SSEU, many members thought 1966 would be even more favorable. The new mayor, John V. Lindsay, appointed former Columbia University social work dean Mitchell Ginsberg to replace the union's outspoken critic, Welfare Department commissioner James Dumpson. Like Schottland, Ginsberg's attitude toward the welfare system was far closer to that of most SSEU members than his predecessor. Ginsberg's first act upon taking office was to end the department's "midnight raid" policy, long opposed by the union and welfare rights advocates. Also, Ginsberg favored phasing out home visit certification, a practice he found dangerous for welfare workers and insulting to welfare clients. However, any hopes for an easygoing relationship between Ginsberg and the union were quickly dashed.[36]

SSEU's first clash with Ginsberg came over enforcement of the 1965 contract clause for semiannual clothing grants for welfare clients. Initially Ginsberg claimed the grants were not part of the contract; later he acknowledged their presence, but argued in one of his closed-circuit TV lectures to welfare centers that control over service levels was management's prerogative and not subject to collective bargaining. It took two years of SSEU lobbying, assisted by pressure from client groups, before the city finally released the funds, and then only with the proviso that the concession did not indicate any willingness to ever again include service levels in a collective bargaining contract.[37]

Within SSEU, the clothing grants were also a hotly debated issue. One group favored attempts by the union to unite with welfare recipients, while others argued that the union should focus more narrowly on matters directly beneficial to welfare workers. In general, recently hired workers, led by union vice-president Judy Mage, wanted more community contacts. Older workers, many of them supporting families, led by union president Joe Tepedino, opposed "community activism," as they called it. The differences between the two factions were not over the justification of the social causes supported by younger members; the older set shared in the belief welfare recipients deserved higher benefits. However, the older members argued it was presumptuous for SSEU to include welfare groups' demands in union negotiations. To do so actually perpetuated what everyone agreed was an outdated notion of welfare worker as protector of the welfare client. Demands such as clothing grants allegedly alienated an otherwise sympathetic city administration and made SSEU look silly in the public's eyes.[38]

Younger workers answered that the union could not expect support from recipient groups unless union demands were widened to include the needs of welfare recipients. In their minds, the clothing grants were only symbolic of the power of a coalition between workers and clients, which itself was a small part of social protest then sweeping the country. The 1966 union election, in large part a referendum on the issue of union involvement in community affairs, resulted in an overwhelming victory for Judy Mage and her activist followers. Joe Tepedino remained as first vice-president (under union rules he could not succeed himself as president), although it is alleged that Tepedino's three-vote victory over the candidate on the Mage slate was arranged by Mage supporters, who feared the union would be divided if there was no spokesperson among union leadership for the more conservative slate.[39]

On December 31, 1966, the hard-won 1965 contract would expire. Throughout the fall and early winter, SSEU and the city squared off against each other just as they had done two years earlier. Once again the city contended that SSEU wanted to bring inappropriate issues to the bargaining table, emphasizing, as Tepedino predicted they would, the union demand for higher welfare grants. However, even though so-called "service level" demands were denounced by the city with great publicity, two more traditional issues actually were more contentious during bargaining sessions.

First, SSEU claimed that caseloads remained higher than stipulated in the 1965 contract; the union wanted additional hiring programs specified in the new contract to guarantee a lower caseload. Second, the 1965 contract had exempted welfare workers from the civil service program, enabling them to gain better sick leave, vacation, and eduational benefits not available to other city workers. The city wanted to coordinate the benefits of all nonuniformed city workers on the basis of a citywide contract soon to be negotiated with DC 37, which that year gained representation rights for a majority of Career and Salary Plan workers. These two demands—caseload limitation and an independent contract—provoked a series of work stoppages and caused negotiations to spill over into much of 1967.[40]

When the two-year 1965 contract expired, city negotiators tried to send the conflict to fact finders, a procedure rejected by the union because, just as in 1965, the city would not allow the mediators to discuss certain issues. Instead, on January 16, 1967, SSEU voted to strike all welfare centers except for the children's center, which would be staffed by volunteers. At least 60 percent of all SSEU caseworkers walked out. Local 371 leaders refused to endorse the walkout, but an estimated 35 percent of Local 371 supervisors and 20 percent of the clerical staff stayed home. The welfare centers closed down when telephone lines were cut during the night and repair crews refused to cross SSEU picket lines.[41]

Three days later Mage announced a temporary settlement mediated by DC 37's new executive director, Victor Gotbaum. DC 37 staffers saw Gotbaum's intervention as an act of generosity, since it was believed a continued strike would have destroyed SSEU and probably returned membership to DC 37's fold. Meanwhile, within SSEU, Mage sustained criticism from members who did not like the union's faith in Gotbaum's mediating role. Mage prevailed and called members back to work, although absenteeism remained high for several days afterward.[42]

Two weeks later SSEU members at the nonresidence welfare center walked out again. According to federal guidelines, caseloads at such special facilities were supposed to remain less than forty per worker. But according to SSEU members, the average caseload was almost sixty. When caseworkers refused to accept new clients they were suspended and the union voted to strike. This time the city attempted to keep the center open by posting police guards at all doors with orders to admit only workers with "pink slips," indicating allegiance to the department. Striking SSEU members soon eluded the system and jammed the workplace so that processing of clients could not continue. Five days later the city agreed to hire more trainees to lower caseloads.[43]

The contract terms remained unresolved. Negotiations dragged on through the spring as both sides debated the terms of the January 18 settlement, which was supposed to send the entire dispute to fact finding. SSEU then called for a novel protest: the work-in. Beginning on June 19, SSEU members were asked to report for work and keep busy doing anything but their regular duties. "Do not answer the phone, do not pick up a pen or pencil, do not do intake [initial interviews with new clients], do not go into the field [to conduct home visits] . . . if pressure mounts too high, go to the bathroom. You cannot be denied your legal right to go to the men's or ladies' room." In a more productive vein, strikers ran classes for one another in Spanish and other skills needed on the job.[44]

Mayor Lindsay's chief labor negotiator, Herbert Haber, declared the protest "illegal and irresponsible"; almost 1,000 SSEU members were suspended from their jobs for "intimidating fellow workers and interfering with service to clients."[45] The strike, which originally had the support of about 70 percent of union members, began to falter. By mid-July, half were back on the job. At the end of the month, SSEU leaders were forced to allow the outstanding contract terms to go to mediation, a process unlikely to favor the union since the disputed issues were outside the scope of bargaining accepted by most labor mediators. Indeed, the agreement signed that September weakened the union's unique contract terms. Only through the intervention of Victor Gotbaum did the union gain reinstatement (at new work locations) for twenty-eight protesters who had been suspended. As Judy Mage explained, the union won only to the extent that it proved it could not be "busted." [46]

Reaffiliation

Some SSEU members had hoped the election of Mayor John Lindsay would benefit the union.[47] Conflict over the 1967 contract dispelled any such hopes; the union was much weaker than after the successful 1965 strike. Yet, on other matters, Lindsay's appointees lived up to SSEU expectations by ending home-visit recertification and replacing Wagner's arbitrary labor relations policy with a uniform collective bargaining structure. Ironically, it was just these two policies, not Lindsay's recalcitrance to SSEU contract demands, that resulted in the demise of the union.

In 1967, the Welfare Department was replaced by the Department of Social Services, one of Lindsay's attempts to streamline city government. The name shift also symbolized a different attitude toward welfare begun when Commissioner Ginsberg eliminated surprise midnight raids on welfare clients. Home recertification was phased out altogether in an attempt to separate the department's role as conduit for state assistance from its function as provider of counseling to those in need. Beginning in 1968, welfare aid was increasingly administered by clerical workers using computers rather than by social welfare workers, who previously managed a specified caseload out of manila folders.

The new welfare system was supported by the union, as in a 1969 memo from union leadership to the membership: "[contractual changes in welfare organization] will not inaugurate a millennium of radical social change. . . . The demand for changing this way of meeting human needs and legal rights has been a basic (and often notorious) goal of this union since its inception." [48] But the change also had the effect of undermining the union's existence. Mass hiring of caseworkers came to an abrupt end. Moreover, SSEU's ability to shut down the welfare system during a strike decreased because SSEU members no longer carried out the key function of recertification. At the same time, however, caseloads worsened because reorganization did not proceed as quickly as planned and the welfare rolls continued to grow.

A second Lindsay administration policy contributing to the decline of SSEU was the development of a citywide labor relations program. Here, too, it was an SSEU initiative, the Schottland report, that set in motion the policies that eventually led to the end of SSEU as an independent union. One recommendation of the Schottland Commission was a study of city labor relations, which Mayor Wagner assigned to the Labor Management Institute of the American Arbitration Association. Their report, released in March 1966, became almost word-for-word the city's collective bargaining law passed in 1967.[49]

Under the new law, labor relations policies were no longer subject to the whim of the mayor. Beginning in 1968, a new governmental body, the Office of Collective Bargaining (OCB), with the now-familiar tripartite structure, oversaw city labor relations (see Chapter 6). OCB's rules diminished the bargaining power of small, independent unions like SSEU. Specifically, OCB ruled out the exceptional SSEU 1965 contract both because it permitted bargaining on such a wide scope of issues and it gave the union benefits in excess of those granted other Career and Salary Plan employees. As a result, SSEU was forced to reaffiliate in 1969 with its one-time nemesis, Local 371.

The move to reunite SSEU with Local 371 probably would not have occurred so quickly had it not been for increasingly hostile relations between welfare workers and welfare recipients. The welfare rights movement was in full force and recipients now carried their protests to welfare offices. At one time many SSEU members had worked closely with welfare activists, helping to organize recipient groups. Now the welfare rights movement was more independent; demonstrations at welfare centers became violent, often disrupting welfare work and even destroying several workplaces. In the 1968 union elections, SSEU members chose Marty Morgenstern as president. Although originally affiliated with the "activist" wing of the union, Morgenstern had been on leave during SSEU's 1967 hiatus. Rather than continue to debate "community activism," Morgenstern urged a new priority, reaffiliation with the labor movement.[50]

A large number of SSEU's most respected members, including Morgenstern, favored merger with DC 37's Local 371, a remarkable turn of events only three years after SSEU's bitter election campaign against the same local. With hindsight, SSEU leaders saw that the new collective bargaining law necessitated the merger; once the city signed a citywide contract with DC 37, it would be impossible for SSEU to sign a separate contract covering so-called "citywide" issues. Rather than explicitly acknowledge DC 37 dominance, advocates of reaffiliation argued instead that it was time for SSEU to rejoin the mainstream of the labor movement. The failure of the 1967 strike, compared with the unmitigated 1965 victory, demonstrated that SSEU could not stand alone. Moreover, Local 371 had changed since the days when union leaders were cozy with city officials. SSEU victory in the 1964 election had forced Local 371 to undertake a complete housecleaning, replacing all of the former officers and making Local 371 among the most militant in DC 37.[51]

Overall, DC 37 was portrayed as a progressive union that had organized clerical workers, hospital aides, and school lunchroom workers, groups previously outside the labor movement. Those who favored reaffiliation pointed out that AFSCME, DC 37's parent body, had led the 1968 Memphis sanitation strike and was the only union on the AFL-CIO Executive Council that regularly protested George Meany's support for the Vietnam War. If SSEU considered itself part of the movement for social change, should the union bypass a chance to affiliate with the union most successful in organizing women, blacks, and other oppressed groups?[52]

Opponents of a merger painted quite a different picture: DC 37 and AFSCME might be liberal compared with other unions, but they were still undemocratic in their structures. Unlike SSEU, control of DC 37 and AFSCME was concentrated in the hands of a few leaders who succeeded themselves in office for long periods of time. Victor Gotbaum, DC 37's executive director, the critics claimed, was handpicked from Chicago by Jerry Wurf to run the New York district council when Wurf became dissatisfied with Calogero Taibi, his original stand-in choice. Union members were not consulted in these changes; despite the presence of a district council president and elected delegate assembly, Gotbaum continued Wurf's tradition of single-handed domination of DC 37. Critics worried that if SSEU affiliated with such a union, it would lose control over its funds and be unable to initiate independent protests. SSEU might even find itself in receivership, takeover of local responsibility by higher union leadership, a step taken against more than 100 AFSCME locals in prior years.[53]

Some opponents of the Local 371 merger argued for affiliation with another union. Exploratory talks took place with a number of unions, including the Teamsters and Sleeping Car Porters, but finally settled on the Fur, Leather, and Machine Workers Union (FLM), a New York–based union with strong roots in the Jewish left-wing tradition. The FLM offered SSEU over $1 million to undertake a campaign to organize public sector workers, a self-acknowledged effort to compensate for

FLM membership in the fast-declining fur industry. FLM president Henry Foner actively courted SSEU, arguing that the FLM shared with them a commitment to active organizing that might rekindle union growth on a scale not seen since the 1930s. But the FLM offer could not gain support from SSEU's Affiliations Committee, comprising an even number of those favoring affiliation with Local 371 and those preferring to maintain an independent union.[54]

By 1968 attendance at mass membership meetings declined; many new SSEU members had experienced only the frustration of the 1967 strike and not the euphoria of the 1965 victory. Even so, subsequent debate about the merger proposals reaffirmed SSEU's commitment to democratic and inclusive decision making. Welfare center newsletters were full of pro- and antimerger letters. Leaflets appeared for each position and the Affiliations Committee itself prepared a newspaper-style report with lengthy statements for each of the three main positions (merger with DC 37, merger with FLM, and no merger).

In a summer 1968 referendum, immediate affiliation with DC 37 was voted down. The Affiliations Committee returned to negotiations with DC 37 and gained a written guarantee of a number of rights SSEU would hold after the merger: hiring and firing of union organizers; funding for an editorially independent publication; independent positions on such issues as the Vietnam War and the Office of Collective Bargaining (these were listed specifically); use of its strike fund for independent strikes; exemption from receivership for four years; and the ability to disaffiliate again after six months if SSEU was unhappy with the merger. Based on these concessions, in January 1969 SSEU members voted by a wide margin—5,207 to 1,390—to merge with Local 371.[55]

The years following the merger proved correct predictions made by both sides in the affiliation debate. SSEU–Local 371 remained an unusual local in DC 37, with relative autonomy, including its own office and newspaper. The union continued to press for client rights and a variety of left-wing causes not supported by either DC 37 or AFSCME. There has been no move on the part of the parent groups to quiet SSEU through the power of receivership.

But even though the tradition of independence remains, SSEU is no longer the trend setter it once was. The presence of SSEU within DC 37 has not caused other locals to emulate its model of participation, nor has it changed the power structure of DC 37, as some advocates of the merger claimed would happen. Nor have any significant policies suggested by SSEU been adopted by the district council as a whole. The relative isolation of SSEU was most clearly demonstrated during the

New York City fiscal crisis when SSEU–Local 371 put forward an alternative strategy for responding to work force cutbacks that received little attention from either DC 37 leadership or other DC 37 locals. The heritage of SSEU is not so much its present form as SSEU–Local 371, but rather its impact on the laws and institutions that today regulate public sector unions in New York City. These will be discussed in the following chapter.

6

District Council 37 and OCB

Consolidation of Collective Bargaining

Comparison is often made between 1930s federal labor relations legislation and the executive orders promulgated for New York City employees by Mayor Wagner. Indeed, the Interim Order of 1954 and the Executive Order of 1958 were both called "Little Wagner Acts" to denote their similarity to the original Wagner Act, the National Labor Relations Act of 1935, sponsored by Mayor Wagner's father, Senator Robert Wagner, Sr. A closer analogy actually exists between the mayoral executive orders and other legislation on the national level, specifically the 1932 Norris-La Guardia Act and Section 7(a) of the 1933 National Industrial Recovery Act, each of which affirmed the rights of workers to join unions but lacked procedures for the enforcement of those rights. Later the National Labor Relations Act provided the structure for private sector union recognition, just as the 1967 New York City Collective Bargaining Law superseded Mayor Wagner's 1954 Interim Order and Executive Order 49 of 1958.[1]

Although analogous in terms of development, changes in labor relations proceeded much faster in the private sector during the 1930s than they did in New York City thirty years later. Only six years elapsed between the Norris-La Guardia Act supporting the right of workers to join unions until 7 million industrial workers were brought under union contracts, whereas fifteen years went by between the Interim Order of 1954, promising that the city would negotiate with public unions, and the first contract for most city employees in 1969.

The rapidity with which unions were recognized in the private sector is explained by the unprecedented outbreak of strikes, sit-ins, and organizing that took place during the mid-1930s. As labor historian Irving Bernstein notes, "In 1934 everybody struck,"[2] prompting the U.S. government to develop a framework for collective bargaining before the labor force became more uncontrollable. Even though militancy grew steadily among New York City employees after 1954, it never reached the scale of the 1936–37 sit-down strikes. As described in Chapter 4, the road to collective bargaining in New York City was slower and more carefully contemplated by city management than the sudden shifts in national policy precipitated by the upheavals of the 1930s.

A second difference between Executive Order 49 and corresponding legislation for private sector workers concerns enforcement mechanisms. Unlike the national legislation, EO 49 did not set up an independent board to determine the means by which unions would be recognized. Instead, Mayor Wagner's Department of Labor determined which unions would be recognized and also bargained with those selected unions. Such a conflict of interest was quite purposeful: during most of Mayor Wagner's term in office he was able to maintain control over union certification, thereby keeping out unwanted unions and preventing any one union from becoming too powerful.

Then, during the summer of 1965, Mayor Wagner initiated a dramatic shift in labor relations strategy. Within two years, ad-hoc recognition of unions gave way to institutionalized certification under the Office of Collective Bargaining. The large number of contracts signed with small unions was consolidated into a few major contracts signed with large unions. As a result, New York City public sector labor relations came to resemble more closely the framework for industrial workers; a "Little Wagner Act" now actually existed for New York City employees.

Tripartism

Chapters 4 and 5 documented why Mayor Wagner's arbitrary rules no longer worked to management's advantage in 1965. Before then, Wagner's system had created a large number of fragmented unions, each competing for limited City Hall favors to be passed on to union members. But as unions changed their strategy from patronage seeking to demands for full-fledged contracts, they began to confront city management rather than curry its favor. Competition between unions now led to increased militancy as unions bid against one another to be the one most aggressively fighting for a favorable contract.

The major example of a union charting this new course was the Social Service Employees Union, which struck city welfare services in January 1965, winning significantly improved wages and benefits later that spring. Among city concessions in the subsequent contract was a promise to establish a commission to study the overall framework of New York City labor relations. Although SSEU had successfully circumvented the restrictive bargaining rules set up by Mayor Wagner, the union believed that formal endorsement of rights won by it would strengthen its own position as well as assist other unions. In July 1965 Mayor Wagner convened a panel under the auspices of the American Arbitration Association's Labor-Management Institute. This group's report, released the following year, became almost word-for-word the 1967 New York City Collective Bargaining Law.[3]

In a curious twist, SSEU whose 1965 contract set in motion events leading up to the 1967 law, later became the most vocal critic of the new labor relations system. In early 1965, SSEU supported the study of city labor relations out of a belief that unilateral and arbitrary mayoral policy kept all unions, including itself, at a disadvantage. But the Labor-Management Institute report boomeranged on SSEU by creating a framework in which the union lost its independent status. The final outcome held an irony for Mayor Wagner as well: one of the panel's recommendations was that collective bargaining be consolidated, with a single union representing all Career and Salary Plan employees. Mayor Wagner would have preferred that a favored union such as Teamster Local 237 gain that role. But by the time the procedures were set up for recognizing this single union, AFSCME DC 37 had won a series of dramatic representation elections, establishing itself as the dominant New York City public sector union.

The Tripartite Report, as the Labor-Management Institute Report was commonly called, stated four times in its three-page preamble that collective bargaining would mean "peaceful settlement of disputes."[4] According to the Tripartite Panel, the document itself was evidence that management could sit down with responsible union leaders and reach agreement on major issues, especially if they were assisted by experts like the Arbitration Association representatives. Future city labor relations would be overseen by an Office of Collective Bargaining, which like the Labor-Management panel would be tripartite in structure, with union, management, and "public" representation.

Despite the unanimity and goodwill expressed in the report, not all unions supported its conclusions. The most vocal critic, SSEU, argued that the proposed labor relations system would stifle the type of activity that enabled the union to gain concessions won in their 1965 contract, including ironically, the commissioning of the Tripartite Panel itself. SSEU articulated such concerns in a variety of forums, ranging from public hearings to picket lines, trying to convince other city employees that the new rules gave one union, District Council 37, an effective monopoly in negotiations. As the only union with citywide bargaining power, DC 37 could unilaterally set time, leave, and pension levels, which the city said had to be uniform for Career and Salary Plan employees. Separate and possibly better contracts such as those negotiated by SSEU would be impossible. Also, SSEU pointed out that Tripartite Panel rules prevented unions from bargaining over service levels, thus undercutting coalitions with city residents that SSEU tried to build. Finally, under the new setup, unions would be required to renounce the use of strikes, a promise that any union leader could easily circumvent, but possibly making it easier for the courts to impose antistrike penalties.[5]

SSEU president Judy Mage and DC 37 executive director Victor Gotbaum engaged in several acrimonious television debates, reportedly even more heated off camera. A DC 37 official countered SSEU's concern about the limited scope of bargaining by arguing that "the rights reserved to management in these procedures are thus no greater than those provided in the contracts of the strongest and most militant unions in private industry." DC 37 accused SSEU of opposing "majority unionism" and favoring instead "negotiation by temper tantrum" or the "political fix." According to DC 37, the Office of Collective Bargaining would provide a fair and equitable system of labor-management relations; by being outside City Hall, OCB would force the city to implement its contracts, a problem with previously negotiated agreements. Furthermore, once there was a citywide contract, there would be fewer so-called "vulture" unions and less need for costly, militant protests.[6]

SSEU formally signaled its opposition to OCB by refusing to join the Municipal Labor Committee (MLC), the organization set up by the Tripartite Panel as labor's mechanism for determining labor representation to OCB. Not suprisingly, Teamster Local 237 joined SSEU in opposing OCB since the plan would cement the leadership role of DC 37, their longtime rival. The Uniformed Sanitationmen's Association, another Teamster local, also opposed OCB, based on their dispute with DC 37 over representation of sanitation department employees, combined with fears that AFL-CIO unions might dominated city labor relations. Within a year, however, both Teamster locals dropped their boycott of the committee when it became evident that they could have more influence by participating in the tripartite arrangement. Of all major unions, SSEU alone continued the protest.[7]

The Taylor Law

At the same time New York City was revising its public labor relations system, Governor Nelson Rockefeller, in response to the January 1966 New York City transit strike, initiated a study of New York State public employees labor relations laws. Although not tripartite in structure, the state commission members shared the institutionalist perspective of the Tripartite Panel's public representatives. George Taylor, well-known mediator of steel industry disputes, chaired the panel and gave the resulting legislation its common name, the Taylor Law. He was joined by John Dunlop and Frederick Harbison, contributors to the seminal institutionalist work *Industrialism and Industrial Man*; David Cole, mediator of city transit disputes fifteen years earlier; and W. W. Bakke, a Yale economist. Taylor, Dunlop, and Cole all served on the advisory committee of the Labor-Management Institute (sponsoring body for the Tripartite Report), further underscoring the ideological similarity of the city and state commissions. The Taylor Report, completed in only nine weeks, was debated in the 1966 state legislature and adopted in April 1967.[8]

A major feature of the new law was its endorsement of union recognition for public workers employed by the state and its counties, cities, public authorities, and school districts. Six states (Connecticut, Delaware, Massachusetts, Michigan, Minnesota, and Wisconsin) had already passed similar legislation, but the Taylor Law received disproportionate national attention because of New York's size and the publicity given the city's transit and welfare workers' strikes. Administration of the new law was assigned to a new State Public Employee Relations Board (PERB), created as a close analog to the corresponding body for the private sector, the National Labor Relations Board. But PERB had the added duty of providing conciliatory services in the event of contract negotiation disputes, jurisdiction not granted to the NLRB. Technically, the Taylor Law superseded city efforts to regulate collective bargaining; localities could set up their own "mini-PERB's," like the proposed New York City Office of Collective Bargaining, only if the local legislation was "substantially equivalent" to the state law. But those framing the Taylor Law and the Tripartite Report shared such similar perspectives that they recommended almost identical criteria for the crucial issues of union recognition, scope of bargaining, and impasse resolution. Thus OCB, with its unusual tripartite structure, was approved as a mini-PERB.[9]

A second provision of the Taylor Law, however, conflicted with the Tripartite Report and, for a time in the summer of 1967, threatened to upset the formation of the Office of Collective Bargaining. The 1946 Condon-Wadlin Act penalized public sector strikers with a three-year pay freeze; the Taylor Law would permit unions to sign remunerative contracts after a strike, but subjected them to stiff fines, including two days' pay for every day on strike and suspension of dues checkoff rights. These provisions aroused impassioned opposition from New York City unions against what they now called the "RAT" (Rockefeller and Anthony Travia) Bill.

The proposed strike penalties also provoked a split within the otherwise compatible institutionalist public representation on the Tripartite Panel. Peter Seitz and Saul Wallen maintained that in preparing the Tripartite Report they fully expected the state to supplement it with penalties against public sector strikes. Vern Countryman and Phillip A. Carey responded that the Taylor Law undercut principles endorsed in the Tripartite Report because, as Carey explained, "without the strike weapon (and mind you, I hope that it will be used rarely and responsibly), you just do not have collective bargaining."[10] In the end, however, the Seitz and Wallen position prevailed; New York City unions were forced to accept the Taylor Law provisions as a condition for being recognized under OCB rules.

Office of Collective Bargaining

Mayoral Executive Order 52 and New York City Council Law 53-1967 formally created the Office of Collective Bargaining on January 1, 1968. Initial OCB jurisdiction covered 200,000 city employees in 200 different labor agreements and over 800 job titles. In subsequent years OCB's responsibility was extended to nonmayoral agencies, including the Health and Hospitals Corporation, the Board of Higher Education, the New York City Housing Authority, and the Off-Track Betting Corporation.

For some OCB functions, the National Labor Relations Board served as a model: both boards determine bargaining units, supervise representation elections, and certify bargaining agents. In other respects, however, OCB has extended responsibilities, including arbitration of contract and grievance disputes, areas not touched by the NLRB except in extraordinary circumstances. OCB also differs from the NLRB in its tripartite structure, with two labor representatives chosen by the Municipal Labor Committee, two city representatives chosen by the mayor, and three "impartial" representatives chosen with the joint consent of labor and city appointees. (The three impartial members also comprise the Board of Certification, which rules on union recognition.) One of the impartial representatives serves as chairperson and full-time OCB administrator. The NLRB, by contrast, consists exclusively of presidential appointees.[11]

Like the NLRB, OCB was given guidelines on how to carry out its decisions. On the matter of negotiations, for example, the New York City Collective Bargaining Law adopts NLRA language requiring that the employer "bargain collectively in good faith."[12] OCB can join negotiations at an impasse by mutual consent of both bargaining parties, or by consent of one party and the OCB director. Then, depending on the complexity of the issues involved, a panel of one to three members is chosen from a list of candidates acceptable to both parties. The panel holds hearings and makes recommendations based on the following criteria: comparison of compensation elsewhere; changes in the cost of living; and the general public interest. These recommendations can be appealed to the OCB director or to judicial review, but otherwise are binding.

An OCB review of the period 1972 through 1975 showed that impasses were infrequently invoked: only thirty-two cases went to impasse (about one in twelve of contracts negotiated under OCB jurisdiction) and only nine were appealed, of which one led to a strike (the case of firefighters described in Chapter 7). OCB chairman Arvid Anderson notes that over two-thirds of the impasse cases did not actually involve a conflict between union leaders and city representatives: a panel decision was requested only to legitimate to union members an agreement already worked out in private. In these cases, OCB impasse procedures resolved conflict between union members and union leaders, not the usually perceived opposition between unions and the city.[13]

Unlike Executive Order 49, the Consolidated Rules of OCB listed criteria for what were "appropriate units" for bargaining. They were to grant "public employees fullest freedom in exercising rights"; to be "in line with the community of interest of the employees"; to take "into account prior history of collective bargaining"; to "have the greatest positive effect on efficient operation of public service"; and to "facilitate bargaining with the appropriate government official."[14] In practice, however, OCB's aim was much simpler. The 1975 Annual Report states, "In the interest of strengthening stability in municipal labor relations," it is a "major objective" to reduce the number of bargaining units in the City.[15] Between 1968 and the end of 1975, the city bargaining units fell from over 400 to 114.[16] Even these numbers overstate the breadth of contracts, since the New York City Collective Bargaining Law, going beyond the requirements of the Taylor Law, limits the scope of bargaining on so-called citywide issues to the one union representing all mayoral agency employees, except for uniformed forces. As a result, most important issues are determined by the dominant union, District Council 37.

The scope of bargaining also was formulated more concretely than it had been under Executive Order 49. Instead of defining the scope simply as the "terms and conditions of employment," the Collective Bargaining Law followed the recommendation of the Labor-Management Institute Report in limiting negotiations to those issues that do not impinge on the "right of the City . . . to determine standards of service to be offered by its agencies; to determine the standards of selection for employment."[17] Furthermore, the report recommended that bargaining not limit city control over levels of service, hiring, firing, or the technology and organization of work. Such detailed restrictions, not leaving much in the way of working conditions open to negotiations, were a response to the 1965 SSEU contract, which had opened up bargaining to such issues as caseload, city hiring procedures (to assure adequate staffing), grants for clients, and the appointment of a commission to study labor relations, the Tripartite Panel.

Not surprisingly, many of OCB's first cases concerned the widened scope of bargaining demanded by SSEU. The union contested sixty-three major topics rejected by the city as not subjects for bargaining, losing the right to bargain for fifty of them. Under Executive Order 52, employees had the right to bargain over "questions concerning the practical impact" of managerial decisions. But in what became known as the "impact doctrine" the board defined it to include only "unreasonably excessive or unduly burdensome workload."[18]

Citywide Contract

Certification of DC 37 as the representative for all Career and Salary Plan employees enabled the union to continue the fast growth rate it enjoyed during the early 1960s. Not until 1971 did DC 37 membership growth level off; since then the union has had to rely on "intensive" organizing, increasing the number of dues-paying members in already existing locals. Although DC 37 reserved its strongest political push for trying to defeat the Taylor Law, the union also continued its identification with liberal causes, inviting Irish activist Bernadette Devlin to visit, supporting community involvement in hospital reorganization, supporting community control of schools, and along with national AFSCME, but few other unions, supporting the 1970 postal workers' strike. The union's career development program continued strong, helping over 1,500 members upgrade their jobs.[19]

In other ways, however, DC 37 had changed. Its base among city employees shifted away from the laborers and motor vehicle operators who once dominated DC 37, but accounted for less than 5,000 of the union's 80,000 membership in 1970. Now membership was largest in hospital workers Local 420 (11,000) and Board of Education Local 372 (8,000).[20]

With a secure membership base, DC 37's main concern turned from organizing workers to negotiating contracts, in particular, beginning in June 1967, the first citywide contract. That contract, finally signed in February 1969, was celebrated by the union as the culmination of twenty years of organizing efforts. At the outset of negotiations, the union demanded a $6,000 minimum annual salary for all full-time city workers (raising pay for some workers by over $1,000), a "twenty-year" pension similar to that won by transit workers after their 1966 strike, decreased workloads, and maintenance of a shortened summer workday. Most items were won by the union; significant concessions were made only on workload rules and the pension plan, for which the union settled on full pension rights after twenty-five years of employment.[21]

In the second citywide contract, for which bargaining began in February 1970, DC 37 attempted to improve the pension plan to the level now granted all other city employees: a full pension after twenty years of service, funded on an equal employer-employee contribution basis. An OCB mediator helped the union and the city reach an agreement in July giving the union the desired pensions, along with 10 percent night differential, retention of summer hours, an upgraded health plan, and a new dental plan, benefits won in exchange for lower wage increases.

Unexpected Strikes

Two strikes marred OCB's early record of peaceful labor settlements. The nine-day 1968 sanitation strike and the two-day 1971 drawbridge and sewage treatment strike each had entirely different origins, but both illustrate the fragility of accommodations reached under OCB rules.

A previous sanitation strike, the one-day 1960 work stoppage, affected city life little more than a major holiday or snowstorm. By contrast, the nine-day February 1968 strike presented the city with a major health problem. On both occasions the strikes came about when Uniformed Sanitationmen's Association president John DeLury was unable to sell a negotiated agreement to his membership. When the existing contract expired in January 1968 and USA delegates voted down the current city offer, the union initiated a work slowdown in which drivers refused to take out trucks with even the slightest safety defects. The city pressed into service the newly created Office of Collective Bargaining, quickly reaching a new settlement, which DeLury expected to present for ratification at a February 2 "victory" rally. But just as in 1960, DeLury was greeted by hecklers and pelted with eggs as he mounted the speaker's platform. The OCB proposal was voted down, as was DeLury's call for a strike vote by mail. Instead, USA members voted for an immediate strike and accosted DeLury as he was escorted from the hall by police.[22]

Technically, DeLury was correct in asking for a mail ballot: it was a prerequisite to obtaining International Brotherhood of Teamster support for the strike. But DeLury did not want a strike and he must have known that mail ballots traditionally are less likely to support a strike. (Voting in the presence of family, union members are less likely to vote for a strike; whereas when the vote takes places in the company of fellow workers, strike fervor sets the tone.) DeLury's good relations with city officials depended on his twenty-year record, blemished only by the short work stoppage in 1960, which could boast continued sanitation service. But as Michael Quill discovered in 1966, in order to appear militant, a union leader must occasionally lead a strike. In 1968 it was DeLury's turn to support a strike he did not want.

An additional complication of the strike was the presidential aspirations of Mayor John Linsday and Governor Nelson Rockefeller. Overall, Governor Rockefeller proved to have more political power, snubbing Mayor Lindsay's request for the National Guard to pick up the trash. Rockefeller also supported a state legislative act giving the state temporary control over the city sanitation department and mandating binding mediation on the city and the union. As a result, sanitation workers won a contract costing about $800 per worker, well over the January OCB recommendations.

This Rockefeller-imposed settlement was conditioned in part by his need to score political points over the mayor. But Rockefeller also received advice from city private sector labor leaders that DeLury was losing control of his membership. Unless sanitation workers received an offer greater than the OCB agreement, a second strike would occur in which DeLury would not be able to convince sanitationmen to return to work as they did on February 11. Mayor Lindsay, on the other hand, was under pressure from other municipal labor leaders not to give sanitation workers more than the mediator's January offer. If sanitation workers were able to strike with impunity, then these union leaders saw no reason why they should support Office of Collective Bargaining–mediated contract talks in return for a promise from the unions not to strike. In the end, most unions continued to work within the OCB framework, although the firefighter and police unions used the sanitation contract as a goal for their own reopened contract negotiations (see Chapter 7).

Unlike the sanitation strike, the drawbridge and sewage treatment strike of 1971 did not arise out of conflict between union members and union leaders. In fact, this strike differs from most recounted here in that it was initiated by union leaders. Prior to the walkout there was almost no warning of an impending strike in union newspapers. At issue was the contract signed by DC 37 in July 1970 granting city employees full twenty-year pensions. Under New York State law, pensions more generous than those given by the state to its own employees must be approved by the state legislature and the governor. Despite prior approval of similar pensions for other city employees as well as for the legislators themselves, the legislature and Governor Rockefeller balked at such a program for DC 37 and Local 237 members. The reason appeared to have been in part narrowly political, since DC 37 traditionally supported Democratic party candidates.[23]

But wider economic concerns were also involved. A state legislature fact-finding panel reported that the proposed pensions far exceeded anything offered to comparable groups of private sector employees. A recurring theme put forward by business leaders throughout the 1970s was that the combined pay and benefits for low-skilled city employees was out of line with comparable remuneration in the private sector. Indeed, there were few other clerical jobs that offered any kind of pension, not to mention the superior kind negotiated by DC 37. Such benefits were threatening to private sector employers of clerical labor, an influential group in New York City's financial and commercial economy.[24]

When the state legislature and the governor balked at approving the pensions, Victor Gotbaum threatened the city with what he called, in a widely quoted remark, "the fattest, sloppiest strike."[25] DC 37 and Local 237 planned the strike together, informing the city early of their plans; a full month before the strike city fire trucks practiced alternate routes in case the drawbridges were closed. Union members, however, were relatively uninvolved. According to DC 37 leaders, the purpose of the strike was to hit at "commuters and business communities because it was the suburban dwellers who were electing and supporting legislators who benefitted from New York City at every opportunity and provided for Rockefeller machinations."[26] In its execution the strike was not so selective: on June 7, 1971, drawbridge operators walked off the job, taking with them vital electrical parts, handles, fuses, and keys, thereby stranding 90,000 vehicles. The following day sewage treatment workers joined the protest, walking off the job and allowing 100 million gallons of untreated sewage to flow into the rivers. Other key but less critical employees were also brought into the protest, including incinerator operators, zookeepers, park workers and truck drivers for the school lunch program.

After two days the strike was called off, leaving the unions with a partial victory. Although DC 37 and Local 237 did not win their stated goal, legislative approval of the pension plan, the city agreed to lobby the state legislature the following year for retroactive approval of the pension. And should Albany still fail to grant the pensions, the city promised to compensate for lost pensions with equivalent benefits in the retirees' health plan, which did not need state approval. A few union members and one official in Local 237 received fines as a result of the strike, penalties that DC 37 executive director Gotbaum refused to fight on the grounds that "if you break the law you must pay for it."[27] He maintained that both unions had sufficient funds to cover any financial burden imposed on members. In fact, union leaders claimed that union membership increased significantly in the days following the strike. Over the long run, however, the pension dispute was lost. In 1973, instead of giving DC 37 and Local 237 the pensions promised two years earlier, the state legislature removed pensions from collective bargaining altogether, making the issue subject to state statutory control. Technically, the provision was temporary, but it has been extended through the mid-1980s.[28]

A New Understanding

Although the 1971 walkout was DC 37's only major strike, the protest came at a time when the union had already shifted to far less militant stands overall. The lack of membership participation in strike planning was symptomatic of a trend toward the decreased involvement of members in union policy. The 1971 strike notwithstanding, DC 37 policy was now oriented more toward accommodation with the city.

During its early years and through most of the 1960s, DC 37 was not reluctant to boast about gains won for members by the union, especially when they came as a result of the union's willingness to threaten militant action. Beginning in 1969, however, DC 37 leaders began to play down outcomes favorable to the union and to express concern for city finances. The union's newspaper noted the "real and serious" nature of the 1969 budget crisis,[29] while executive director Gotbaum pointed out during negotiations in 1970, "This union has never acted irresponsibly in presenting demands to the City; nor have we lacked sympathy for the Mayor's financial position."[30]

DC 37's new spirit of cooperation was best expressed in productivity deals, contractual arrangements in which management and the union hoped to increase employee output. Productivity deals had already been stipulated for many city workers, beginning with the transit contracts of the 1950s. The city brought Career and Salary Plan under productivity guidelines in 1971 as a way to maintain service while cutting back on employment. Joint city-union committees were empowered to enforce minimum work levels based on "prevailing work standards," aligning city employee productivity with that of workers in the private sector. Of greatest concern to the city was street maintenance, a highly visible city function, earmarked by the Bureau of the Budget for "deadly serious" attack in which the Department of Transportation was asked to "cut bodies" and "risk strikes."[31] The city wanted to change prohibitions on "out of title" work that prevented lower-paid workers from filling in at higher-paying tasks such as driving trucks. More repair crews were assigned to night shifts, undesirable from the point of view of workers, but 60 percent more efficient according to the city. Reports issued afterward concluded that the pothole quota was 90 percent met in 1971 and bettered by 9 percent in 1973, although much of the anticipated saving was lost because of the need to pay steamroller drivers at double-time rates and others a 10 percent nighttime differential.[32]

Other productivity programs simply meant more work effort by city employees. In the Parks Department, for example, workers were assigned to roving crews covering several parks, which allowed the department to eliminate 35 percent of the cleaning crews—and to significantly reduce park maintenance. Methadone and child guidance clinics were ordered to serve larger numbers of patients per day. Motor vehicle operators, asphalt deliverers, lead inspectors, and city record filers had their quotas increased. The city reported increased productivity through new technology when park maintenance and sign production equipment was mechanized. Other aspects of the productivity program targeted employment practices such as increased use of part-time help, subcontracting, and efforts to cut down on employee absenteeism. The latter involved a computer search to identify departments and individuals with high rates of absenteeism.[33]

Mayor Lindsay was careful to acknowledge that no productivity program would work without cooperation from municipal unions, noting that there was now a "new understanding on the part of municipal trade union leaders as to the accountability that is required to the public and the need for productivity changes and advances."[34] This "extraordinary response," as Mayor Lindsay called it, is particularly evident in the DC 37 newspaper, *Public Employee Press*, where members read how "it is time that we proclaimed to all who will listen that we want to produce to our fullest potential . . . we welcome an opportunity to sit down with the powers that be and discuss changes that will produce more meaningful work goals"; "without efficiency there can be no fiscal soundness. We need both, and the Union has a deep obligation to help achieve both."[35]

Such language contrasted markedly with union newspaper rhetoric of earlier years, which boasted: "DC 37 wage increases double private industry's"; "DC 37 can take pride in the fact that its wage packages have tended to average ten percent per year"; "We have just begun to fight"; "If we have to strike, we will strike, law or no law."[36] By 1971 union leaders no longer trumpeted such accomplishments, preferring instead to emphasize how much the union was willing to concede, even when the consequence was reduced services for city residents and, in some instances, greater work effort for union members.

During the 1970s, New York City labor relations settled into a framework quite different from that of any earlier period. Changes begun by Mayor Wagner in 1965 were now fully incorporated into the structure of the Office of Collective Bargaining. Responsibility for union recognition and bargaining rule making had been taken out of the mayor's office and given to the tripartite OCB.

In several respects, however, there is continuity between labor relations before and after OCB. In fact, there is even a suggestive comparison between DC 37, the union that benefited most from OCB, and the Transport Workers Union, the union that gained most from Mayor Wagner's 1950s approach to union recognition. Both the TWU and DC 37 were accepted by the city as bargaining agents in preference to more costly alternatives. Favored TWU leadership was chosen over more left-leaning, militant competitors, while DC 37 was considered a superior replacement to bargaining with small splinter unions such as SSEU. Notably, at the time of their respective certifications, neither the TWU nor DC 37 had actually led a full-scale strike. Finally, in terms of internal structure, DC 37 and the TWU were both unions controlled by well-ensconced individuals who faced little organized opposition within their respective unions.

The importance of this confluence in city strategy as well as the similarities of internal union structures will be considered in Chapters 9 and 10. First, however, Chapter 7 will examine the growth of the police and firefighter unions, organizations that provide interesting contrasts to the TWU and DC 37 in their maintenance of an undiminished level of militancy after recognition by the city and in their achievement of active participation by union members.

7
Police and Firefighters
First Organized, Last Recognized

Police and firefighters, along with street cleaners, have the longest tradition of labor organizing among New York City employees. But unlike the street cleaners, who were forced to start new unions every time the city defeated an organizing drive, the police and firefighters each maintained essentially the same union since the 1890s. As described in Chapter 2, the Patrolmen's Benevolent Association has been the dominant police union ever since it was founded in 1894, while the Uniformed Firemen's Association, officially founded in 1917, was a direct outgrowth of the Firemen's Mutual Benevolent Association, first organized in 1893.

In addition to their long heritage, the PBA and UFA also differ from other New York City public unions in terms of member participation. To be a police officer or firefighter is to be a member of the PBA or UFA; both unions sustained high membership rates even though membership was always voluntary and at times subject to disciplinary action by the department. In fact, police and firefighters were the last group of city employees to enjoy formal city endorsement of their right to join unions and bargain collectively for contracts.

A further differentiation of the PBA and UFA from other New York City public unions was the active rank-and-file role in union decision making. Here, too, there is an irony: although police and firefighters ultimately determined union policy, in no other unions were there as many conflicts between union members and union leaders. UFA and

PBA presidents consistently faced contentious elections and frequently were voted out of office, even after they had successfully led negotiations for a generous contract. A detailed look at the recent history of the PBA and UFA provides an instructive contrast to the histories of other New York City unions.

"The Wishes of the Lowest Echelon"

Chapter 2 recounted the history of the PBA through the end of World War II, when the police force returned to its full complement, bolstered by large numbers of new recruits. Two successive elections for PBA president pitted Raymond Donovan, who wanted the PBA to openly declare itself a labor union, against John Carton, who preferred the old association model without ties to organized labor. Although Carton won and began a long incumbency, lasting from 1947 until 1958, the presence of activists like Donovan eventually pushed the PBA toward more militant stands.

In 1951 Donovan directly threatened the PBA by joining the United Patrolmen's Association, a CIO affiliate that Transport Worker Union head Michael Quill had long wanted to organize in the Police Department. At the time the PBA once again suffered from its periodic internal disarray. When union leaders were charged with pocketing ticket and journal sales from PBA dances, Carton responded by expelling the four members who made the allegations. When the United Patrolmen's Association membership reached 3,200, out of 25,000 police, enough to represent a serious challenge to Carton's leadership, police commissioner George Monoghan stepped in to end the threat. To prevent any future charge of embezzlement, he banned dance fund raisers. To take care of the CIO threat, he announced that any police officer joining a union would be disciplined: the United Patrolmen's Association was considered a union, while the PBA was not. Clearly the definition was one of convenience; despite its formal existence as an "association," the PBA acted like a union in defending the interest of police.[1]

Contemporary observers interpreted Commissioner Monoghan's preference for Carton and the PBA, over Donovan and the CIO, as a means to keep the police from adopting the confrontationist stance increasingly prevalent in the labor movement, especially in CIO unions. By contrast, Carton had become adept at accommodation. As one PBA leader observed, Carton's greatest asset "was his ability to ingratiate himself with the commissioner and the mayor."[2] Carton himself wrote in the association newspaper at the time of the CIO threat that it was necessary for him to maintain friendly relations with the commissioner because otherwise "we would have to get tough with the very people who are trying to raise the money to pay us a salary increase."[3] Under Carton's leadership, police won pay increases totaling more than 50 percent over a ten-year period; in return, Carton kept police out of the activist labor movement.[4]

By 1958 a number of trends converged to make it more difficult for Carton to operate with what Mayor Wagner's labor negotiator called Carton's system of "petition, pressure, and political involvement."[5] PBA members noticed that other city workers were now organized into unions, engaging in public protests and winning substantial pay improvements. The sanitation workers even signed a contract with the city, a success Carton never achieved. The final blow to Carton's authority came with the appointment of a new police commissioner, Stephen Kennedy, a man who did not believe in trading favors with the PBA, thus leaving Carton without his major source of power. Now perceived by his members as ineffective, Carton was voted out of office, primarily by younger police officers who wanted a more militant PBA, a direction advocated by Carton's replacement, John Cassese, PBA president from 1958 until 1969.[6]

Not surprisingly, Commissioner Kennedy, with his antagonism toward employee representation, and John Cassese, elected to give the PBA a more militant outlook, were on a collision course. However, only a few days after Cassese's election victory, their relationship was complicated by the entrance of a third party: the Teamsters announced a campaign to organize a new police union. Jimmy Hoffa, national Teamster president, summed up the situation: "The only thing New Yorkers liked less than Jimmy Hoffa was death and taxes."[7] Cassese used the threat of the Teamster union to boost his case as an alternative to what he called the "efforts of outside unions," which would bring the police force to the "very brink of chaos."[8]

Mayor Wagner agreed and supported the PBA in a court case that granted the association the right to dues checkoff already enjoyed by other city labor groups. Wagner's original order concerning dues checkoff contained a clause specifically excluding police. But it was circumvented, as in the 1951 anti-TWU deal, by declaring the PBA to be an association, not a union. With dues checkoff, Cassese obtained 95 percent participation from eligible Police Department employees, an extremely high membership rate for a union without mandatory membership, thus ending the possibility of competition from the Teamsters. Dues checkoff also freed PBA leadership from the time-consuming task of collecting dues from members who often worked various shifts and thus were difficult to contact.[9]

Within the Police Department itself, Cassese continued to encounter stiff opposition to the PBA from Commissioner Kennedy, who argued, "How in the name of all that's holy can you run a department on the wishes of the lowest echelon?"[10] Kennedy accused the PBA of using "Marxist rhetoric"[11] and installed secret tape recorders in squad cars to find out who was using the radio to broadcast anti-Kennedy remarks. However, the issue that most rankled PBA members was Commissioner Kennedy's crackdown on moonlighting. When fines were imposed on officers caught with second jobs, the PBA ousted Kennedy from his honorary membership in the association and offered to pay the fines of penalized members. Kennedy responded by ceremonially tearing up his PBA card and threatening to dismiss anyone who accepted PBA funds to pay their fines. The association then escalated what had been a war of words to a ticket-writing slowdown, cutting parking violations by 20 percent and prompting Kennedy to penalize the police force with increased, undesirable foot patrol duty. Although a moderate protest by the standards of later years, the ticket-writing slowdown signaled a change in PBA policy. The days were over when the police commissioner could claim his "door was always open";[12] no longer could he sidetrack protests by meeting individually with over 200 police officers per year.[13]

Kennedy won the battle over moonlighting, but in 1961 the PBA celebrated his resignation, a move prompted by Mayor Wagner's fear of a potential election rival. The new commissioner, Michael Murphy, took a much more conciliatory attitude toward the PBA, initiating a long sought after grievance procedure. For the first time police could formally appeal complaints to an authority outside the department. The PBA won a nearly 15 percent pay increase, compensating for stagnant wages of previous years, but nonetheless the largest pay increase won by police under either the Wagner or Lindsay administrations.[14]

In March 1964 Mayor Wagner extended Executive Order 49 to cover the Police Department. The proclamation did not change relations between the PBA and the department significantly; in fact, in an interview ten years later, Commissioner Murphy could not even remember how or when it was introduced. But the new order formalized what had been de facto collective bargaining between the PBA and the city for the previous five years. The city was now legally bound to deal exclusively with the PBA. And in order to keep its certification as the police bargaining agent, the PBA was committed not to affiliate with any labor organizations with members outside of the police department.[15]

"Will I Die for $2.43?"

As in the PBA, an influx of young recruits following World War II
pushed the Uniformed Firefighters Association toward more militant tactics. Chapter 2 described the 1945 censure of UFA president
Vincent J. Kane for his too cozy relationship with the fire commissioner. Kane's successors moved the union steadily away from such
currying of favor, culminating in an unprecedented public demonstration. The issue was a new work schedule. Firefighters, having finally eliminated twenty-four-hour shifts, now demanded a forty-
hour work week. When the UFA took their case to the public and
called a demonstration outside City Hall, fire commissioner Edward
F. Cavanagh expressed shock at "wanton attacks on the Mayor," in
slogans such as "Talk is cheap to city officials"; "Hey, Wagner will I
die for $2.43?" and "Prove to us you are not afraid." [16] Cavanagh
ordered the department to study films of the demonstration so he
could dismiss those in what he termed the "lunatic fringe." [17]

Protests escalated further in 1960 when scuffles broke out in a
picket line. A fire battalion chief had threatened to punish UFA leaders because they wore parts of their uniform during the demonstration. Two hundred firefighters trying to break through police lines to
enter City Hall were stopped only when the labor commissioner appeared and agreed to negotiate a compromise. [18] In 1962, the UFA began daily picketing of City Hall, ending it because of the Cuban mis-
sile crisis and a city offer to renegotiate its previous "final" offer.
Thus, by the early 1960s, the UFA joined the PBA in moving away from
an accommodationist stance with their supervisors and was prepared to engage in protests in order to achieve its goals. [19]

Intra-union Conflict

Contrary to the experience of other New York City unions, the PBA
and UFA continued their militant tactics into the 1970s. In the TWU,
USA, and DC 37, for example, bargaining became a relatively peaceful
process during which union leadership consolidated its power. In
both the PBA and UFA, however, continued conflict between union
presidents, union delegates, and rank-and-file members prevented
the centralization of power in the hands of ensconced union leaders.
As a result, contract bargaining between 1966 and 1973 was so tu-

multuous that by the time an agreement was reached, it was already time to negotiate the next contract. Two issues predominated: (1) parity, the established pay ratios among uniformed employees; and (2) the reintroduction by the city of schedule changes long opposed by police and firefighters.

In the first such contract in 1966, the UFA and PBA combined forces to negotiate a $375 wage increase over two years. The PBA delegates assembly accepted the settlement, but the UFA membership overruled their advisory negotiating committee and voted down the contract at a mass meeting by a three-to-two margin. Negotiations resumed, only to be disrupted by a contract signed in February 1967 with sanitation workers, granting them a wage increase of $450, or $75 more than the offer previously accepted by police. According to UFA and PBA leaders, city labor commissioner Herbert Haber had promised during the fall 1966 negotiations that no other city employees would receive more than the tentatively accepted settlement. UFA and PBA union leaders, who had recommended the $375 contract, were now embarrassed by the sanitation agreement and demanded that the city reopen police and firefighter negotiations. The city agreed to send the dispute to a nonbinding fact-finding commission. The following month it recommended that workers give up two days of vacation leave in return for longevity pay hikes of $100 per ten years of service, thus boosting the overall contract nearer to the amount received by sanitation workers.[20]

UFA and PBA members responded angrily to the report, especially new recruits, who would not receive any wage increases. At a membership meeting attended by 6,000 firefighters, the UFA voted to take a mail ballot strike vote. While the UFA counted ballots, the PBA picketed City Hall. The city then increased its offer: if the unions would agree to a twenty-seven-month contract (instead of twenty-four months), the city would raise wages and add an extra day of vacation leave. This contract was accepted by union leaders and members. The city claimed the contract package, totaling over $600 per worker, did not represent an increase over the previous offer because the contract period had been extended. But the almost 50 percent increase in the city's pay offer in exchange for only a 12.5 percent increase in the contract's duration was an obvious union victory.[21]

Even with the extended contract, almost immediately it was time to negotiate another contract. Once again, the sanitation contract set the standard, this one raising wages by $800 following the February 1968 strike. After rejecting a $700 offer in July, PBA and UFA leaders agreed to a $1,367 contract offer in October. During the 1966 negotiations, firefighter rank-and-filers forced negotiators back to the bargaining table; this time PBA delegates took the lead by voting down the proposed contract 160 to 140. An Associated press poll showed that the membership opposed the contract by a larger margin. PBA president Cassese then proposed that the union accept Mayor Lindsay's plan for impartial arbitration. But again the delegates refused to go along, instead preparing for protests to begin immediately.[22]

The PBA response took place in two stages, first a slowdown in which police scrupulously reported all street defects, including potholes and broken curbs, and refused to issue traffic citations or drive vehicles with the slightest safety defects. Second, a sickout was coordinated among PBA members, in which five groups took turns reporting sick on a different day of the week. Absenteeism rose to 20 percent for the week of October 20. Felony arrests fell 20 percent and the number of towed cars was off by 25 percent. On October 24, the city obtained a supreme court injunction against the slowdown and sickout and Cassese announced that, as police, "we cannot in good conscience violate the law." PBA members went back to work.[23]

Meanwhile the UFA initiated its own slowdown in which members refused to do nonemergency duties during the week of October 24. UFA leaders urged a membership mail ballot on the contract. UFA delegates initially disagreed and voted a full strike in two weeks if no new agreement could be reached. But after several more meetings, a mail ballot was narrowly approved. Voting, conducted in mid-November, resulted in 70 percent ratification of the contract.[24]

PBA members still did not want to settle; the same contract accepted by firefighters was rejected by a three-to-one margin, also in a mail ballot. The city and the union went back to the bargaining table, finally reaching a settlement agreeable to PBA rank-and-filers in early 1969. It included two new key items: a 5 percent night pay differential and a new parity clause. The meaning of "parity" in the contract would be debated by the PBA and the city for the next three years; it served to make the 1969 contract, intended to be a two-year settlement, a short-lived respite in city-union conflict.[25]

Squaring the Trapezoid

Parity between New York City's uniformed service workers dates back to the 1930s, when a pattern was established in which firefighters and police received equal base pay, while sanitation workers received 90 percent of that amount. In a similar manner, supervisors in each department earned salaries a set percentage above base pay for patrolmen and nonofficer firefighters. Police sergeants traditionally earned more than patrolmen by a ratio of 3.5 to 3.0, while fire lieutenants received 3.9 to 3.0 more than firefighters.[26]

For a number of reasons, actual take-home pay did not always correspond to the parity ratios. Exact comparison between police and firefighters was difficult because firefighters worked a longer work week and were paid overtime at a different rate. Sanitation workers often had higher paychecks because they were frequently called in for emergency snow removal. And finally, benefits varied between the three groups. Despite such discrepancies, the underlying ratios guaranteed that higher status was associated at least with higher base pay.

The starting point for the 1969–72 parity dispute was an inconsistency built into the pay ratio for police and fire officers that soon embroiled all city employees with salaries set by parity. In 1967 police sergeants demanded that their parity ratio be raised from 3.5–3.0 to 3.9–3.0 because they occupied a supervisory position equivalent to fire lieutenants, who already received the 3.9-to–3.0 ratio. Some observers attribute the claim as much to concern about status as pay. The dispute was sent to an OCB impasse panel chaired by David Cole, mediator for transit disputes twenty years earlier. In the midst of the 1968 PBA contract dispute, the panel recommended a compromise parity of 3.7 to 3.0, acceptable to the sergeants and the city.

But the city's contract with the PBA called for a 3.5–to–3.0 ratio, which the city agreed to honor. City labor commissioner Haber claimed that PBA president Cassese promised not to invoke the parity clause any further should the sergeants receive another pay raise. Cassese remembers no such agreement.[27] In any case, the sergeants, who were still behind the fire lieutenants, brought the city before another OCB impasse panel, chaired by another former transit mediator, Theodore Kheel. This time they won the 3.9–to–3.0 parity, thus exacerbating the city's mutually exclusive parity scheme, still committed to a 3.5–to–3.0 ratio for patrolmen. If put into practice, parity would cause wages to spiral indefinitely as each group demanded its contractually based ratio. Furthermore, the ratchet effect applied to fire lieutenants and firefighters, since their wages were also tied to the parity formula.

In theory the parity inconsistency could lead to a wage spiral upward or downward. But because of the city's initial unwillingness to negotiate out of a situation that neither side considered tenable, parity became a mechanism for the rank and file to fight for wage increases. In March 1970, the city attempted to fight the PBA's parity clause. Immediately, the union sent out a referendum on a possible job action, which, despite another court injunction, gained approval from over 70 percent of the police force. In a series of stormy meetings the delegate assembly then debated whether to call a strike or carry their case to the courts. After first putting the city on three days' notice before a job action would begin, the assembly reversed itself and postponed any action pending a court ruling. Obtaining a decision from the courts proved difficult. The state supreme court ruled in favor of the PBA, only to be overruled on city appeal by the appellate division. Finally, in January 1971, in the middle of negotiations for a new police contract, the court of appeals sent the case back to a lower court for new hearings.

Escalating Protest

The court decision set in motion a series of protests, first by police and then later by firefighters, on a scale not yet experienced in New York City. After learning about the ruling, PBA members did not wait for a delegate assembly vote. Beginning with the 4:00 P.M. shift, a wildcat sickout quickly spread throughout the city. According to one patrolman, "Nobody was leading it; nobody could have stopped it." [28] Department supervisors and union delegates rushed to the Bronx and Brooklyn precincts where the protest began, but by the time they arrived, the call to protest had spread over patrol car radios. Even among those who stayed on duty there was an informal slowdown, described by one policeman as follows: "I'm going around like the dumb cop I'm supposed to be. I can't ignore crime, but I'm not going out of my way to find it." [29]

The sickout began to have an effect the following day. The arrest rate fell dramatically, illegal parking increased, and according to some reports, there were delays in responses to emergency calls. Although some feared major riots, they were unlikely to occur because police who called in sick frequently stayed near their precinct stations, saying they would work if major disorder ensued. The PBA received support from welfare and transit police: on the third day of the sickout, over 50 percent of the guards in the Department of Social Services refused to report for work and large numbers of transit police—estimates range from 25 percent by the Transit Authority to 80 percent by the union—called in sick. On the fourth day of the sickout, the PBA delegate assembly voted 229 to 112 to have police return to work. PBA lawyers advised the assembly that they were likely to win the parity dispute after further court appeals.[30]

Such counsel proved correct when a second supreme court hearing awarded parity to the PBA. The court was not convinced by city arguments that the 1969 contractual parity clause was invalid because the union had not lived up to its no-protest obligations under the contract. Realizing the hopelessness of their case, the city elected not to appeal a second time and to settle out of court. Reaching an agreement took another year and a half, so by the time a pact was signed it required the resolution of a number of new issues, including the 1972 contract. It also meant coming to terms with all the other groups of uniformed workers in order to end the lock-step of parity. A settlement of over $2,000 in pay raises for police and firefighters finally ended the dispute in July 1972.

That agreement also resolved the issue of scheduling, a matter dormant when the parity dispute first arose, but once again at issue during the 1969 mayoral campaign. John Lindsay proposed a "costless" way of fighting crime: the fourth platoon, an extra shift during the evening and nighttime high-crime hours. Police officers vigorously opposed the plan because it would require additional time away from their families. Suddenly the PBA found itself on the wrong side of the crime issue. No longer could they count on the pro-police proclivity of the state legislature; intensive PBA lobbying proved futile and the legislature repealed the 1911 law mandating the three-platoon system. The union tried to stop the fourth platoon in the courts, but their case was weak, limited to an argument that the proposed duty chart changes violated their contract. On April 28, 1969, the supreme court ruled the fourth platoon could be implemented immediately.[31]

Both PBA president Cassese and the Police Department were under pressure to resolve the matter quickly. Cassese was losing his stronghold on the union presidency, and his chief aide, Norman Frank, was under investigation for alleged misdealings involving the Health and Welfare Fund. (Later investigations revealed that Frank paid himself as a broker and investment counselor for the fund.)[32] Police commissioner Leary was afraid that unless the issue was settled quickly, Cassese would be replaced by a PBA president elected specifically to prevent the fourth platoon.

However, time was short. Rumors spread among police about a wildcat action. Once it occurred, neither Cassese nor Leary would be able to compromise easily. In this charged atmosphere, the two worked out a settlement in which the fourth platoon would be staffed by volunteers, a proposal previously rejected by the city because "volunteers can always unvolunteer." But now the PBA agreed to help recruit police to the fourth platoon, and with the 5 percent night pay differential as inducement, the PBA provided sufficient volunteers. After all the fanfare, the fourth platoon lived a short and inconsequential life. Despite Lindsay's election slogans, it appeared to do little to decrease crime. In 1970, when volunteers dropped off, the platoon was allowed to fade away.[33]

Just prior to the 1971 police sickout firefighters conducted one of their own. It was prompted not by the parity dispute, but by the expiration of their contract. Beginning in 1971, UFA bylaws required a job action if no contract was signed. So, at the end of December 1970, when the union and the city were still far from agreement, the union received membership ratification of a work slowdown to begin January 1, during which only emergency services would be performed. The firefighters officer association (UFOA) agreed to help the UFA by asking officers not to report violations of department rules by UFA members. Soon the department was far behind on inspections and repairs. The city obtained a court restraining order against the slowdown, imposing fines on the union if it continued. As a result, UFA president Michael Maye recommended calling off the slowdown and accepting a city offer to go to mediation.[34]

When negotiations stalled again in April, the union called another slowdown. This time fire trucks were to follow department rules by obeying all traffic laws, including stop signs and stoplights. One week after the slowdown began, union leadership hailed as a victory a contract proposal from an OCB arbitrator. UFA membership, however, was less pleased; they voted down the contract because it delayed the initial wage hike until July and it rearranged the duty chart so that night duties would be less widely spread. In June Mayor Lindsay further complicated negotiations by announcing a productivity program, including cutbacks in the fire department. UFA president Maye now responded, "If one firefighter is laid off, we will consider the entire force laid off."[35] A second November city productivity program, which would increase firefighter rotations during peak hours, caused UFA members to petition for a mass membership meeting, where they voted to begin an immediate slowdown and sickout.

The slowdown was conducted in a manner similar to the January protest. Firefighters flooded the department with hundreds of grievances daily, far more than the usual one or two. Workers protested insufficient rest periods between calls, lack of time to perform inspections, and trucks with worn tires, or lacking protective devices against street harassment. The sickout had even greater impact. By

November, over 200 new sick claims were filed daily. Initially the department granted most such claims, but as the work force became depleted, physicians were called in to staff seven-day-a-week clinics to check on everyone claiming to be ill. By the end of the month, only 15 percent of those filing claims were granted sick leave.[36]

In mid-December UFA president Michael Maye called a membership meeting to vote on a new contract settlement. The union won a major demand, increase in the night pay differential from 5 percent to 10 percent. But other terms, including city reorganization of some fire companies, were less favorable. UFA members complained that they were being asked to vote without seeing a full written copy of the contract. In a heated atmosphere punctuated by fistfights, the contract was ratified by a narrow 5,274 to 3,897 margin.[37]

When the city signed this firefighter contract in December 1971, PBA negotiations were still stalled. As in firefighter bargaining, the city tried to tie wage increases to productivity changes and personnel cutbacks. Police were asked to accept a new duty chart and one-man patrol cars. The delegate assembly twice rejected contract offers with these clauses. In June PBA president Ed Kiernan narrowly won reelection. In May the delegates had finally accepted a contract including the new duty chart, but without one-man patrol cars. PBA members first rejected the contract, but then accepted it after intense lobbying by Kiernan.[38]

A few days later the PBA and the city settled the parity dispute with lump-sum payments of over $2,000. For the first time in several years, there were no outstanding formal disputes between the PBA and the city. Even so, peaceful labor relations once again proved ephemeral; the contract had taken so long to negotiate that it was due to expire in two months. Bargaining began immediately for the succeeding contract.

"Twelve Feet Tall"

While the PBA went back to the bargaining table, attention shifted to the firefighters, who, in 1973, called their first-ever full-scale strike. At the time observers were surprised by the degree of militancy among firefighters, since they had just signed a favorable contract and won the substantial parity settlement. Still, UFA members voted to oust president Michael Maye in favor of Richard Vizzini, who urged even more aggressive representation of firefighter interests. Following his campaign promises, Vizzini led UFA negotiators out of talks that September and called for a strike authorization vote. Mediation efforts failed and the union rejected a last-minute city offer on the grounds that it included the productivity plan rejected two months earlier.[39]

On November 6, between 8:30 A.M. and 2:00 P.M., almost all New York City firefighters walked off their jobs. Partial service was provided by fire officers who nonetheless declared themselves in support of the strike. One Brooklyn firefighter stated proudly, "When I walked out, I felt twelve feet tall and I thought we had a real union."[40] The strike ended when supreme court justice Sidney Fine threatened to impose $1 million fines per day against the union and to issue contempt citations against each individual striker. UFA leaders now agreed to a city proposal to submit the dispute to arbitration.

One week later the impasse panel recommended a one-year contract with $700 wage increases for the first six months and $250 more after the next six months. The city refused to accept the proposal on the grounds that the initial increase was too high and that a longer contract was needed. They countered with a thirty-month contract offer with $200 paid retroactively to the expiration of the old contract and $600 in each of the succeeding two years beginning January 1974. The union suggested a $2,000 one-year contract. On November 14 the two parties compromised on a $1,450 contract lasting two years, with $750 paid the first year and $700 the next year, for an average wage increase of 11 percent.[41]

The willingness of the union to settle so quickly and the ability of the city to reject the panel recommendations was influenced by a rumor that spread soon after the strike: the UFA membership mail ballot had been against a strike, even though the union leadership called it "overwhelmingly" in favor. The ballots had been counted by the Honest Ballot Association, which did not report the discrepancy between the ballot results and UFA statements. A reporter from radio station WNEW received what he termed a "confidential" tip, prompting an investigation by the district attorney's office. On November 16 the Honest Ballot Association revealed that the vote indeed had been 4,119 to 3,827 against a strike.[42]

UFA president Vizzini readily conceded that he had misrepresented the vote. His counsel explained, "He lied for the benefit of the union to maintain his position in bargaining."[43] In terms of procedure, Vizzini defended his actions by arguing that city intransigence changed the situation after the membership vote. In fact, the day before the strike, members gave a unanimous voice vote approval to the strike. According to a newspaper survey of firefighters, there was little anger at Vizzini and no call for his resignation. The strongest criticism came from others in the labor movement. Victor Gotbaum assailed Vizzini for committing "one of the most destructive acts in recent memory for a trade unionist."[44]

The State Labor Relations Board investigated the case, finally concluding that there had never been an analogous situation; nothing in the law required union members to endorse a strike before union leaders could call one. As will be discussed in Chapter 10, the board overlooked the many situations when union members voted to strike, only to be overruled by union leaders. The city never protested such a situation as a failure to follow democratic decision making. There were, of course, laws against the strike itself: union leaders and individual strikers were subject to criminal penalties as well as the more commonly enforced Taylor Law. In addition, fire commissioner John T. O'Hagan announced new procedures; to "reemphasize discipline," promotions were suspended and dissident firefighters were reassigned to new companies.[45]

The city's threat to enforce stiff penalties eased when contract concessions were gained from the union. On December 4 Vizzini and three other UFA officers pleaded guilty to Taylor Law violations. They promised supreme court justice Fine to do all in their power to obtain member compliance with the court's no-strike injunction and to support a bill before the state legislature creating binding impasse procedures for future contract negotiations. In return, Justice Fine postponed a decision on the city's request for $1 million Taylor Law penalties and loss of dues checkoff for two years. In January, after Commissioner O'Hagan signaled a "return to normalcy" and lifted the suspension of promotions, Justice Fine announced the Taylor Law penalties. The union was to be assessed $650,000. In return for their "guilty" plea, UFA officers received no personal penalties. Other criminal indictments against them remained outstanding until May. Again, the officers pleaded guilty and received three-year probationary sentences in return for a three-year no-strike pledge.[46]

When police and firefighters went out on strike during the 1970s, every group of city workers had now been involved in a work stoppage; police and firefighters were no longer exceptions. As with other city employees, the reasons for the sudden upsurge in police and firefighter militancy are unclear. Statements by workers themselves suggest that effective protest by other groups and city service recipients, combined with a feeling of declining respect, caused police and firefighters to overcome the stricture that public safety workers could not strike. For police in particular, the first work stoppage was significant because it involved a technical violation of the law. During the 1968 sickout, PBA president Cassese called police back to work once a court injunction was issued; by 1971 police were willing to engage in a full-scale sickout.

PBA and UFA contract negotiations during the early 1970s contrast with the situation of other city unions. At a time when other city workers were forced to accept less advantageous contracts and productivity deals, the police and firefighter unions won large pay increases and continued to defeat most city demands for work-rule changes. Why were the UFA and PBA so different?

One school of thought puts blame on city negotiators, in particular, their ineptness in tolerating conflicting parity rules, thus sending the city on an upward wage spiral.[47] Yet while the parity dispute ultimately cost the city dearly, the length of time it remained in dispute did not result from lack of recognition of the ratchet effect. Agreement could not be reached because city officials took a rigid stance against pay increases, thus provoking continuous pressure by rank-and-filers on their union leaders not to settle the parity paradox by compromising wages and not to agree to new work rules.

With the benefit of a long-term historical perspective we can see that the PBA and UFA members have a tradition of being actively involved in union negotiations, ready to disagree with settlements reached by union negotiators. In this atmosphere of distrust, PBA and UFA officials were continuously in jeopardy of being voted out of office, a condition one might think would lead to a divided and thus weakened union. But clearly the reverse was true: during the period 1966 through 1972, these disputative unions were able to obtain remuneration superior to that gained by other unions. And at the same time, the PBA and UFA protected work rules that were being compromised by other unions in productivity bargaining.

A second anomaly in the situation of the PBA and UFA is the role of city rules for collective bargaining. As noted earlier, these unions were the last to be recognized for the purposes for bargaining, yet they are the oldest and most consistently effective of all New York City public unions. The major impact of city policy on the PBA and UFA was to prevent them from allying with the rest of the labor movement. Repeatedly city officials were willing to give preference to these two unions over unions affiliated with other organized groups of workers. One wonders how much stronger, and perhaps less elitist, the PBA and UFA might have been had they been allowed to cooperate with other unions. Chapters 9 and 10 will explore such issues. Chapter 11 will then summarize events after 1973 during the New York City fiscal crisis, when the police and firefighter unions continued to be the most contentious—and most successful—of all city unions, but even so were able only partially to contain erosion of contract gains won during prior years.

8

United Federation of Teachers

The Making of a Bureaucracy

As discussed in chapter 2, Henry Linville's Teachers Union, formed in 1913, quickly became the largest and most influential local in the American Federation of Teachers. Even so, the New York group was beset by charges of "un-American" influence and never attracted more than 5 percent of the city's teachers. A bitter split in 1935 between a CIO faction (which kept the name Teachers Union) and an ardently anti-Communist AFL group (renamed the Teachers Guild) sapped organizing energies of both unions. The post–World War II teachers strike wave in other U.S. cities never took hold in New York; the Teachers Guild and Teachers Union continued to oppose each other as much as they did the Board of Education. During the subsequent anti-communist hysteria, the Board of Education banned the Teachers Union from negotiating meetings and fired hundreds of its members from their jobs, leaving the weak 1,800-member Teachers Guild as the only voice for New York City teachers.[1]

Discontent under the Surface

Yet, as for other groups of city employees, the 1950s were deceptively silent in terms of workplace unrest. Even in the absence of successful union organizing, protests took place throughout the decade. Most involved high school teachers, for whom a major source of discontent was 1947 "single salary" state legislation. Its intent was to alleviate the shortage of elementary schoolteachers by raising their pay. But by replacing an automatic differential for high school teachers with a bonus for those with graduate degrees, high school pay fell on a relative basis. Between 1929 and 1950, raises for high school teachers covered only half the increased cost of living; during the same period, average U.S. wages rose more than 50 percent after taking inflation into account.[2]

High school teacher unrest boiled over in two lengthy protests during the 1950s: a fifteen-month boycott of all extracurricular activities beginning in 1950, followed by a four-year boycott beginning in 1954. Lacking leadership from either a strong Teachers Guild or Teachers Union, teachers organized themselves under the auspices of the High School Teachers Association (HSTA), a group founded in 1900 but largely moribund until the 1950s. Students, fearful that the boycott would force cancellation of prom night, rallied to the defense of teachers with large protest rallies, prompting Mayor O'Dwyer to call for an investigation of "subversive" powers behind the student revolt. The first boycott ended when the board obtained a court order backing their right to dismiss teachers who did not follow principals' orders to do after-school work. Rather than risk a confrontation on this decision, the HSTA called off the protest in return for a small salary increase and extra pay for sports coaches, who had joined the protest through their own separate organization.[3]

Still upset about their low pay, high school teachers called a second boycott in 1954, refusing all after-school assignments, although this time without support from the sports coaches. Three years later the board brought back yearbooks, dramatics, and school newspapers by agreeing to extra pay of $8.75 per session. The HSTA attempted to keep the protest alive in order to win pay for club activity as well, but teachers returned to these duties when ordered to do so by their principals.[4]

The Teachers Guild and Teachers Union responded to HSTA protests with typical ideological fervor and tactical fratricide, opposing high school teacher elitism on the single-pay issue and initiating their own competing activities. In an embarrassingly copycat maneuver, the Teachers Guild announced a "Minimum Service Program" in which teachers refused extra tasks such as hallway patrol and bulletin board display making.[5] The Teachers Union further splintered teacher unionism by supporting a new group, the Grass Roots Movement, which Teachers Guild leaders dismissed as a front for the now blacklisted Teachers Union. Whatever its origins, the Grass Roots Movement relied on TU organizational expertise, which recommended a 1930s-style organizing drive to capitalize on the election of Mayor Robert F. Wagner, son of the 1935 Wagner Act senator. After gathering together representatives from 200 schools at all levels, the group drew up salary demands and planned an April rally to be followed by a strike if a pay increase was not forthcoming.

The Teachers Guild countered with slightly different salary proposals, a similar strike threat, and even a demonstration one day before the Grass Roots meeting. Guild leaders claimed their rally, coinciding with city hearings, offered teachers a valid reason for being absent, whereas TU adventurism jeopardized teacher jobs. In any case, by itself, each demonstration was disappointing and smaller than those of the past. No strike occurred and salaries continued to stagnate, increasing for the typical high school teacher by only 5 percent between 1954 and 1959.[6]

Evening Teachers Strike

The final high school protest of the 1950s was the most impressive of all: a small group of HSTA members closed down the evening high school program, winning a nearly twofold increase in their wages. Leading the protests were Samuel Hochberg and Roger Parente, HSTA vice-president and secretary, respectively. Both men came from union backgrounds, Hochberg as a one-time member of the Teachers Union and Parente as the son of a building trade union officer. They advocated an evening teacher strike, not just to gain improvements in the notoriously low pay for evening teachers, but also to demonstrate the feasibility of a militant strategy they hoped would be adopted later by all high school teachers.

As a testing ground for future organizing drives, evening teachers made an ideal target: working at only sixteen schools citywide, and prone to after-work drinking parties, they formed a ready-made cohesive group. Discontent ran high over paltry pay, only $12.25 for a three-hour session, yet because most evening teachers also taught during the day, they were not fearful of losing these second jobs in a strike. Parente and the HSTA attorney, Harold Israelson, designed a double-endorsement petition campaign in which a mass resignation went into effect only after teachers signed their names for a second time. Once a large majority of the evening teachers signed for the first time, everyone would see that they had the support of their peers. Even though Parente preannounced the strike with great fanfare, school officials were stunned; in February 1959 so few teachers reported for work that the board was forced to close all evening programs. Three weeks later the evening teachers returned with an immediate 47 percent raise, to be followed by an additional 24 percent pay increase the following fall.[7]

The lesson of the newfound solidarity among evening teachers was not lost on Teachers Guild leaders, in particular the guild's full-time organizer, David Selden. Raised in Michigan, Selden experienced firsthand the effect of CIO organizing among auto workers and, while a United Auto Worker labor educator, helped launch the Dearborn AFT local. After four years on the road as the AFT's "eastern organizer," the union assigned Selden the only slightly less overwhelming task of building up the New York City local.[8] Beginning with a basis of just 1,500 members, in five years Selden attracted only a few hundred new members, causing him to conclude, "It would take more than a hundred years to enroll a majority of the teachers."[9] Selden attributed slow growth in part to the Teachers Guild's ideological purity, which caused them to deny support to elitist groups like the HSTA. Along with guild board member Ely Trachtenberg, also a socialist and former auto worker, Selden convinced guild leaders to underwrite the cash-poor HSTA with telephones, mimeograph machines, and a "Guild Coffee Mobile" to comfort evening teachers on the wintertime picket line.[10]

Then, motivated by the success of the evening teachers, and also by HSTA threats to organize in the Teachers Guild's junior high school stronghold, young guild activists Selden, Albert Shanker, and George Altomare initiated surreptitious merger talks with friendly HSTA leaders. The high school group, now renamed the Secondary School Teachers Association (SSTA), was divided on a merger: Parente in favor; Hochberg skeptical, arguing for an HSTA organizing effort among junior high teachers; and the conservative SSTA president Emil Tron, fearful that either proposal would diminish his authority. After initially maintaining control over SSTA policy, Tron blundered by refusing to endorse a guild call for a one-day work protest in April 1959. Even though this protest never took place (the guild called it off after gaining a modest $120 pay increase), Tron's lack of solidarity with an organization that had supported the recent evening strike dismayed large numbers of SSTA members, who subsequently resigned from the organization.[11]

Hochberg then recanted his original antimerger position and accepted guild assistance in maintaining contact with dissident SSTA members, eventually building up a mailing list for a new organization called the Committee for Action Through Unity, or CATU. In March 1960 CATU members of the SSTA joined with the Teachers Guild to create another new group, with guild leader Charles Cogen as president and Hochberg as deputy president. This new union, Local 2, the United Federation of Teachers, would later grow to be the largest single union local in the United States.

The UFT

Between 1960 and 1962 labor relations for New York City teachers were recast from a structure of fragmented unions without serious consultative rights to fully recognized collective bargaining for a single union, the UFT. Increased size alone does not account for the UFT's success. The merger of CATU with the Teachers Guild boosted membership, but only by several hundred. By November 1960, at the time of the union's first strike, the UFT had fewer than 5,000 members (out of more than 40,000 teachers); a year and half later, when the union signed its first contract, membership had not grown significantly. Only with this contract in hand did the UFT mushroom in size, gaining hundreds of new members weekly, reaching 16,000 in 1965, thereby finally surpassing the combined Teachers Union–Teachers Guild membership several decades earlier.[12]

Early success of the UFT is less attributable to numbers than the changing characteristics of its members. A comprehensive study of New York City teachers by sociologist Stephen Cole found three traits strongly associated with militancy: young, male, and Jewish teachers were most likely to have participated in UFT strikes.[13] As individual correlates of activism these characteristics are readily explainable: male teachers, especially in the high schools, felt that their wages had eroded in comparison with similarly educated men; young teachers who had not experienced the Depression were less fearful of losing their jobs; and Jewish teachers were more likely to be members of left-wing pro-union political parties. Between 1940 and 1960, New York City school teachers increasingly fell into these three groups. The larger number of young teachers is noticeable in the number of teachers on the low end of the promotion ladder: only 7 percent in 1940, but more than 30 percent in 1960. The percentage of men increased steadily throughout the century, especially in secondary schools, rising from 36 percent in 1940 to 49 percent in 1960. In most years prior to the Depression, less than 25 percent of new teachers were Jewish; after 1940 over 60 percent of all new teachers were Jewish.[14]

Teacher backgrounds also varied within the school system: high school teachers were most likely to be male and Jewish and thus, not surprisingly, were most militant during the 1950s. Elementary school teachers were disproportionately female and also worked under more authoritarian work rules. With hardly a chance to talk to one another (they typically spent their lunch hours supervising the student cafeteria), elementary school teachers tended to be less unified in their opposition to principals' authority than were high school teachers.[15] Junior high teachers held a middle ground subject to authoritarian work rules, but were predominantly male, Jewish, and younger than their high school counterparts. About half were "full-time substitutes," working year after year at lower pay than regularly appointed teachers. As late as 1962, over 50 percent of UFT members, including key leaders Shanker and Altomare, came from the junior high schools.[16]

What focused the simmering discontent among teachers into effective union organizing was a reorientation of the Teachers Guild away from the interunion conflict that had plagued its organizing drives since 1935. The origins of this shift in guild policy can be traced to the 1953 election of Charles Cogen as guild president and the appointment of David Selden as national AFT representative in New York City. Cogen's victory was a defeat for a relatively conservative group associated with Rebecca Simonson, although as before, "conservative" guild members were the right wing of a spectrum skewed far to the left, ranging from left-liberals to various socialist and communist groups. Simonson herself recollects that she hardly knew a Republican in the guild.[17] Cogen, a social studies teacher at Bronx High School of Science and later chair of the department at Brooklyn's Bay Ridge High School, served as an unpaid union official, content to leave strategy making to paid staff like Selden. As a result, Selden exerted considerable influence, which he used to nudge the union toward a more open-door policy. He brought in labor relations experts to convince union members that a full-fledged collective bargaining contract could be won if the Teachers Guild would endorse other labor groups instead of wasting energy undercutting the competition. Many guild members found such strategies threatening; they were unwilling to risk the autonomy or possibly the existence of their beloved, albeit tiny, organization in a representation election that might be won by another group.[18]

Despite such difficulties, by 1959, Selden had succeeded in building a nucleus of support for change; the merger with CATU provided the impetus to put new policies into effect. Although technically an equal combination of the Teachers Guild and CATU, the UFT—or "New Guild," as some members called it—actually was controlled by former guild members. What CATU brought to the UFT was a sense of outreach. Selden explained to guild board members, "We are buying the franchise in order to organize in the high schools."[19]

Prior to 1960, guild decision making was an extremely open process: any member could question union policy by introducing agenda items to the executive board or delegate assembly. Cogen's strict sense of fair play meant that new ideas received a hearing, even though the guild's multiple sectarian groups seldom cooperated sufficiently to actually implement a policy change. Recollection by participants and union records indicated a shift after the merger toward stricter agenda setting by union leadership and more frequent decision making outside the open process of the board or assembly. Running a true labor union, as opposed to the debating society orientation of the Teachers Guild, no doubt necessitated more efficiency in operation. Nonetheless, given the degree of centralization that developed in the UFT a few years later, this early trend away from participatory democracy is significant.[20]

"Can't Somebody Blow the Whistle on These Guys?"

Two major caucuses squared off within the UFT. On one side, Cogen, supported by Selden, Shanker, and Altomare, advocated that the union use its connections with the AFL-CIO's New York City Central Labor Council to obtain a promise from the mayor for a representation election. The opposing faction, led by CATU organizers Parente and Hochberg and Teachers Guild members Ben Mazen and Lou Heitner, favored a representation election but objected to the union's reliance on the good graces of elected officials.[21]

Pessimism about the reliability of city promises proved correct. During the fall of 1960, with no move on the part of the city or board to call a representation election, Cogen was forced to threaten a strike. The Hochberg-chaired strike strategy committee recommended a November 7, 1960, strike deadline, a decision supported by the membership in a 2,896-to-117 vote on October 19. A strike might still have been avoided had not the board inadvertently played into the hands of the militant wing of the UFT by backtracking even further on previously made promises, first by suggesting still more committee hearings on the need for collective bargaining, and then later with a board counsel ruling that a representation election might not be possible after all. On Monday, November 7, one day before the Kennedy-Nixon presidential election, a reluctant Cogen declared the UFT out on strike.[22]

The Board of Education reported no more than 5,000 strikers, although union officials point out that these estimates omitted at least 5,000 full-time substitutes, among the most militant union members. Even so, the effect on the school system was minimal. On Tuesday Cogen called teachers back to work, thus avoiding a possible confrontation when voters would have to cross picket lines to enter school polling places. Although practically inconsequential to the schools, the strike substantially altered the future of the UFT. First, Charles Cogen, who openly expressed his dislike for strikes, gained the unlikely image of a militant union leader, willing to take the risk of a major strike. Second, the strike established the UFT as the unrivaled voice for city teachers, enabling the UFT to defeat the National Education Association in their upcoming representation election fight and dealing a final blow to the Teachers Union, which appeared to backtrack on its tradition of militant support for collective bargaining. The TU refused to endorse the strike on the grounds that no protection would be provided for TU members, who perceived themselves as still susceptible to political retribution from the board. Whatever the merits of these concerns, the TU never regained its status as the union most willing to take militant positions.[23]

Teachers Union leaders further charged that the strike was mere posturing on the part of UFT leaders, who had worked out a deal with city officials. While these allegations did not diminish the public image of the UFT as a powerful union, they were partly correct. Cogen had no intention of carrying the strike over to election day, counting instead on the assistance of private sector labor leaders to mediate an accommodation with Mayor Wagner. UFT leaders met the International Ladies Garment Workers Union president David Dubinsky to devise a settlement acceptable to the mayor and the union. Under their proposal, a committee clearly sympathetic to unionization of teachers—composed of Dubinsky, Amalgamated Clothing Workers union president Jacob Potofsky, and Central Labor Council president Harry Van Arsdale—would make recommendations for a settlement.[24]

Cogen's problem was in selling this procedure to members of his own union. Even though the fact-finding report released in January favored the union's demands, UFT delegates complained of being asked to endorse the report before seeing the full text. Cogen wrote to

Van Arsdale, "When we tell our members and Delegates that assistance is being given, not all of them accept this assurance." [25] Van Arsdale indeed had helped UFT leaders gain access to city officials, but at the same time he had been publicly critical of the November strike. Both Van Arsdale and AFL-CIO president George Meany worried that Cogen could not control his own members. [26] When it became apparent that the November strike would occur despite opposition from Cogen and AFT national president Carl Megel, Selden reports Meany asking, "For Christ's sake, Harry [Van Arsdale]. Can't somebody blow the whistle on these guys?" [27] After the strike Van Arsdale promised there would be "no recurrence." [28] Cogen's critics in the UFT argued that labor leaders like Van Arsdale, who were not known for supporting democracy within their own union, would limit the UFT to political deal making instead of more effective rank-and-file militancy.

Once again, the doubts about the strategy of relying on friends in high places appears to have been warranted. Cogen told the AFT Executive Committee in December that, with the help of Van Arsdale and Central Labor Council secretary Morris Iushewitz, the UFT could win collective bargaining by May 1961 and dues checkoff rights by September of that year. [29] The fact-finding report released in January was favorable to the union, as expected, endorsing collective bargaining for teachers. The panel's main concern was not the pros and cons of bargaining, but whether or not the UFT would necessarily win the representation election over the non-AFL-CIO National Education Association. [30] In February, the board appointed a committee of "Inquiry in Connection with Collective Bargaining," including private sector labor relations experts George Taylor, David Cole, and Walter Gellhorn, all of whom had participated in setting up the city's transit collective bargaining system. Their report urged the Board of Education to follow the Board of Transportation's example in recognizing unions for its employees.

The Cogen timetable faltered when the board indicated it would not accept collective bargaining without the stipulation that contracts would be "terminable at will by the Board." Such bargaining, of course, was unacceptable to the UFT since agreements would be binding on only one party, the union. The situation might have stalemated indefinitely had the union not the good fortune to benefit from a Board of Education scandal over construction contracts. [31] Kickback payments were found to be so pervasive that the old board was disbanded and a new one chosen, this time with a decidedly pro-labor union bias, including as one of its members Central Labor Council leader Morris Iushewitz. During its first week in office, the new board

reversed the old board's position on labor relations and began to implement the Inquiry Committee's recommendations. Two elections
had been planned: first, a referendum among teachers on whether or
not they favored collective bargaining, to be followed by a second
vote on which union they desired as their representative. UFT leaders
did not like the idea of two elections because it would give opposing
unions an opportunity to rally support. But rather than postpone voting any longer, the UFT went along with the procedure, campaigning
on the slogan "Yes is for the teachers, no is for the board." In June 1961
teachers voted by a three-to-one margin in favor of collective bargaining. A union representation election was scheduled for December.[32]

UFT versus the NEA

Estimates by UFT leaders suggested that the union could count on
sweeping the secondary schools, where even before the campaign began 10,000 of 19,000 junior and senior high teachers favored the UFT.
The representation election would be tougher among elementary
teachers, where the UFT had only 2,300 members, or 12 percent of the
work force.[33] Historically, the obvious opponent for the UFT was the
Teachers Union, which after appeals to the Department of Labor's
hearing officer, Nathan Feinsinger, was permitted on the ballot, thus
overturning its non-grata status in force since 1950. The decision gave
the TU only a few weeks to rally support, prompting a TU request to
postpone the election by ninety days, a motion denied by Feinsinger.
But even with more campaign time, the once-largest teachers union
probably could not have won many votes. Teachers Union election
material could only boast of union successes won two decades earlier, pale claims next to the more recent UFT victories.[34]

The only effective opposition to the UFT came from the Teachers
Bargaining Organization (TBO), a hastily created coalition of small
groups loosely affiliated with the National Education Association.
Nationwide the NEA was much larger than the AFT, enrolling over
700,000 teachers, or almost half of the nation's instructional staff,
some ten times the national membership of the AFT. But in New York
City the NEA was weak and could create a credible opponent to the
UFT only by pulling together many formerly independent groups.
Many of them had traditionally opposed collective bargaining, an obvious handicap in campaign debates over which group would most
actively represent teacher interests.[35]

Much of the UFT campaign focused on the conservative tradition of these small organizations, as well as the nonmilitant heritage of the NEA, which the UFT maintained was inherently pro-management in orientation. Indeed, over 70 percent of those who made up NEA Executive Committee, Board of Trustees, and Board of Directors were administrators—although it was also true that UFT president Cogen himself was a supervisor and thus ineligible to vote in the upcoming election. UFT flyers pointed out that the NEA had not been as strong as the AFT in fighting racial and religious discrimination. Particularly embarrassing to the NEA was the continued presence of segregated locals in the South (long after the AFT had expelled such groups) and an NEA-sponsored trip from which Jews had been excluded at the request of some Middle Eastern countries.[36]

The TBO campaign featured a platform calling for equitable salaries, an attempt to recall the reputation of the HSTA for supporting salary differentials between elementary and high school teachers. To win the sympathy of the hotly contested elementary teachers, the TBO emphasized that their proposal for graduate degree bonuses would apply to studies likely to be pursued by elementary school teachers, generally courses toward a masters in education rather than in specific disciplines. The TBO also suggested that the UFT would be subject to the control of the organized labor movement, thus tainting the teachers' "independent professional status." (The UFT did in fact have considerable support from the labor movement: $5,000 directly from the UAW and ILGWU, a $38,000 grant from the AFL-CIO's Industrial Union Department, with $10,000 in monthly interest-free loans available from the Amalgamated Clothing Workers Union's Amalgamated Bank.) Finally, the NEA argued that the UFT was strike-happy, pointing out that Hochberg had threatened a second strike during 1961. Because public sector strikes were illegal under the Condon-Wadlin Act, the TBO claimed strike threats undermined a teacher's "responsibility of inculcating respect for the institutions of democratic society and adherence to the laws through which it operates."[37] As an alternative, the NEA proposed "legal effective militancy," a vague strategy easily parodied by the UFT. On December 11 the result was 20,045 for the UFT, 9,770 for the TBO, and 2,575 for the Teachers Union. A postmortem by the NEA attributed the UFT's success to the reputation of the TBO as a weak organization compared to the UFT's recent history as a militant advocate for teachers.[38]

First Contract

As the certified bargaining agent for teachers, the UFT could now demand serious collective bargaining. When negotiations proceeded slowly with the Board of Education, UFT leaders sought intervention from Mayor Wagner. At a key meeting on February 24, 1962, the mayor guaranteed that the city would finance a settlement $10 million more than the amount then offered by the Board of Education. In return, the mayor asked that the union forgo a strike.[39] As the strike deadline neared, union membership voted 2,544 to 2,231 to carry out the strike. Cogen had not wanted a strike in the first place and now he was asked to lead one without the overwhelming pro-strike vote that typically precedes any strike. UFT leaders later alleged that, given this double-bind, Cogen transgressed his usual commitment to democratic decision making and tried to have the Executive Board overrule the membership. When the board refused, the strike was on. More than 20,000 teachers, or about 50 percent of the work force, stayed home, thus, unlike the November 1960 strike, seriously affecting the school system.[40]

Pressure on Cogen to end the strike was intense: AFL-CIO president George Meany called to encourage Cogen to do so; New York labor leaders David Dubinsky and Harry Van Arsdale let their disfavor be known; and the labor representative on the Board of Education, Morris Iushewitz, openly called the strike an "unmitigated disaster."[41] Moreover, the union faced a court injunction, threatening fines and jail terms if the strike continued. As a result, Cogen called teachers back to work the next day even though a new agreement had not been reached. According to David Selden, the settlement reached the next day included extra money advanced by the state with the approval of Governor Rockefeller at Selden's instigation. The final contract included $9.2 million more than the board's earlier offer, just within the range proposed by the mayor in February.[42]

Union dissidents were bothered as much by the manner in which the contract was negotiated as by its terms. As one dissident later described his reaction, "I waited outside the hotel, unable to find out how the negotiations were going, while UAW officials freely walked in and out of the meeting."[43] Two hundred teachers met to discuss their dismay over the agreement, suggesting that in the future union leaders pledge their willingness to fight court injunctions by going to jail if necessary.[44]

Opposition to the UFT leaders also focused on a new Board of Education demand that the union agree to a no-strike clause as part of the contract under negotiation. Although a standard feature of most U.S. labor contracts, the dissidents felt that in combination with a June 30 expiration date for the contract, the no-strike clause would leave the union powerless to act during the spring, when the budget was set. TWU president Michael Quill urged the UFT to accept the no-strike clause, noting that it was included in TWU contracts. UFT leadership, still sensitive to the criticism that they were too responsive to other union leaders, replied that the UFT "deeply resents your [Quill's] unwarranted interference in the crucial struggle now in progress between the teachers and the Board of Education."[45] But the board would not accept a contract without a no-strike pledge, so UFT leaders conceded that point, quieting rank-and-file displeasure with a "no contract, no work" policy. Thus the union affirmed its right to strike *after* the contract expired and did not accede to the board's intention of a principled stand against all teacher strikes. The contract gained final approval in September 1962.[46]

In the midst of these conflicts, Roger Parente, leader of the 1959 evening teachers' strike, formed a slate to run against Cogen for control of the UFT. Opposition leaders later agreed that Parente, who won only 30 percent of the vote, was a weak candidate and that Ben Mazen, author of the union grievance plan, or Samuel Hochberg might have had a better chance of unseating Cogen. Others suggest that the opposition moved against him too quickly and that after two successful strikes, Cogen was unbeatable even though he had initially opposed both strikes.[47]

Cogen's substantial victory also signaled a change in the union's decision-making processes. Prior to the 1960s, when the Teachers Guild had few negotiating rights, it was not necessary for the union to reach quick decisions on many issues. Typically, several factions bitterly opposed one another with no single group possessing so much power that it could prevent participation by any other. Some UFT members urged the union to adopt proportional representation as a means to institutionalize continued recognition of minority positions. Under such a plan, adopted in several U.S. municipalities and in some European countries, seats in representative bodies such as city councils, parliaments, or in the case of the union, the Executive Board, would be allocated on the basis of proportional votes received by each political party or caucus. In this way minority groups are assured of representation, whereas in a winner-take-all system a majority party might easily win all of the seats. Incumbent UFT leaders rejected proportional representation, adopting instead a slate system in which caucuses put forward slates of candidates, thus all but guaranteeing complete domination of the Executive Board by the victorious caucus. Thereafter dissent in the union's ranks was significantly reduced.[48]

Bargaining Rules

When the Board of Education recognized the UFT in 1961 and signed the first contract with the union in 1962, several key decisions were made about the structure of collective bargaining: the exclusivity of representation; the size of the bargaining unit; and the scope of permissible bargaining. The principles adopted during these early years were to guide teachers' collective bargaining not only subsequently in New York City, but also in other U.S. cities and even abroad.

First, the board had to decide whether to recognize one single labor union, or to allow teachers to be represented by any number of unions—that is, whether to grant exclusive or multiple representation. Almost all U.S. private and public sector bargaining operated at the time—and still does—on the principle of exclusive representation. In late 1960, the New York City Board of Education, claiming that exclusive representation would violate teachers' freedom of choice, canceled previously announced plans for a representation election, thus unwittingly prodding the union toward its November strike. The Commission of Inquiry appointed by the board in February 1961 reached an entirely different position, arguing in their report, released that spring, that exclusive recognition of one union would minimize competition between unions and would result in easier bargaining for management.[49] (UFT representatives carefully made this point during hearings on the issue.)[50] This was precisely the same argument used in granting exclusive recognition to the TWU (see Chapter 3), a not surprising coincidence since three of five Commission members—George Taylor, David Cole, and Walter Gellhorn—had also consulted with the city on transit labor relations.

The Commission of Inquiry found it more difficult to make a decision about the size of the bargaining unit. Just as in deliberations about the transit system ten years earlier, the consultants had to decide whether all employees should belong to the same unit. For teachers, one obvious division would be between primary and secondary teachers as suggested by some former members of the Secondary School Teachers Association. The commission's report recommended that the question of separate units be decided by a vote of the teachers themselves. Such elections were common practice in the private sector under the National Labor Relations Act when determining whether to include professional employees in the same unit as nonprofessional employees. It was more unusual, however, to adopt separate units when all employees were judged to be professionals and they held similar jobs, as was the case with primary and secondary school teachers. In any case, the Board of Education rejected the commission's recommendations, prompting the Commission's members to resign, although soon afterward the scandal-plagued board itself was displaced. The new Board of Education passed the decision on unit determination to the city's Department of Labor, which recommended the more common practice of a single unit for all teachers without holding a referendum on the question.[51]

An equally important decision about the structure for collective bargaining—the scope of bargaining—was left vague in both the commission's report and the 1962 contract. The issue could no longer be ignored during the 1963 contract talks when the union demanded the right to negotiate about educational policy, claiming democratic management of the schools as the union's ultimate goal.[52] Money items were settled before the beginning of the school term in September 1963, with a pay increase small enough to be covered out of the board's contingency budget.[53] But the board and union struggled throughout the fall to resolve matters of working conditions. Union officials remember Cogen as quite dubious about greater union say in running the schools (he was a supervisor); but as a result of pressure from more radical members he became caught up in a debate with school superintendent Calvin Gross over a letter Cogen wrote to *Newsweek* in which he stated that the union's aim was a "tremendous increase in the share of control in the administration of the school system."[54] Gross responded that such an interpretation put the negotiations in jeopardy and demanded a further clarification in the contract that "no measure of administrative control shall be exercised over any operation of the school system by the United Federation of Teachers."[55]

Such management proclamations notwithstanding, the union had gained considerable influence over school policy. The negotiations in September 1963 already conceded to union members additional conference time, more preparation periods, duty-free lunch periods, and provision for hiring of substitutes. (When substitutes were unavailable, teachers often had to double up their classes.) The final contract conceded three additional issues of "administrative control," setting a precedent for subsequent negotiations. First, in response to union demands the board agreed to change its hiring procedures by seeking more applicants from the South, the goal being an increase in the number of black teachers. Second, the board affirmed its intention to develop a program for "difficult" schools based on consultation with the union. And finally, the board agreed to include limits on class size in the contract, a particularly crucial administrative matter since it could incur considerable costs.

Like the social workers in SSEU (see Chapter 5), teachers argued that better working conditions for teachers and improved education for students were not separate issues: smaller class size would serve both goals. The board tried to characterize class size limits as a barrier to alternative teaching that required flexible scheduling. But since the union was willing to allow for exceptions for the purpose of team teaching or other such experiments, cost was obviously the board's real concern. Even if the contract simply reiterated New York State rules limiting teacher workload in high schools to thirty students per class, the board would need to hire many additional teachers. The state education commissioner admitted that the city frequently violated class size regulations, either through outright disregard of regulations or by having a few small classes balance out large ones. Nearly three-quarters of high school classes and more than half of elementary school classes exceeded state standards.[56]

The 1963 UFT contract limited junior high school class size to thirty-five (lowered to thirty-four in 1964) and high school class size to thirty-nine (with a target of thirty-seven by 1965). These limits were to be implemented only "insofar as possible" and could be exceeded if there was a shortage of space or if implementing the target would lead to double sessions or, most important, if the total excess in a particular grade was less than 50 percent of the maximum. Thus, if other classes were within the size limit, then the remaining class could be as much as 50 percent over the legal maximum. Nonetheless, the clause on class size served as a model for other U.S. teacher unions.[57]

Shanker's Hegemony

In 1964 Charles Cogen left his position as UFT president to assume leadership of the national union, the American Federation of Teachers. Albert Shanker, a man more willing than Cogen to assert his dominance over the union, obtained nomination for UFT president from the union's Unity Caucus, the group that had supported Cogen against Hochberg and Parente. Product of a New York City union family, Shanker earned a University of Illinois masters degree in philosophy before returning to New York for a short stint as a Queens junior high teacher. Almost immediately he joined his teaching colleague George Altomare and neighbor David Selden in the Teachers Guild. In 1959 Shanker gave up teaching entirely for a job as AFT national representative assigned to the New York local, and thereafter was a key policy maker in the Cogen-Selden caucus. Shanker's major opponent for control of the union was Ben Mazen, a teacher at the Bronx High School of Science who was also a lawyer, an architect of the union's grievance procedures, and a longtime opponent of the Unity Caucus. The 36 percent of the vote received by Mazen in this election would be the high-water mark for Shanker's opponents.[58] In elections up until 1985, when he announced that he was serving his last term, Shanker won by lopsided margins of four to one or more.

Contract negotiations in 1965 were indicative of changes that had occurred in the UFT since 1963. Cogen's opponent, Roger Parente, predicted that the June expiration date of the 1963–65 contract would undermine the union's previous commitment to no work without a contract.[59] Indeed, when Shanker asked for a strike vote on June 30, 1965, no strike could be called until September, when school would again be in session. Three days before school was to open, union members were assembled in the Randall's Island stadium and told that "the best contract negotiated in New York City or anywhere else in the country" had been obtained by union leaders. Because the contract raised minimum salaries by only $100 there were scattered cries of "strike, strike," then in extraordinarily light voting the contract was accepted by a 3,392-to-616 margin.[60]

The apathy apparent in the 1965 contract vote was a short-lived reaction. During the succeeding three years, teacher labor relations were as tumultuous as in any other period. Two characteristics of the teacher work force identified by Stephen Cole as being associated with increased militancy were on the upswing during this time.[61] First, the school system hired a large number of young teachers, over 4,000 annually after 1965, an addition of almost 10 percent to the total staff every year. Second, the number of male teachers increased, in particular after graduate school draft deferments were eliminated (teaching was a draft-deferred profession); in 1968 alone, the Board of Education processed 2,000 requests for deferment notifications to be sent to draft boards.[62]

Teacher unrest of the late 1960s differed from earlier periods of militancy in that it took place at a time of unprecedented teacher dis-

satisfaction with their jobs. The civil rights movement and urban unrest created what one AFT leader called an "explosive mixture" in
which "teaching, especially conventional teaching," became "frus-
tratingly demoralizing and at times even hazardous."[63] Such discontent manifested itself in several wildcat protests during 1967:

- At Junior High School 98, 79 teachers submitted their resignations
  and only 36 of 126 teachers reported for work, saying they needed
  protection from violent students. UFT vice-president for junior
  high schools John O'Neill warned that this grass-roots protest was
  likely to spread.
- Teachers walked out of PS 194 to protest inadequate heat. They returned when the custodian agreed to turn up the thermostat.
- Nearly all 50 teachers at PS 284 in Brooklyn refused to work for
  half an hour after receiving what they termed "offensive literature" in their mailboxes. They returned to class only upon order of
  the district superintendent.[64]

Facing such simmering unrest, Shanker could not approach 1967
bargaining in as lackadaisical a manner as he had in 1965. In order to
put pressure on the Board of Education, Shanker urged a mass resignation campaign in which pledges to resign would be submitted to
the board in advance of contract negotiations. Because of the high
level of discontent in the schools, the union had no trouble gathering
signatures. On August 12, four weeks before the school term was to
begin, a panel of labor experts proposed a settlement, including significant raises over two years totaling $1,200 for new teachers and
$1,050 for others. The plan was rejected by both the UFT bargain-
ing committee and the membership. So, on September 11, 46,000 of
58,000 teachers refused to meet their classes, technically a mass resignation, but in actual fact the UFT was once again on strike.

For the first time a UFT strike created a major disruption in the
schools. When 80 percent of the teaching force did not report for
work, most schools closed. This time union leadership did not call
off the strike after only one day, as they had in 1960 and 1962. Members were too upset to respond to any claims that a reasonable settlement could be reached through poststrike negotiations. Noteworthy
in view of later events were the attempts by some teachers to cooperate with community groups in setting up "freedom schools," serving
over 6,000 students, yet receiving only token endorsement from UFT
leaders. Overall, such efforts by rank-and-file teachers were insufficient to prevent some community groups from warning striking

teachers that they would not be welcomed back to their jobs. Such confrontations took place primarily between black community residents and white UFT teachers.

On September 20, 1967, Mayor Lindsay announced settlement of the money issues with a pay scale of $150 higher than that recommended in mid-August by the mediators. But on the following day Shanker claimed that the board reneged on a promise to set aside funds for More Effective School (MES) programs, a union-initiated attempt to improve education through smaller classes with special attention to needy students. The program was to be financed out of a fund that would be monitored by both the union and community groups. One reason Shanker had to be careful about such specific items of the contract was that union dissidents had gained passage of an amendment to the union constitution requiring that the entire contract be made available for at least twenty-four hours before members could be asked to ratify it. It took another ten days before the board and union signed a Memorandum of Understanding, including funding for the MES proposal. With strong endorsement from Shanker, teachers approved the pact 18,171 to 3,442.[65]

Three key UFT officials publicly opposed the settlement: UFT founder George Altomare, junior high school vice-president John O'Neill, and black UFT Executive Board member Richard Parrish. They argued that, despite Shanker's reopening of negotiations, funding for MES was still inadequate. The board pledged $10 million for MES out of a $1.2 billion budget. The dissidents further alleged that a key demand in the strike, teacher input on educational policy, had not been pressed for sufficiently. Earlier that summer delegates had voted in favor of a demand for workplace democracy, including the election of principals and other supervisors and placement of union members on the Board of Education. The demands were quietly dropped by UFT leaders.[66]

The defection of the three Executive Board members did not alter union policy. Instead, the strike dramatically improved Shanker's image as a forceful leader, giving him greater control over the union and enabling him to demand allegiance or resignation from dissenters. Shanker's unbridled authority over UFT policy was critical in the union's subsequent conflict, the Ocean Hill–Brownsville strikes of 1968.

The Union and Community Control

No crisis in recent New York City labor relations history evokes such despair as events at Ocean Hill–Brownsville in 1968. Nominally a dispute over the rights of a locally constituted school board to choose its own teachers, the conflict became a symbol of urban strife, enmeshing not only the UFT (three citywide strikes in 1968), the city Board of Education (replaced in May 1969), and the local Ocean Hill–Brownsville board (disbanded in 1969), but also pitting civil rights groups against one another, including such traditional allies as the New York Civil Liberties Union, the Anti-Defamation League, and the Congress of Racial Equality (CORE). The short-term outcome of the dispute was a total victory for UFT leaders who wanted to end the experiment with community control. However, an equally critical legacy of Ocean Hill–Brownsville was long-lasting hostilities between various participants, ranging from the absurd—as when the UFT attempted to prevent the appointment of a Brooklyn College provost on the grounds that her research on Ocean Hill–Brownsville had been antagonistic to the union—to serious ongoing racial polarization in Brooklyn.[67]

For the historian, such emotionally charged involvement by participants means problematic recall. In a 1980 oral history interview, Charles Cogen commented freely on a number of controversial union matters, but when asked about the Ocean Hill–Brownsville strikes, answered, "I don't remember."[68] (He was UFT president until 1964 and AFT president from 1964 until 1968.) Others, of course, are more willing to recollect; several full-length books and dozens of articles, many of them by participants in the events, attempt to analyze—or more commonly to assign blame for—the most controversial issues raised by the strikes. Were teachers fired or simply transferred from the local school district? How prevalent was anti-Semitism among supporters of the community district? Were UFT leaders racist in their opposition to community control of schools, or just protecting the rights of union members? The critical underlying issues, such as black-white relations, the appropriate role for community control, and the quality of inner-city education, received less attention and remain unresolved to this day.[69]

There also has been little discussion of the effect of the Ocean Hill–Brownsville conflict on its chief antagonist, the UFT. Events during 1968 reinforced two significant trends already evident in 1967: first, control of the union by Albert Shanker; and second, alienation of the union from community groups. Whereas the 1967 teacher strike bolstered the image of president Shanker to UFT members, the 1968 protests went farther and almost completely undercut the effectiveness of all opposition groups within the union. The purge of dissidents that followed the strikes weakened a large number of groups opposed to Shanker's leadership, including Unity Caucus Executive Board members who expressed dismay at union policy; followers of the Hochberg-Parente-Mazen group allied in the UFT's Staff Party; a caucus of black teachers led by longtime UFT activist Richard Parrish; a group with ties back to the Teachers Union; and nonaffiliated teachers who elected to cross picket lines. Members of all these groups suffered ostracism from the UFT, thus exacerbating the trend already under way toward one-man control of the union.[70]

A second consequence of the demise of these opposition groups was that there remained no counterbalance to increasing union antagonism toward community groups. Before 1968 two contradictory approaches to community participation existed side by side within the UFT. On the one hand, beginning with the first contract in 1962, the union had worked with community groups to upgrade education on the principle that educational quality was inseparable from the issue of teachers' working conditions. Despite strong opposition from the Board of Education, every UFT contract contained some form of commitment by the board to new programs and additional funds for poor neighborhoods.

Moreover, the union had a long history of alliance with the civil rights movement, beginning with the expulsion of southern segregated units from the AFT during the 1950s. Later the New York City UFT specifically endorsed the Freedom Marches of the early 1960s, sending four busloads to the 1963 march on Washington, and protecting teachers who boycotted classes during the 1964 pro-integration protest. In 1965 the UFT supported the Civilian Review Board of police, putting the UFT in opposition to many white New Yorkers and some of the other municipal unions. As recently as the 1966–67 school year union members joined parents in protests over inferior conditions at some schools, while in Harlem the union worked closely with community groups and the Ford Foundation—both later bitter opponents of the union—to advocate for experimental community control of schools in the neighborhood surrounding IS 201. Even in Ocean Hill–Brownsville, the UFT endorsed the community-control experiment, albeit reluctantly, providing two representatives to the project's governing board.[71]

At the same time that both rhetoric and deed seemed to place the UFT on the side of the civil rights movement, a second union attitude toward minority groups was also evident. In March 1967 the UFT

Executive Board proposed "a program to remove disruptive children from regular classrooms," a response to teacher complaints of uncontrollable students. However valid the merits of teacher concerns, the union's solution was perceived by community groups as unnecessarily harsh because it permitted teachers to remove so-called disruptive students from a class with only minimal rights of appeal by parents. Dissident UFT members pointed out that there were alternative means for dealing with disruption in the classroom, ways that would not antagonize minority groups, who viewed the proposed program as specifically aimed at black and Hispanic children. Nonetheless, Shanker vigorously pursued the issue, and then, during the 1968 strike, further alienated minority group leaders by suggesting that children should not attend alternative schools run by community leaders because of "undesirables" in the classroom, by which he clearly meant outspoken black activists. Overall, prior to 1968 one can find elements of support and opposition by the UFT for civil rights; after events at Ocean Hill–Brownsville UFT policy hardened against minority group demands.[72]

Conflict at Ocean Hill

The proximate cause of the strikes in the fall of 1968 was the dismissal of nineteen teachers from the Ocean Hill–Brownsville local school district, an experiment serving 10,000 students in the easternmost section of Brooklyn. The elected twenty-one-member board was burdened with two critical handicaps. First, Ocean Hill sat in limbo between two communities, Brownsville and East New York, so its community board did not have the solid community base found in other designated experimental districts. Second, all of these experiments, even the ones with strong initial community support, suffered from lack of basic financial wherewithall. UFT president Shanker, who played a key role in dismantling the local board, nonetheless understood this limitation. He characterized the superintendent's attitude toward the community in a mock monologue: "Now look, I know that you've been working with the union and you want two things. You want local control and you want More Effective Schools. Well, More Effective Schools cost a lot of money. I'm willing to give you half a package. I'll give you local control."[73]

Utilizing one of the few powers they possessed, the Ocean Hill–Brownsville board sent telegrams on May 8, 1968, to nineteen teachers, stating, "The governing board of the Ocean Hill–Brownsville demonstration school district has voted to end your employment in the schools of this district. . . . You will report Friday morning to Personnel. . . ."[74]

The actual text of the letter was soon lost in newspaper accounts about "fired" teachers, a misrepresentation fueled by the UFT, which added the further misleading allegation that these teachers faced service in Vietnam if not returned to their jobs at Ocean Hill. Only eighteen months before the UFT had worked closely with community groups to plan the demonstration projects; now the UFT characterized community control as "mob rule," operating through "terror and threats," and that cooperation with Ocean Hill amounted to "appeasement of small groups threatening violence." "Your school will be next," warned union leaflets.[75]

The bitterest confrontation, however, came over union charges of anti-Semitism against community leaders in Ocean Hill and the Afro-American Teachers Association. Crudely anti-Semitic leaflets had been distributed in the community and placed in teachers' mailboxes, but the culpability of the local community board itself was never proved. In fact, it was later shown that the union doctored some leaflets to make them appear to have been Ocean Hill products. The worst leaflets received wider distribution as a result of UFT publicity (copies were sent to all members and a total of 500,000 printed) than ever could have been managed by their authors.[76]

The local board was scarcely blameless in its rhetoric. In May 1968 Rhody McCoy, the Ocean Hill–Brownsville administrator, said of the supposedly transferred but not fired teachers, "Not one of these teachers will be allowed to teach anywhere in this city, the black community will see to that."[77] And, the Afro-American Teachers Association, whose president, Albert Vann, taught in Ocean Hill–Brownsville, published an editorial in its November 1968 newspaper asking, "How long shall the Black and Puerto Rican communities of New York City sit back and allow the Jewish-dominated United Federation of Teachers to destroy our every effort to rescue our children?"[78] Thus, responsibility for the union's animosity certainly rests with the community groups as well; such deliberately provocative statements played into the hands of those union leaders who opposed community control.

In actual practice, however, both anti-Semitism and involuntary transfer of teachers were red herring issues. A majority of the teachers hired as replacements by the community board were white and Jewish. And polemics aside, both Shanker and McCoy were later to agree that transfer of incompetent teachers without formal hearings was a common practice liked by no one, but continued with tacit approval of the union (which wanted to avoid costly hearings) and administrators (who rid themselves of undesirable teachers, albeit often in exchange for another school's reject). UFT dissidents maintain that the practice continues up to the present day.[79]

From the opening salvo at Ocean Hill in May 1968, UFT leaders used the situation to attain more general goals than just the return of the nineteen teachers. Shanker highlighted the board's alleged firing to convince state legislators to defeat a bill on school decentralization that many thought was close to passage. By charging that community-controlled school boards would use "tax money to teach children to hate," the union gained alternative legislation, essentially postponing decentralization decisions for another year.[80]

During the summer the local board found itself backed further into a corner when a trial examiner ruled that none of the charges against any of the teachers was valid. The board still refused to take back the teachers, setting the stage for a series of strikes beginning when school first opened in September. The events of the succeeding ten weeks were tortuous (see note 69 for references with chronologies). At several points compromise appeared near at hand, only to be rejected by Shanker, who insisted that the local board be replaced and the experiment in community control be severely curtailed.[81]

The dispute dragged on through three separate strikes, which closed the schools most days through mid-November. Only then, with the return of the transferred teachers to their classrooms and the imposition of a trusteeship takeover of the Ocean Hill–Brownsville district, did the UFT call off their protest. The following spring the state legislature replaced the existing community-control experiments with boards representing much larger areas and with limited authority. Elections in these districts resulted in only 17 percent black representation and eventually in UFT-supported candidates winning control in most districts.[82]

Inside the UFT

Teachers were angry and alienated from their profession during 1968; resignations ran five times the normal level.[83] And the vast majority of teachers viewed the union as the best source of protection. Despite organized opposition to the strike, only 9,000 teachers crossed the picket lines in 1968, fewer than had done so during the

1967 strike.[84] As a result, in the years after the 1968 strikes Shanker's control over the UFT went unchallenged and his willingness to make unilateral deals with management did not affect his public image as a militant labor leader. Shanker himself noted an analogy between decentralization of the school system and decentralized authority within the union:

> If local school boards are represented in negotiations, then teachers at the local level within the union will also demand to be represented at the bargaining table. You're going to have about a hundred people involved in negotiations . . . people will make beautiful speeches . . . then, close to contract time, the superintendent and I will walk off in a room together and will either arrive at an agreement or we won't, because it will never be done in front of a mob like that, just never.[85]

Shanker maintained his hegemony in the UFT through a series of structural changes that made opposition extremely difficult. His base of support rested with the Unity Caucus, which imposes discipline on all union officials below the rank of president. A descendent of the party-line caucuses of the Teachers Guild, the Unity Caucus today has ties to the Socialist Party, USA, but primarily was the vehicle for a line of authority from Shanker downward in the union. With few exceptions, all UFT officers are elected from the Unity slate. Gaining access to the union's election ballot is difficult since it requires a petition drive for over 1,500 signatures, subject to careful scrutiny by the Unity Caucus–dominated elections committee. Under slate voting, UFT members can vote for several dozen candidates with a single mark, thus assuring that Shanker and the caucus will sweep into office supportive officers and Executive Board members.[86]

Dissidents also accuse the election committee of manipulating the timing of the elections so that they follow close on the heels of paychecks, a strategy likely to favor incumbents if those paychecks include retroactive pay from a contract recently negotiated by union leaders. Moreover, it is difficult for opposition candidates to publicize their positions. Union newspaper space is available, but only in the issue before the election, which union dissidents charge is mailed so late that union members often vote before learning about non–Unity Caucus candidates. As a result, opposition candidates to Shanker have done poorly in every election since 1968, receiving 10 to 15 percent of the vote.

Occasionally union positions are determined by a membership vote in the UFT, but in such instances critics again allege undemocratic procedures by union leaders. During the 1960s dissidents attempted to have the union go on record against U.S. participation in the Vietnam War. According to supporters of the resolution, the ballot was mailed so that younger members (who were more likely to oppose the war) received ballots last and consequently had fewer days to return them. Voting on negotiated contracts was also subject to manipulation through the practice of presenting contract summaries written by union leaders themselves as the basis of voting, thus abandoning the principle of requiring that there be sufficient time for members to read the entire contract. In 1963, for example, David Selden kept the union's printer on standby so that members could read a copy of the just-negotiated contract when they voted at a Randall's Island rally.[87] In 1967, dissidents demanded that the full contract be available for scrutiny, but the practice was later dropped.

According to the UFT constitution, union policy flows from the membership through the legislative body, the delegate assembly. Once a source of lively debate and control over union affairs, after 1962 the assembly was dominated by a single caucus. Theoretically, delegates represent over 1,000 chapters, but in actual practice the assembly functions as a rubber stamp for decisions already made by a handful of UFT leaders. The 75-member Executive Board votes in the assembly, constituting a large Unity Caucus–disciplined bloc of votes out of the 400 who typically attend meetings. As one former Unity member explained, discipline on the Executive Board is stringent because anyone who dares vote incorrectly is "threatened with removal from the slate, an act which under our present system is tantamount to removal from office."[88]

Union leaders set the agenda for delegate assembly meetings and new items can be introduced only by a two-thirds vote, requiring near unanimity from the non-office-holding delegates present. Debate on any resolution that does reach the floor is controlled by Shanker, who, critics note, would often treat rival opinions with sarcasm and scorn or, when opposition was sufficient, would not call on known opponents. If a resolution opposed by Shanker somehow slipped through the delegate assembly, it could be reintroduced at a later meeting when more Unity Caucus representatives were present, or as in the case of the union's resolution on Vietnam, it could simply be ignored by union leadership.

As the delegate assembly positions became effectively sinecures, the importance of other union offices increased, particularly the Executive Board, dominated by slate-voted Unity Caucus members, and the Administrative Committee, appointed by the Executive Board. In contrast to the early 1960s, when debate in the delegate assembly was accessible to all union members, today the Administrative Committee, the main source of union policy, keeps no public minutes, and even the toothless assembly publishes its minutes in abbreviated form, and belatedly at that. As they did in the early 1960s, critics suggest proportional representation on the board as a means for enabling minority positions to receive a hearing. Shanker remained opposed to proportional representation, maintaining that where it exists, as in the Federal Republic of Germany, proportional representation enables "extremists" to have a platform for their views.[89]

Chapter chairs and district representatives, those union officials who directly serve teachers, are the primary means by which teachers interact with the union. The role of chapter chairs and their relationship with union leadership vary widely; in many high schools, for example, there are active chapters often openly hostile to union leadership. But while such chapters are typically the ones most concerned with teacher rights, they are also in conflict with the next level in the union hierarchy, the district representative. Nominally elected by chapter chairs in each district, according to critics these representatives are actually handpicked by union leadership. Only former or present chairpersons are eligible and they must be nominated by five incumbent chairs. Many elections for representatives go uncontested because chairs are afraid to nominate opposition candidates out of fear of future retribution. The district representatives' contact with the district office and with union leadership gives them control over processing of grievances and assignment requests, key services that the chapter chairs would like to provide to teachers in their schools. Unfriendly relations with the representative can jeopardize such powers, so even if a chapter chair is not a member of the Unity Caucus, it typically pays to go along with those in power. Grievances can be pursued independently of the union, but the Board of Education is thought to shunt aside any grievance not supported by the union.

Some counterbalance to Shanker's domination of the union does exist at the school or chapter level. Through tenacious presence at assembly meetings and occasional use of the courts, these activists have won some victories. Access to teacher mailboxes, for example, was a key union victory in the early 1960s. But then, in collusion with school principals, union leaders used the right to exclude anyone but chapter chairs from using the boxes. After a lengthy grievance procedure, dissidents won the right to distribute literature in mailboxes and now circulate independent newsletters at many schools.[90] Still, such efforts hardly offset the barrage of official union publications; a teacher may receive division and caucus newsletters as well as UFT, New York State, and national AFT newspapers, all promoting the Shanker–Unity Caucus position. When asked by Roger Parente in 1965 for space to respond to criticism of his position, Shanker answered, "Democracy does not—and never did—require the Democratic Party to purchase time for the Republicans."[91]

Shanker's tight grasp over the UFT helps him maintain office in the national union as well. Delegates from the UFT give Shanker control over New York State United Teachers (NYSUT), which in turn represents a solid one-third of the votes in the AFT. Since 1972, voting at conventions has taken place with open ballots, so union leaders know which delegates follow caucus discipline. The penalty for not following instructions can be loss of support from the statewide organization—a serious threat to representatives from small school districts. Dissidents enjoy telling the story of how they once heard a Shanker floor manager (there is one for every twenty-five delegates) who lost track of an issue suddenly shouting, "Shanker says hands up." Dissidents took up the chant to the embarrassment of caucus followers.[92]

The growth of New York City teacher unions encapsulates many of the trends already identified for other city employees. In the same way that DC 37 emerged as the focal point for militancy among Career and Salary Plan workers during the 1950s, the Teachers Guild brought together activists from its own ranks and from the High School Teachers Association. Active, democratic participation by members and two strikes gained the UFT the first citywide contracts for teachers, and won teachers dramatic increases in their pay. Salaries jumped from a range of $4,010–$8,400 in 1959 to $9,700–$20,350 in 1975, a 26 percent increase for the average teacher, after taking inflation into account.[93]

One might have expected the teachers union to maintain a highly participatory organization resembling the Patrolmen's Benevolent Association or the Uniformed Firefighters Association. Like police and firefighters, teachers hold similar jobs to one another (most UFT members are classroom teachers) and they work in close contact with one another with relative ease of communication. However, in the years since 1962, the UFT has been transformed into a union dominated by one leader, Albert Shanker, and thus more closely resembles DC 37, the Transport Workers Union, or New York's Teamster affiliates. As a result, teachers have a union that is only superficially democratic; Shanker, and his successor, Sandra Feldman, are elected, but rank-and-file teachers have little impact on union policy. One consequence is that the union can no longer mobilize support from students, parents, or community groups, as did the Teachers Union, the Teachers Guild, and even the UFT during its earlier, more democratic years.

These problems haunted the union during the 1975 fiscal crisis. Chapter 11 will describe how the UFT was one of the few unions to strike against the austerity program imposed on the city. But this protest, without strong backing from union leaders and conducted without cooperation from parents or community groups, merely exposed the irony of the weakly positioned, yet potentially strong union. First, however, Chapters 9 and 10 will review all of the preceding case studies, summarizing how management strategies affected New York's municipal unions and then comparing the internal structures of these unions.

9

Managing Discontent
Changing City Strategy

Although spanning a century of New York City history, the preceding chapters suggest a remarkable continuity in labor relations over those years. Consider, for example, the Sanitation Department: managers of the 1890s would feel at home in today's department, where the problem of productivity is addressed by imposing workload quotas—just as it was in the nineteenth century. Sanitation union leaders of the past would also feel a sense of déjà vu, albeit an uncomfortable one, if brought to the bargaining table in 1980. Just like today's leaders of the Uniformed Sanitationmen's Association, union officials of the Joint Council of Streetsweepers in 1920 were caught between a rank and file demanding militant action and city managers who expected union leaders to enforce workplace discipline.

Traditional accounts of New York City public sector unionism focus on the turbulent late 1960s, reaching contradictory conclusions. Conservatives typically argue that the strikes of that period correspond with John Lindsay's mayoralty: strikes began literally the day he took office, January 1, 1966, with a ten-day transit walkout.[1] Institutionalists make just the opposite claim, arguing that formal collective bargaining rules, wisely put in place by Mayor Lindsay, actually led to a decrease in strikes because the Office of Collective Bargaining peacefully settled labor-management disputes.[2]

Both sides can cite evidence in support of their positions. Without doubt, many of the city's bitterest strikes occurred during Lindsay's terms in office: transit (1966), teachers (1967 and 1968), sanitation (1968), drawbridge and sewage treatment plant operators (1971), police (1971), and firefighters (1973). But institutionalists can point to a decline in strikes after 1968, when OCB began its mediating function. Moreover, technically OCB was not responsible for the teachers strike (because teachers work for a nonmayoral agency not covered by OCB) or the drawbridge operators strike (because their dispute was with the state legislature about a pension bill).

The narrow focus of the debate, purporting to determine the effectiveness of Lindsay's labor policies, causes those on both sides to ignore decades of relevant history and consequently to leave unanswered questions about the origins of recent policies. Quite simply, unions were organized and management granted bargaining rights to them well before 1954, although on an informal, ad-hoc basis. More substantially, the shifts in management's approach to unions noted in both conservative and institutionalist accounts was in fact only a codification of past policies and did not represent a major shift in management's strategy for dealing with unions. None of the so-called landmark statutes of 1954–68 were without precedent in New York City's relations with labor unions.

The extensive and continuous historical tradition of management strategy in New York City's public sector can be best understood by considering first how management recognized unions and, second, how management negotiated with those unions.

Company Unions

Recognition strategies in New York City have a long tradition of management efforts to influence labor's representative in negotiations. The most brazen interference was the company union, organizations created by management itself, a strategy that had its greatest impact in the then privately owned transit system. Following a 1916 strike, the Interborough Rapid Transit Company organized the Brotherhood of the IRT, an unabashed company union that gave the company the appearance of enlightened labor relations—"our men are satisfied," declared company ads—while actually setting up a legal barrier to authentic unions, which were legally blocked from negotiating with the IRT on the grounds that workers had already signed a binding contract. Although initially successful in displacing the Amalgamated

Transit Union from the IRT, the brotherhood served as a meetingplace for workers who secretly continued trade union traditions and in 1926 called another strike.

In the city's public sector, there were two instances of company unionism. The Employees Conference Committee set up for police in 1915 failed almost immediately when police refused to join it. An 1890s company union, the Committee of 41 for streetsweepers, received considerable attention and later served as evidence for institutionalists that public sector "unions" could be advantageous to management. As in the case of the transit system, an unforeseen outcome was a nucleus of disgruntled employees who went on to form a true union, Teamster Local 658, and led street sweepers in their 1906 strike.

Tarnished by abuse, company unions were banned by the National Labor Relations Act and never again surfaced as such in the city public sector. Nonetheless, the principle remained that certain types of unions could be beneficial to management. When union organizing rekindled during Mayor La Guardia's administration, the city tried to sidetrack an undesirable CIO union by preemptively recognizing an AFL union as the sole bargaining agent for sanitation workers. Chapter 3 described how Mayor La Guardia and his sanitation commissioner, William Carey, arranged for recognition of the Joint Board, an AFL affiliate, in preference to dealing with a CIO union that had ties to the TWU and militant leftist groups. Later, Mayor Wagner's administration typically favored Teamster union leaders who were satisfied with occasional services granted to members, in preference to unions demanding participation in collective bargaining. As a result, even though Wagner endorsed union membership for city employees with his 1954 Interim Order, it was not until 1958 that the first group of city workers actually signed a city contract and not until 1967 that the majority of city employees came under a negotiated agreement.

Some Leaders Are Better than Others

During the 1940s and 1950s, city management also played favorites *within* unions; administrators helped favored union leaders take control of unions and turn union policies in a direction more advantageous to management. The most overt use of this strategy occurred in 1948 when Mayor O'Dwyer helped oust the more militant leaders from the TWU in order to solidify the power of Michael Quill, a leader willing to accede to city demands. At the same time, left-leaning leaders of the United Public Workers, a union with an apparent majority in the Welfare Department, lost their jobs because of city pressure. As a result, the union faltered and eventually was replaced by AFSCME Local 371, a union far less antagonistic to the Welfare Department administration.

Moderate union leaders in the Patrolmen's Benevolent Association, Uniformed Sanitationmen's Association, and Local 237 of the Teamsters also received help from the city in defeating dissident movements within their unions. In these cases management assisted or hindered union leaders with selective work assignments, job transfers, or enforcement of sick leave rules. Favored union leaders received credit for helping an employee resolve a grievance or gain a desirable job assignment or work location. Meanwhile, less favored union leaders had little influence with management and sometimes were themselves transferred to outer boroughs where they would have little contact with fellow workers.

Often the city rationalized its efforts to assist less militant unions or less activist union leaders as necessary limitations on Communist party influence. Transit officials openly urged the expulsion of Communists from the TWU and the Board of Education prohibited all consultation with the allegedly Communist-led Teachers Union. Union leaders, including TWU head Michael Quill and CIO president Phillip Murray, joined the anti-Communist bandwagon, expelling Communist-influenced unions, including the United Public Workers, who had organized a potentially powerful coalition of New York City transit workers, teachers, social workers, and hospital employees.

Even though selective favoritism often was couched in terms of anti-Communism, in actual fact the city was willing to overlook a "red" background when it suited their purposes; labor militancy was the real city fear, not party sympathy alone. Thus, while supposedly ridding the transit union of Communists, Mayor O'Dwyer went out of his way to help Michael Quill, even though Quill was purposefully ambiguous about his political affiliation. Similarly, the city seemed to have few qualms about dealing with the pharmacists of Local 1199 until that union began organizing the potentially much larger group of hospital aides. And even though Teamster locals had hired organizers with possible Communist party affiliation, Mayor Wagner continued to favor them over AFSCME District Council 37.[3]

Management favoritism defeated the left-leaning UPW-affiliated unions, but it could not end rank-and-file dissidence. Just as the company unions early in the century fostered resentment among city employees, discrimination against militant unions sometimes provoked antipathy toward the favored ones. Disaffection among subway motormen, for example, escalated when the city supported Michael Quill in exchange for union concessions. When the city cemented its bond with Quill in 1954 by giving the union exclusive recognition in exchange for contract concessions, the motormen formed their own association and went out on strike in 1956 and 1957. Social workers also were upset with the cozy relationship established between Welfare Department officials and Local 371, a union favored by the city after the 1950s ouster of the UPW. They responded with a new organization, Social Service Employees Union, which won representation rights in 1964 and led strikes in 1965 and 1967. During the first teacher contract negotiations, Mayor Wagner tried to have union leaders agree to call off their strike and moderate their demands in return for city recognition of the union. United Federation of Teachers president Charles Cogen did limit the 1960 and 1962 strikes to only one day, but his private arrangements with AFL-CIO labor leaders caused a rank-and-file rebellion that forced union negotiators to stiffen their resolve on workplace issues until they won key concessions on class size, hiring procedures, and new school programs.

City favoritism also backfired when short-term goals caused the city inadvertently to assist a union that proved disadvantageous to management in the long run. SSEU, for example, received unexpected support when Mayor Wagner wanted to create competition for Jerry Wurf's AFSCME Welfare Department Local 371. Similarly, because the city was interested in stopping an organizing drive by Jimmy Hoffa's Teamsters, the Patrolmen's Benevolent Association won the important right to appeal grievances to an independent, nondepartmental panel.

Blatant favoritism had its drawbacks, both in terms of backlash among city employees and bad publicity for reform-minded Mayor Wagner; by contrast, manipulating the structure of bargaining units could help desirable unions, while maintaining the impression of legal fairness. Considered in isolation, questions about the size and nature of bargaining units seem arbitrary and uninteresting. Should subway motormen be covered by the same contract as bus drivers? Should nurses at Bellevue Hospital be covered by the same contract as nurses at Metropolitan Hospital? Such questions frequently determine the outcome of union recognition campaigns.

Bargaining units in the private sector are set by the National Labor Relations Board. Labor lawyers sometimes criticize NLRB policy for being inconsistent, but at least these critical decisions are made by an independent party.[4] In New York City, however, prior to OCB rule setting, bargaining units were set by management, the same group that then negotiated with unions in the chosen bargaining units. One need not believe in conspiracy theories to see that management probably would manipulate these units to their own advantage. In policy statements, city officials presented unit determination as a matter of principle: how can the city best uphold democracy, self-determination, fairness, and efficiency in deciding who should be covered by which contract? The sudden shifts in the city's position belie the real goal of bargaining power.

Divide and Conquer—or Big Works Best?

In the early 1940s the transit system permitted multiple representation in which competing unions attempted to bargain simultaneously for the same groups of employees. As Mayor La Guardia explained, "The right of petition and hearing will be available to all employees and groups of employees without distinction or discrimination."[5] In other words, granting exclusive bargaining rights to one union, even one with majority support like the TWU, would deny minority unions their right to petition the government. At the same time, however, the City Sanitation Department granted exclusive recognition to an AFL union, the Joint Council, which had only scattered support among workers. When asked about the discrepancy in policy, city administrators responded that the Sanitation Department could pursue independent labor relations policies, an obviously disingenuous argument because only a few months earlier the city invoked the transit system nonexclusivity rule to deny bargaining rights to the United Public Workers, a CIO affiliate with majority support in the Welfare Department.

In general, however, fragmented bargaining units with small, competing unions were the preferred strategy. As Mayor Wagner's labor relations commissioner, Anthony Russo, explained, "There was a conscious policy of Wagner's to get a lot of unions involved rather than create one strong union."[6] Between 1954 and 1964, the mayor's ability to manipulate the size of bargaining units and the timing of representation elections enabled him to prevent any one union from becoming predominant.

When militant protest by subway workers escalated during the 1950s, transit officials abruptly changed their minds about bargaining units. In a complete reversal of principles advanced only a few years before, they now adopted the advice of noted institutionalist labor consultant David Cole, who argued that "it is not implicit in industrial democracy that every group or sub-group be represented separately. . . . If each dissatisfied segment were free to secede and create a competing organization whenever it wished to do so, then the organization would be spoiled, next fragmented and finally pulverized."[7] TWU president Michael Quill added that "the elimination of splinter groups and the new contract [in 1954[promise greater stability in dealings between transit labor and management that has been known for years."[8] Management agreed and granted a single unit to Quill despite continuing protests from motormen and other subway workers.

Such logic was applied to nontransit employees during the 1960s. Just as subway workers had been increasingly militant during the late 1940s and early 1950s, so, too, were teachers and civil service workers by the mid-1960s. When confronted by UFT demands for recognition, the Board of Education first considered separate bargaining units for primary and secondary teachers. However, a panel of outside consultants, all of whom had helped adjudicate disputes in the city transit system, recommended a single unit specifically to prevent "me-tooism" between the always-competitive elementary and high school teacher groups.

Career and Salary Plan employees had multiple representation, a system that initially kept unions such as AFSCME, the Teamsters, and Communication Workers of America competing with one another. By 1965, however, the still relatively small AFSCME DC 37 park laborer, motor vehicle operator, and zookeeper locals all won contracts with substantial wage increases, and SSEU social workers also gained unprecedented workplace rights. To make matters worse for management, in 1964 Mayor Wagner miscalculated the outcome of an election among hospital workers with the result that one union, District Council 37 of AFSCME was likely soon to gain representation rights for a majority of Career and Salary Plan workers. Such a majority would allow the union to bargain over so-called "citywide" issues, primarily time and leave rules, which previously were ruled nonnegotiable on the grounds that such topics had to be uniform for all Career and Salary Plan employees. SSEU affiliated social workers briefly sidestepped the restriction; now management was eager to curtail such practices because SSEU's contract quickly became a standard that other unions tried to achieve.

Although city officials were not eager to grant DC 37 the right to citywide bargaining, experiences with other large AFSCME locals in Philadelphia and Cincinnati suggested that consolidation of bargaining units could redound in management's favor.[9] When the Philadelphia single bargaining unit was formalized in 1957, Mayor Richardson

Dillworth noted, "Municipal management has been plagued with wasteful union competition over grievances and a lack of centralized union responsibility required for stable and efficient collective bargaining." Similarly, in Cincinnati a single AFSCME unit was recognized in 1960 in order to stop a United Mine Workers organized drive. As a Cincinnati official explained, the city would no longer "serve as a battleground between two rival groups." [10]

Beginning with the 1966 Tripartite Panel Report, New York City officials began to plan for a collective bargaining structure in which one union would represent most nonuniformed mayoral agency city employees—almost all employees except police, firefighters, teachers, and transit and sanitation workers. As a result, city strategy shifted away from recognition matters and refocused on negotiation strategies. In this regard three topics were of primary concern: the scope of bargaining, the enforcement of contracts, and productivity deals.

We Can't Talk about That

For the private sector, the National Labor Relations Act sets only broad guidelines about what can and cannot be negotiated in union contracts. A few subjects are prohibited outright: discriminatory practices, criminal arrangements, and in some circumstances so-called "hot cargo" agreements in which the employer is pressured to handle only union goods. A similarly short list of topics is mandatory for bargaining: wages, hours, and working conditions. Everything else is permissible if both sides agree to negotiate. [11]

Public sector labor law makes use of language similar to that of the NLRA; as of 1981, thirty-two state laws defined the scope of bargaining as "wages, hours, and working conditions," and many use the divisions "mandatory, permissible, and prohibited" to delineate what may be negotiated. Typically, however, the scope of bargaining is far more restrictive than in the private sector: many more topics are prohibited from the bargaining process. In particular, the definition of working conditions is narrowly defined in many state laws, giving state governments greater managerial freedom than comparable private sector employers. [12]

Current New York City collective bargaining law is characteristic in its attempt to limit the scope of bargaining. Soon after the Social Service Employees Union won major working condition concessions in 1965, bargaining laws began to include language giving the city "complete control over the organization and technology used in performing work." The 1966 Tripartite Panel Report specified the following as outside the scope of bargaining: hiring, firing, supervision, standards of service, organization of work, technology, and whatever maintained "efficiency" of operation. The 1967 New York City Collective Bargaining Law adopted similar language, which the Office of Collective Bargaining subsequently attempted to enforce in a restrictive manner, determining, for example, that staffing levels are bargainable only when they have a "practical impact" on employees, possibly affecting their health and safety, as in the case of two-person patrol cars for police. In general, the courts have backed OCB, at times imposing even stricter requirements on bargainable topics.[13]

Teachers, although employed by a nonmayoral agency and thus not covered by OCB, also encountered an increasingly restrictive scope of bargaining. As with other city workers, initially the scope was set by tradition, a legal loophole that teachers used to raise issues of school standards into negotiations. School officials issued policy statements supposedly prohibiting any "measure of administrative control" by the union.[14] But during the first two UFT contract negotiations, pressure from union dissidents resulted in concessions on class size, additional board hiring of black teachers, increased number of substitutes, and funding for experimental compensatory education programs—all clearly matters of administrative control. In 1967 discontent within the union once again forced UFT leadership to press for the More Effective Schools program, although only minimal funds were allocated. Since then, the board and the UFT have followed the uneasy truce outlined in Chapter 8, in which union leaders are consulted about policy issues, yet do not present an active challenge to declining school standards.

Enforcing the Contract

Formalized collective bargaining helped management regain its contractual prerogatives at the workplace. Gaining employee cooperation was another matter and one that involved unions beyond the signing of a contract. City negotiators routinely expected union officials to make one guarantee about the workplace—that there would be no work stoppages for a contract's duration. Such an agreement was by no means unusual; almost every private and public sector U.S.

labor contract includes a no-strike clause. Article 10 of the New York transit workers' first contract in 1954 is characteristic: "During the term of this agreement there shall be no strike, sit-down, stoppage of work, or willful absence in whole or part from . . . employees authorized by any of the unions." In a typical use of the no-strike clause, the Transit Authority ordered the TWU to stop a 1955 Brooklyn wildcat bus strike. The authority sent the TWU a telegram reminding the union of Article 10, adding, "[It] is a matter of union responsibility to comply with its contract and not to resort to work action or violation thereof."

During the early days of the UFT, some activists argued that the union should not sign a contract containing a no-strike clause, especially in a contract expiring at the end of a school year, when a strike could not be called for at least three months. Significantly, TWU president Michael Quill interceded, advising UFT leaders that a no-strike clause was standard practice in collective bargaining. Quill's advice proved counterproductive at a time when UFT leaders were trying to convince rank-and-filers that AFL-CIO leaders like Quill would help the UFT win better contracts. UFT president Charles Cogen fought a rear-guard battle, protesting Quill's interference, while union organizer David Selden worked out a compromise. The union signed the no-strike clause while simultaneously committing itself to a "no contract, no work" philosophy, implying an automatic strike if a new contract was not negotiated by September after the old contract had expired.

In the private sector, courts interpret a no-strike clause as a binding commitment on the part of union officials to prevent unauthorized walkouts by their members. For public sector unions such contract clauses are backed by an additional legally enforceable restriction, state legislation. New York's Taylor law, for example, bans *all* public strikes, even in the absence of a contractual no-strike clause. Neither the Taylor Law nor no-strike provisions succeeded in preventing strikes. In fact, as with other aspects of labor law, no-strike penalties have been applied to the advantage of favored union leadership.

Compared to union leaders, rank-and-filers who take leading roles in strikes are more vulnerable to the threat of fines and imprisonment simply because they are city, not union, employees and they do not have substantial financial resources. Leaders of the Motormen's Benevolent Association, for example, were rank-and-filers dependent for their livelihood on subway jobs. Heavy fines and repeated court appearances proved sufficient motive for MBA leaders to try to block a second subway strike in 1957 by refusing to call a strike vote meeting. (The strike occurred anyway, and MBA leaders went to jail even though it had been beyond their power to prevent the strike.) Union officials generally were less worried about being jailed; in fact, they could use their "martyrdom" to rally support for themselves. However, large fines and loss of dues checkoff could be used to gain leadership compliance, as occurred after the 1973 firefighter strike. In this case, the city threatened the relatively small union with a $650,000 fine, suspension of promotions for strikers, reassignment of strikers to new companies, and criminal indictments against union leaders. Not surprisingly, UFA officials promised to do all in their power to follow the court's no-strike injunction and later signed a three-year no-strike pledge.

In addition to the implicit bias against rank-and-filers, no-strike clauses also were enforced selectively to help favored unions. In 1960, Mayor Wagner refused to call a one-day sanitation worker walkout a "strike," thus sidestepping supposedly mandatory Condon-Wadlin penalties. Similarly, the TWU avoided these severe sanctions after the 1966 strike by obtaining special state legislative dispensation. After the 1980 transit strike, the union gained reduced Taylor Law penalties by playing on government fears that dissident union members might win control of the union if maximum penalties were enforced.

Varying enforcement of the law after the five teacher strikes (1960, 1962, 1967, 1968, and 1975) confirms how no-strike penalties kept rank-and-file dissent in check. City officials were pleased that UFT president Cogen called off the first two strikes after one day each, despite pressure from union members to continue the protests. As a result, the ostensibly mandatory Condon-Wadlin wage freeze was not applied. Flexibility in enforcement continued under the Taylor Law. The 1968 walkouts that closed schools for most of September, October, and November incurred the UFT only minor penalties and union members received pay compensating for the lost days through an extended school year. By contrast, the much shorter three-week 1967 strike brought $150,000 in fines against the UFT and loss of automatic dues checkoff, costing the union an estimated $500,000 in servicing expenses and lost dues. Similarly, the 1975 strike also resulted in loss of dues checkoff for the union and, because of a 1969 Taylor Law amendment, allowed the board to demand double pay penalties against union members for every day of the strike. Both the 1967 and 1975 strikes took place at the insistence of the rank and file, so the consequences of severe penalties bolstered the position of union leadership, who had argued that the strike would be counterproductive.

Union-Enforced Productivity

Management enlisted union leaders not only to keep employees on the job, but also to make sure that they acquiesced to work-rule changes. Usually labeled "productivity deals," these arrangements had early precedents in transit labor relations. Each TWU advance— exclusive recognition of the union (1954), agreement on memoranda of understanding (1950), and signing of formal contracts (after 1954)— all hinged on union support for work-rule changes. Chapter 3 detailed how TWU leadership guaranteed the enforcement of new sick leave rules in 1954, first by agreeing in secret that the rules would be changed, then by quelling protests when the new rules were announced, and finally by promising management a set amount of savings due to decreased sick pay, an amount apparently to be subtracted from other items in the contract if employees did not in fact reduce their sick leave absences.

Under the rubric of productivity, transit management asked the TWU for tacit approval of changes in transit service, most of them reductions in services (and thus not in fact true productivity increases), including the closing of subway lines without new construction, delayed maintenance programs, and elimination of second conductors on subway trains. Like the work-rule changes, transit management wanted cooperation from union leadership in order to minimize protests that might occur because of cooperation organized by the TWU's left wing between transit employees and rider groups. Favoritism toward those in the TWU who would go along with service reductions, combined with red baiting within the union and from the city administration, eliminated those union leaders who favored the employee-rider coalition.

Productivity deals established by Mayor Lindsay were never as contentious as those earlier in the transit system. Labor-management productivity groups were organized primarily in cooperation with District Council 37, a union that publicly proclaimed its commitment to productivity. But with the exception of the SSEU–Local 371 reconstitution of the welfare system, productivity efforts produced few results until 1975. Then, pressured by the fiscal crisis, productivity deals again took center stage (as will be described in Chapter 11), this time with truly negative consequences for both city employees and residents.

Understanding Strategy

All management strategies—unit determination, scope of bargaining, union enforcement of contracts—call into question traditional explanations of New York City labor relations. Conservatives, working with a model that emphasizes the deleterious effects of unions, were aghast when city officials chose to grant representation rights to large groups of employees in the 1967 collective bargaining law. But conservatives overlooked the long and successful tradition of single-unit bargaining for sanitation and transit workers dating back to the 1940s. Coupled with favoritism in the original choice of union representation, the single unit could guarantee that management would deal with the most advantageous union. And because exclusive representation precluded any other union from building a base of support, a more militant union could never take over. Competitive unionism, as occurred among teachers during the 1950s and among social workers during the 1960s, is all but impossible in today's large, exclusive bargaining units.

Conservatives also fail to see the new collective bargaining rules as strategically important. By restricting the scope of bargaining, city officials blocked the possible spread of contracts dealing with workplace and service delivery issues as negotiated by SSEU. Labor contracts are not simply capitulation to the monopolistic power of unions, as conservatives describe them. Union enforcement of work-rule changes clearly increases managerial authority and diminishes the employee workplace control that exists even without a union. In summary, the conservative verdict against Mayor Lindsay cannot be sustained; tripartite-controlled collective bargaining ended the pattern of strikes by small unions and increased city workplace dominance.

Institutionalist analysis of collective bargaining is more complex; in their careful documentation of rules, institutionalists identify the strategic importance of bargaining units, a restricted scope of bargaining, and union enforcement of contracts. Institutionalist theoretician Richard Lester, in his book *As Unions Mature*, notes the collaborative aspects of what he calls "mature" union-management relations.[15] For New York City, OCB documents the strike-free environment brought about by unchanging large bargaining units.[16]

Certainly institutionalists offer a corrective to conservative bias against unionism; when carefully designed, collective bargaining can serve the interests of management. But institutionalist thought rarely states its goal so baldly, referring instead to "stability" in labor relations without explaining that stability is defined as management's ability to continue production, not an employee's sense of secure employment or remuneration. Institutionalists make it clear that unions can be molded not only to represent their members, but also to insure that management directives are carried out at the workplace. However exhaustive the institutionalist cataloguing of these collective bargaining practices, typically they ignore concomitant effects on unions. Favoritism toward particular union leaders and creation of bargaining units inimical to membership control over their own unions are played down in institutionalist theory. These issues conflict with the expressed institutionalist view that unions are democratic representatives of workers' interests. Chapter 10 will explore the serious consequences of management strategies on the internal affairs of New York City unions.

10

Union Response

Shaped from Above and Below

Management strategies have a readily apparent legacy in New York City. Even when strategy shifted, as it did periodically from union busting to union favoritism, management's role was widely reported and relatively unambiguous. By contrast, the task of tracing labor influence is more problematic. Often without any public voice, New York City employee unrest was limited to informal and thus difficult-to-document responses at the workplace. Even with union representation, opposing "labor" viewpoints typically were present as different unions and different groups within unions competed to speak for city workers. Yet despite the sometimes muted and often divergent character of labor's voice in the preceding case studies, they suggest several historical patterns, the first being simply a long tradition of speaking out.

A Century of Militancy

Labor's role was typically reactive, responding to management-initiated decisions. The adversarial role of labor resulted from work structures that gave management unilateral control over hiring, pay, the pace of work, and methods for delivering city services. In a social system so dominated by these work structures, alternatives are difficult to imagine. But when public sector jobs first arose, other work relations were possible, of which firefighting provides the clearest example. In the early nineteenth century, competing volunteer fire companies served New York City, just as they do today in many small towns and rural communities. Typically cooperative ventures, these volunteer units relied on unpaid labor and collective decision making. Since mid-century, however, New York City firefighting involved wage labor with nondemocratic supervision. Thus firefighter organizations necessarily responded to management initiatives, rather than participating in democratic decision making about the structure of work.

Hierarchical decision making has its most pervasive influence at the workplace itself, where in the absence of consultation, worker input frequently takes the form of resistance to managerial authority. "Cooping" (unauthorized work breaks), coordinated work sharing (allowing one worker to relax), prearranged sick leaves (in which employees take turns being absent), and even sabotage have been noted in a variety of city jobs. Repeatedly management reports singled out such informal protest as just as detrimental to productivity as more publicized strikes. But it is impossible to measure systematically the extent of these informal workplace actions; organized protests provide the only empirical measure of worker dissatisfaction.

Table 10.1 lists worker protests, including all of those sponsored by unions, as well as wildcat activity that was on a scale widespread enough to be recorded. Clearly labor militancy dates back well before the late-1960s strikes emphasized in the conservative-institutionalist debate. The protests occur cyclically: street sweepers engaged in protests early in the century; transit workers were militant from the 1930s through the 1950s; park laborers, motor vehicle operators, and hospital workers led protests in the late 1950s and early 1960s; social workers went on strike in the mid-1960s. Labor militancy has a long history in New York City.

Significantly, each set of protests preceded a shift in city labor relations strategy. Strikes by the Knights of Labor occurred before the 1896 formation of the Committee of 41. Transit worker activism prompted the 1948 recognition of the TWU. It was reaffirmed by the 1954 and 1957 representation elections and the management-assisted 1958 MBA-TWU merger, in each case following wildcat protests. For teachers, a series of high school protests and then two UFT-led strikes predated the 1962 contract. Finally, collective bargaining rules promulgated between 1965 and 1968, and decried by conservatives as the cause of subsequent labor protests, were in fact preceded by less well-known strikes by laborers, gardeners, motor vehicle operators, zookeepers, and social workers. Thus, not only does the conservative perspective err in attributing labor protest primarily to the Lindsay era, it also misspecifies the order of events. Collective bargaining cannot be the cause of worker unrest, because major strikes and other forms of protest took place before collective bargaining was adopted for each of these city employee groups.

Not surprisingly, national historical trends correlate with events in New York City. Transit worker militancy, for example, is linked to the contemporaneous Depression-era industrial worker protests; the success of TWU organizing mirrors the rise of other CIO unions in auto, rubber, and steel plants. In this case, private sector union organizing introduced a strong union heritage that continued when transit employment moved fully to the public sector. Similarly, increased militancy and union organizing among Career and Salary Plan workers during the 1960s drew on the civil rights movement, prompting black (and mostly female) hospital, clerical, and school cafeteria employees to be more outspoken, to protest, and to support one another through the union. Here again, an exogenous social movement translated into a union campaign that served as a model for other city employees, including, for example, police, who were not often in sympathy with the civil rights effort itself.

Job characteristics also appear correlated with militancy. Employees in clearly delineated jobs who work in single city departments—street sweepers, police, firefighters, and transit workers—were among the first groups to form unions. Employees with relatively high-skill job classifications frequently were the instigators of protest. Social workers and subway motormen, for example, both among the better-trained nonsupervisory employees in their respective employment areas, were the leaders of strikes later joined by less-skilled employees. Teachers, a group with both homogeneous jobs and relatively high skill level, indeed were among the first to strike and win a full-fledged union contract.

However, counterexamples quickly confound any simple theory about the source of worker activism. Laborers in the Career and Salary Plan were an unlikely group to lead the resurgence of union organizing during the Wagner administration. These workers were largely unskilled; they did not have a tradition of union organizing from the 1930s on which to build a new union; they were primarily of Italian background and thus were unlikely to join unions as an outgrowth of the civil rights movement; and probably most inimical to unionism, they worked at widely separated locations, a barrier to communication and solidarity. Nonetheless, these laborers comprised a majority of DC 37 membership through most of the 1950s and

TABLE 10.1
Protests by New York City Municipal Employees: 1950–1980

Year	Workers Involved	Union	Support Action?	Activity	Issue and Outcome
1950	High school teachers	HSTA	Yes	Boycott of after-school activities	Low pay; won increased pay
1954	High school teachers	HSTA	Yes	Boycott of after-school activities	Low pay; won pay for after-school activities
1955	Subway motormen	TWU	No	Call in sick; refuse overtime for several days	City attempted to decrease lead time between trains; those calling in sick are suspended
1955	Bus drivers	TWU	No	Refuse overtime for several days	"Downgrading" of bus drivers; union orders back to work; some bus runs saved
1956	Subway motormen	TWU; MBA	No; yes	One-day strike; over 50% participation	Protest against low pay, sick leave changes; ten-day prison sentences for leaders, rescinded for no-strike pledge
1956	Subway maintenance workers	TWU; ATU	No; yes	One day "standup" strike; 500 participate	Protest downgrading; 68 workers suspended
1957	Subway motormen	TWU; MBA	No; yes	Week-long strike; 50% participation at maximum	Protest sick leave, downgrading, low pay, no recognition for MBA; win pay increase; MBA joins TWU
1958	Sanitation workers	USA	Yes, but only after protest	Clock in one hour late	Dissatisfaction with contract offer; win pay increase, benefits reduced
1959	Gardeners	DC 37	Yes	Eighty-day strike	Want union recognition; fail
1959	Career and Salary Plan workers	DC 37	Yes	One-day "leave of absence" by estimated 2,600–8,000	Protest city budget without pay increase; gain publicity
1959	Evening teachers	HSTA	Yes	Strike evening classes	Protest low pay; win substantial pay increases

Year	Worker group	Union	Legal	Action	Outcome
1960	Teachers	UFT	Yes	One-day strike	Protest no collective bargaining; win promise to consider
1960	Police	PBA	Yes	Ticket writing slowdown	Protest policy on moonlighting; no change in policy
1961	Zookeepers	DC 37	Yes	Two-month strike	Want contract; win one with favorable terms
1961	Welfare guards	DC 37	No	Strike	Protest low wages; workers suspended
1962	Motor vehicle operators	DC 37	Yes	Ten-day strike; 4,000 participate	Protest contract offer; win favorable contract
1962	Teachers	UFT	Yes	One-day strike	Protest contract offer; win first contract
1963	Asphalt plant workers	DC 37	?	One-hour work stoppage	Protest schedule changes; no change in policy
1965	Social service workers	SSEU; DC 37	Yes; yes	One-month strike; 5,000 participate	Protest contract offer; win favorable contract
1965	Social service workers	SSEU	Yes	Refuse to do recertifications	Protest caseload; win promise of reduction
1966	Transit workers	TWU	Yes	Twelve-day strike; 30,000 participate	Protest contract offer; win favorable contract
1967	Social service workers	SSEU	Yes	Five-day strike	Protest suspensions in workload protesters; win promise of reduction
1967	Social service workers	SSEU	Yes	One-week work-in	Claim city not following promise; win reinstatement of protesters
1967	Teachers	UFT	Yes	Three-week strike	Protest pay and workplace issues, win favorable contract, except minimal workplace concessions
1968	Teachers	UFT	Yes	Three strikes on most school days over three months	Protest local control transfer of teachers; win end to local control plan

TABLE 10.1 continued

Year	Workers Involved	Union	Support Action?	Activity	Issue and Outcome
1968	Sanitation workers	USA	Yes	Nine-day strike; 10,000 participate	Protest contract offer; win favorable contract
1968	Police	PBA	Yes	Five-day sickout; informal slowdown	Protest contract offer; go back after court injunction
1971	Police	PBA	Yes	Four-day sickout; estimated 25%–80% participation	Protest parity ruling; win favorable outcome
1971	Drawbridge operators; sewage treatment operators	DC 37; Local 237	Yes; yes	Two-day strike; 5,000 participate	Protest pension plan; win partial settlement; strikers fined
1971	Firefighters	UFA	Yes	Slowdown on three occasions	Protest contract offer; win first contract
1973	Firefighters	UFA	Yes	Strike for 5½ hours	Protest contract offer; win favorable contract, but sign no-strike pledge
1975	Sanitation workers	USA	Yes	Slowdown, strike, sabotage	Protest layoffs; initially rehired; later laid off
1975	Teachers	UFT	Yes	Strike	Protest layoffs, contract; layoffs enforced; win contract
1975	Firefighters	UFA	Yes	Sick-out	Protest layoffs; layoffs enforced
1976	Police	PBA	No	Block bridge, refuse to follow orders	Protest layoffs; compromise contract in 1977
1980	Transit workers	TWU	Yes	Strike for 12 days	Protest contract offer; win compromise contract
1980	Police	PBA	Yes	Slowdown	Win contract with some concessions

led the first protests of the Wagner era by any city employee outside of the transit system. For teachers, in-depth poststrike interviews revealed yet other correlates with militancy; male, Jewish, and Socialist teachers were most likely to have participated in the strike. But then why were street sweepers alone among civil servants in carrying forward the Knights of Labor tradition after the 1890s, and why were most other civil service professionals slow to organize unions? Further research might investigate these apparently contradictory patterns of militancy.

Union Leaders versus the Rank and File

Whatever the origins, employee unrest did not necessarily manifest itself measurably in the form of organized protests. For much of the time period studied, there existed no organization through which the protest could proceed. Table 10.1 indicates a second reason for unexpressed employee unrest: union leaders did not always voice rank-and-file concerns, often taking a conservative posture relative to their members. Many protests initially were opposed by union leaders and took place only after continued insistence by the rank and file. Such intra-union conflict sometimes had the support of organized groups within the union, such as the Motormen's Benevolent Association and the American Transit Union in 1956 and 1957; but even in these situations the protests had a spontaneous character and were not in any sense controlled by MBA or ATU officials.

Further evidence for the rift between union leaders and union members is the repeated incidence of contracts voted down by the rank and file after approval by union leaders. Table 10.2 lists these occurrences. Excluded are contracts negotiated by union leaders but presented to membership without leadership endorsement. It is standard practice for union leaders to gain membership rejection of a contract in order to demonstrate to management that more concessions are necessary if a settlement is to be reached. The conservative predilections of union leadership are confirmed by comparing Tables 10.3 and 10.4, listing, respectively, strikes supported by union members but not authorized by union leaders, and actions supported by union leaders but not the rank and file.

It is possible that some strike votes were simply maneuvers by union officials, designed to gain a better contract with only the threat of a strike. If not repeated too often, the strategy might gain higher

TABLE 10.2
Examples of Rank-and-File Rejection of Decisions by Union Leadership

Year	Workers Involved	Union	Issue	Outcome
1954	Transit workers	TWU	Change in sick leave	Sick leave changes remain in effect
1956	Transit workers	TWU	Contract	MBA, ATU lead protests
1958	Transit workers	TWU	Merger of MBA and TWU	Merger takes place
1960	Sanitation workers	USA	Contract	Members reject contract
1961	Welfare guards	DC 37	Wage agreement	Reject negotiated agreement; strike
1962	Firefighters	UFA	Contract	Members reject proposed agreement
1965	Welfare workers	SSEU–DC 37	Contract	SSEU rejects settlement approved by DC 37
1966	Firefighters	UFA	Contract	Members reject proposal from leadership
1967	Social service workers	SSEU	Contract	Members reject proposal from leadership
1968	Sanitation workers	USA	Contract	Members reject proposal from leadership; strike
1968	Police	PBA	Contract	Members reject proposal from leadership
1971	Firefighters	UFA	Contract	Members reject proposal from leadership
1972	Police	PBA	Contract	Members reject proposal from leadership
1975	Sanitation workers	USA	Layoffs	Members protest union's settlement incorporating layoffs
1975–1977	Police	PBA	Contract	Repeatedly reject contract settlements

TABLE 10.3
Examples of Union Leadership Overruling Rank-and-File Vote for a Strike

Year	Workers Involved	Union	Issue	Action by Union Leadership
1955	Transit workers	TWU	Sick leave	Orders workers not to protest
1956 and at two-year intervals except for 1966, 1980, 1982	Transit workers	TWU	Contract	Strike voted by members; not called by leaders, except in 1966, 1980. No strike threat in 1982.
1956	Laborers	DC 37	No recognition	Local votes strike; leadership calls it off
1958	Sanitation workers	USA	Contract	Leadership shortens protest
1960	Sanitation workers	USA	Contract	Leadership shortens protest
1961	Motor vehicle operators	DC 37	Contract	Members call for strike; leadership calls it off
1962	Social service workers	DC 37	Contract	Members vote for strike; leadership calls it off
1980	Uniformed workers	PBA, UFA, COBA	Contract	Members vote for strike; leadership calls if off

TABLE 10.4
Examples of Rank and File Overruling Union Leadership
Vote for a Strike

Year	Workers Involved	Union	Issue	Action
1966	Firefighters	UFA	Contract	Delegate assembly votes for a strike; membership votes to accept contract
1973	Firefighters	UFA	Contract	Union president falsely represents membership vote for a strike

wages and benefits for employees without the cost of lost work time
or strike penalties. Subsequent refusal by union leaders to carry out
the strike would be explained as a strategic necessity. A lost strike,
after all, is worse than no strike, since it means lost pay, a bad contract, and members disillusioned about the effectiveness of their
union. Perhaps union leaders think of longer-term benefits than their
members and are less willing to "bet the union" on a strike that is not
assured to win significant concessions.

Taken as a whole, however, Tables 10.2, 10.3, and 10.4 suggest that
differences between union leaders and the rank and file typically
were neither a matter of bluff nor differences about strategy. During
the early stages of union organizing drives, union leadership typically was more aggressive than the rank and file, urging employees
to take the risk of union membership and to participate in union-
sponsored rallies, petition drives, or on occasion even strikes. Later,
however—the pivotal time appears to be the point of official union
recognition—we find union leaders counseling restraint to an in-
sistent rank and file. The preceding chapter offered an explanation
for this shift in behavior: city management strategies repeatedly re-
enforced the differences between the two groups. These management
strategies were:

- favoritism toward unions with the least militant outlook;
- favoritism toward union leaders least accountable to their members;
- introduction of exclusive representation to assure continued dominance by these favored unions and union leaders;
- introduction of large bargaining units, which often meant a union
leadership out of touch with union membership;

- uniform citywide personnel practices mandating bargaining with only large unions;
- a limited scope of bargaining preventing unions from forming coalitions with service recipients;
- no-strike provisions and productivity deals promoting union leadership cooperation in enforcing management rules.

Each of these management efforts thwarted control over union affairs by union members, a consequence mentioned infrequently in traditional analyses of New York City labor relations. For conservatives, the lacuna is to be expected, given the lack of attention to internal union affairs in their overall perspective.[1] More curious is the institutionalist silence on the subject of democracy in New York City municipal unions.[2] For the private sector, institutionalists developed a sophisticated literature on the internal structure of unions, including rank-and-file participation.[3] Moreover, U.S. labor legislation, basically a product of institutionalist influence, directly addresses union democracy by setting rules concerning union elections and union finances. No other extragovernmental organization faces such strict standards for democratic participation. Union activists justifiably complain that the U.S. Department of Labor and the National Labor Relations Board are lax or selective in their enforcement of union democracy requirements. But even so, no business, social, religious, or other social institution is required to meet even minimal democratic requirements, as are labor unions.[4]

For the public sector, institutionalist-inspired labor legislation itself takes a remarkably inactive stance with regard to union democracy. In contrast to the National Labor Relations Act, which now sets forth standards for private sector union behavior, the New York City Collective Bargaining Law contains only minimally explicit directives for the internal affairs of city public unions. It requires only that unions bargaining with the city file a no-strike pledge (as mandated by New York State law); that unions do not discriminate on the basis of race, color, creed, sex, or national origin; and that unions do not advocate the violent overthrow of the government. Police and firefighters are also limited to joining unions confined to their own professions. Otherwise New York City bargaining law is silent on the internal affairs of unions and does not attempt to require union democracy, as the law does for the private sector.

Management policies, however, as distinct from explicit legislative law, do not remain aloof from internal union affairs. In fact, informal and thus less noticeable interference, significantly altered the structure of today's municipal unions. Beginning with Mayor La Guardia's recognition of a bargaining agent for sanitation workers and lasting into the current period of OCB rule making, city policy consistently favored particular types of unions. Earlier city rules were biased toward blatantly undemocratic unions, while recent collective bargaining laws have favored large, bureaucratic, and thus less democratic unions. Only social workers, firefighters, and police unions emerged relatively unscathed from this management influence. By first reviewing the internal structure of these democratic unions, we can see by contrast the absence of member participation in almost all other New York City municipal unions.

Union Democracy

The Social Service Employees Union stands as a model of union democracy, an exception to the city's success in repressing democratic unions. Initially, SSEU gained city Labor Department recognition only because Mayor Wagner wanted to provide competition to the fast-growing unions organized by Jerry Wurf, especially DC 37's Welfare Department Local 371. Once granted the right to compete for certification, SSEU was able to win extraordinary contract terms, a success directly attributable to its fiercely democratic character.

Union democracy was strong by several measures: meetings were well attended; contract negotiations involved large numbers of rank-and-file representatives; and union leadership positions reflected different factions within the union. All these elements of democracy can be traced to union structures that fostered membership participation: new member orientations; daily taped telephone messages at union headquarters about union events; and workplace newsletters, which served as a debate forum about union policies. Rotation of power was assured by union bylaws prohibiting union officials from succeeding themselves in office. Eventually SSEU was forced to merge with DC 37 when city bargaining rules limited the ability of independent unions like SSEU to negotiate on their own. Still, many of the democracy-enhancing institutional structures remained, as illustrated by the decision-making process for the merger itself. The debate was carried out with self-conscious effort to make it public; all sides (those wanting to affiliate with DC 37, those advocating affiliation with a different union, and those opposed to any affiliation) had access to union publications in a lively year-long forum.

SSEU's unusual bargaining strength was directly attributable to these democratic structures. Widespread commitment by membership to the union enabled SSEU to hold out through the cold January 1965 strike. The union's diligent enforcement of contract terms was possible because of close communication between workers on the job and union leadership. Similarly, the alliance between Welfare Department employees and welfare recipients developed as a result of outreach by union members. As described in the previous chapter, OCB rules were a direct response to SSEU successes, attempting to prevent duplication of SSEU-style contracts.

Police and Firefighters

The Patrolmen's Benevolent Association and the Uniformed Firefighters Association also maintained democratic structures in their respective unions, a perhaps surprising trait in workplaces with paramilitary lines of command. But there have always been widely acknowledged feelings of solidarity among police and firefighters, even between those on street duty and their officers. The perceived and actual dangers of the job contribute to a sense of camaraderie, as does ease of communication through two-way radios and the free time each group has to talk with co-workers. Police tend to develop the well-known commitments to their partners, and firefighters speak of their second "family" at the firehouse, with whom they prepare meals, play games, and watch television during the sometimes long hours between calls.

For firefighters, the strong commitment to unionism dates back to the nineteenth century, when city efforts to outlaw firefighter associations caused the group to go underground as an even more unified organization. The PBA, which allowed the police commissioner to join as a symbolic member, was more amenable to currying favor with management until the 1950s. But the unbridled authority of Commissioner Stephen Kennedy, coupled with post–World War II hiring of better-educated, younger recruits, put the PBA on a more confrontational course, winning benefits for its members through collective strength rather than favored access to the commissioner's office.

As with SSEU, recent PBA and UFA successes are directly attributable to the unions' democratic structures. The sense of solidarity on the job carries over into the union through delegate assembly representatives, each directly accountable to cohesive work groups operating out of police stations or firehouses. The democratic tradition is best illustrated by debates within the PBA and UFA about *how* to make decisions. When strikes were under consideration during the 1970s, the union had to decide between mail votes, which would guarantee wide participation, versus votes taken at a mass meeting, which would allow for last-minute input by members in response to changing management offers. Both procedures were used on different occasions, and the rank and file helped determine which was appropriate.

Leadership turnover in the PBA and UFA is sometimes equated with weakness, that is, leadership that cannot count on a membership following. Indeed, during the period 1975–80 alone, a new president took office four times in the PBA and three times in the UFA. By comparison, no other New York City union changed leaders more than once during this time period, and then because of death or retirement. Such insecurity at the top did not detract from union bargaining power; like SSEU, the PBA and UFA negotiated relatively advantageous contracts. Police and firefighter base pay, for example, nearly tripled between 1955 and 1973. Also, the unions successfully challenged city efforts to change work rules, delaying for many years reducing staffing of police cars and fire trucks. Repeatedly union officials were sent back to the bargaining table by a recalcitrant rank and file; as DC 37 executive director Victor Gotbaum characterized the task of newly elected union presidents: "When you assume leadership, life imposes a much tougher responsibility on you. You now have to produce."[5]

Another PBA and UFA attribute is less pleasant from a civil liberties point of view. Both unions lobbied against fairer treatment for women, homosexuals, blacks, and other minority groups. In terms of the police or firefighter forces themselves, the unions fought to preserve entry criteria based on strength, height, and mental tests, which according to court rulings kept women and some ethnic groups from qualifying. The PBA provoked additional enmity in black and Hispanic communities by opposing the Public Review Board during the 1960s, and in later years by consistently defending what appeared to be serious police abuse during the arrest and confinement of minority group suspects.

Unlike in other city municipal unions, PBA or UFA leaders have not attempted to advance their membership's understanding on issues of race or gender. Indeed, given the democratic nature of both unions, leaders are sometimes elected precisely because they will carry out the racist or sexist beliefs of union members. A full analysis of police and firefighter political views remains to be completed. Based on this study, however, we can note that management policies ruled out coalitions between the uniformed services and other city workers.

The PBA and UFA were encouraged to stay outside the national labor movement, while individual firefighters and police were prevented from joining unions that had members outside the forces themselves. It is not unreasonable to assume that closer cooperation with other city employees, many of them female or minority group members, would have had a salutory effect on police and firefighter views on race and gender.

Authoritarian Unions

Other city union leaders typically were under less pressure to produce. At the opposite end of the spectrum from the SSEU, PBA, and UFA were unions with dominant leadership and much less democratic participation. Some union officials built up virtual fiefdoms: for example, John DeLury, president of the sanitationmen's union from 1938 until his retirement in 1978, and Henry Feinstein, head of another Teamster affiliate, Local 237, from its inception in 1952 until 1960 (in 1965 his son, Barry Feinstein, took over). Leadership in these two unions operated largely without membership consultation; only when union officials capitulated in an obvious manner, as in the case of the USA's 1960 and 1968 contracts, did the threat of a rank-and-file revolt force union leaders to change their position.

Both the USA and Local 237 had management's blessing during their early organizing efforts. The USA got its start when Mayor La Guardia preemptively recognized them over a more militant CIO affiliate in 1941, while Local 237 received Mayor Wagner's favorable treatment in preference to DC 37 locals. No doubt city officials would rather not have dealt with unions at all, but the authoritarian-structured USA and Local 237 were unlikely to lead strikes, or if they did—as in 1968 and 1971, respectively—dominant union leaders could be counted on to bring workers back to their jobs and squelch any dissident rank-and-filers who might want to continue the protest.

The price of favored treatment for both these unions was high. Despite a reputation for supposedly tough bargaining, Local 237 contracts have never been "target" contracts, instead Local 237 successes all came on the coattails of DC 37. On one occasion, the 1968 USA contract was leading one in that it contributed to the city's parity dispute with police and firefighters. But this possible exception actually proves the rule because it followed a nine-day strike in which, at the insistence of an angry rank and file, USA leadership departed from its traditional friendly relationship with the mayor's office. In the past that strategy had helped keep the usa the sole bargaining agent, but had not won significant contract concessions.

In terms of leadership turnover, Local 100 of the Transportation Workers Union resembles the usa and Local 237. Michael Quill dominated both the local and national twu union from its founding in 1936 until his death in 1966. At that time Quill's chosen successor, Matthew Guinan, took over, serving until 1979. As in the case of the usa, Quill unilaterally determined union policy, even when opposed by a majority of union members. And like the usa, twu leadership owed its dominant position to assistance from city officials, who in 1948 helped him ease out a left-wing faction and, between 1956 and 1958, imposed bargaining rules and undertook an eavesdropping campaign that insured the eventual demise of various splinter groups within the twu. Quill craftily exacted a price for his willingness to suppress militant trends; ultimately, in order to undercut the repeated rank-and-file challenges, transit contracts had to be relatively generous. In each case, however, wage increases were granted only after the city was assured that dissident, militant groups were squashed, and that union leadership was willing to help management enforce work-rule changes.

The Odd Unions

Between the poles of democratically run unions (sseu, pba, and ufa) and more authoritarian-structured unions (usa, Local 237, and twu) lie the ambiguous cases of District Council 37 and the United Federation of Teachers.

Membership control in dc 37 is minimal: the key union position is executive director (the president has little power), a job filled by Jerry Wurf from 1948 through 1964, followed by Wurf's handpicked successor, Victor Gotbaum, until his announced retirement in 1986. (For a short time Wurf tried to maintain control of the district council through a surrogate, Calogero Taibi, but quickly surrendered the reins to Gotbaum when he found he could not manage both dc 37 and the national union.) Within the district council, many locals maintain open, well-attended meetings, with active participation by large numbers of members. But decisions about important policies, and anything that affects the union as a whole, is determined by the executive director and his staff. Thus, prior to contract negotiations, individual locals meet to draw up "demands," but because most DC 37 members come under the citywide contract, the only meaningful negotiations take place at the union's highest levels.

DC 37's social outlook also derives primarily from leadership decisions. Nonetheless, DC 37 earned a well-deserved reputation for providing pathbreaking member services in legal aid, education, and health care. Moreover, the union's unwavering support for civil rights and the peace movement, in which Wurf was often the lone left-wing opposition on the AFL-CIO Executive Council, earned the respect, if not approval, of other unions. Into the 1980s DC 37 stands as one of the few stalwarts continuing traditional labor support for full employment, peace, and civil rights coalitions.

Such political views were no doubt consistent with those of DC 37's largely low-paid, female, and black membership. In 1986, income for DC 37 members averaged about $20,000 (prorating part-time employees at a full-time equivalent).[6] Yet, in contrast to the PBA and UFA, which consistently advocate divisive positions (they oppose racial, gender, and sexual preference equality), DC 37 policies do not follow from membership involvement. In fact, the irony is that DC 37 advocates democratic participation by the powerless everywhere *except* in its own internal structure. Thus the union that actively strives to increase participation in outside electoral politics is itself organized on a basis that minimizes the ability of rank-and-filers to directly influence union policy. The large bargaining unit, purposefully designed by city officials, is in part responsible for decision making from the top down. But DC 37 leaders themselves must share the blame for the transformation of a once-dynamic union based on actively mobilized membership into one that strives to restrain membership unrest. AFSCME president (and former DC 37 executive director) Jerry Wurf recognized the change from confrontation to cooperation:

Up until now militancy has often been needed to deal with employers who would not listen, deal fairly or allow their employees to peaceably organize. We are entering a new and different stage in the development of labor relations in state and local governments. . . . We are responding to it by consciously moving from confrontation to cooperation. The experimental and voluntary phase of public employee unionism is over.[7]

A second anomaly of DC 37's public face and internal policies concerns coalition building. To the outside world, DC 37 is a model citizen, lending its name and funds to a variety of causes that affect the union only indirectly. Several DC 37 leaders are active in the Democratic Socialists of America, a group that argues the need for working people around the world to unite for peace, equality, and justice. Yet when it comes to cooperation with New York City community groups or service recipients, DC 37's zeal is remarkably diminished. The social workers Local 371 – SSEU continues to provide a counterexample, although on a much smaller scale than when the SSEU was an independent union.

The United Federation of Teachers shares several characteristics with DC 37. Albert Shanker has dominated UFT policy since 1964 when he was first elected president, until 1986, when he stepped down as UFT president (but not AFT president). The UFT resembles DC 37 in its predominantly male leaders for a majority female union, although, in contrast to DC 37, UFT leadership shares the white and Jewish background of its membership. The major similarity between the two unions lies in leadership commitment to nonconfrontation with the employer. Compare Wurf's philosophy of bargaining, quoted above, with that of Albert Shanker:

I see the same thing [a sense of maturity] in teacher–school board relationships. In New York City, the longest such relationship, there is much more cooperation than there is conflict. . . . In other communities where that relationship is just beginning, or where there is the first contract, or first conflict, they will go through the few rounds before conflict is taken care of and they develop that mutuality of interests that generally comes about and is recognized by both sides.[8]

Whereas in DC 37 the shift away from active protests could be accomplished simply by leadership decisions, in the UFT it required major structural changes in the union. Even though Charles Cogen was president of the teachers union from 1952 through Shanker's election in 1964, Cogen did not enjoy one-man rule, as did Wurf in DC 37; instead, numerous competing union activists determined union policy through the democratically run delegate assembly. Chapter 8 documented the slow erosion of democracy in the assembly and other structures, such as the union newspaper and grievance process. As in DC 37, pockets of independent dissent remain in the UFT, especially among high school teachers, but thus far they act only as a check on union leadership excesses.

As might be expected, the 1975 fiscal crisis uncovered the strengths and weaknesses of each union described here. Internal union tensions that had been papered over for many years could no longer be suppressed when suddenly severe cutbacks in pay, benefits, and employment were on the bargaining table. Chapter 11 will examine how each union—the unstable but democratic PBA and UFA, the authoritarian USA, Local 237 and TWU, and the ambiguously situated DC 37 and UFT—responded to the new challenge.

11

The Fiscal Crisis and Beyond

There were storm warnings before the New York City fiscal crisis hit in the summer of 1975. Major banks had already expressed doubts about their willingness to refinance city debt and thus sold off New York City bonds in anticipation of a city default.[1] In June, however, the crisis struck with unexpected force; default suddenly appeared inevitable when the city was unable to honor $792 million in maturing securities. In fact, in all but legal terms the city declared bankruptcy, placing its finances under quasi-receivership, monitored by corporate and bank leaders.

The price demanded for the bailout was massive reduction in city spending, including a three-year 17 percent reduction in the police force, 16 percent cut in firefighting personnel, and over 25 percent layoffs in such "nonessential" services as health, higher education, and parks.[2] To insure that the cutbacks were put into effect, political control shifted to the Emergency Financial Control Board, on which elected officials had a nominal majority but were subject to veto power by the so-called "public" bank and corporate representatives.

For city employees, the fiscal crisis abruptly reversed the trends of previous years. After decades of an expanding labor force—60 percent growth between 1954 and 1970—there was now a 20 percent cut in employment, leaving those on the payroll demoralized, wondering when they too would receive pink slips.[3] Contracts of the 1960s and 1970s, with their constantly increasing wages, were replaced by a wage freeze. And following a string of union victories on key workplace issues, the fiscal crisis caused decisions to go in management's favor: increased summer work hours, one-person patrol cars for police, and decreased staffing of firefighting equipment and sanitation trucks. Without doubt, by 1978 New York City employees were significantly worse off in terms of wages, benefits, and working conditions than they had been three years earlier.

One might expect that these wrenching reductions in city employment and pay levels would dramatically change public sector unionism. Yet neither a more than 15 percent loss in membership nor repeated unfavorable contracts had much effect. As the fiscal crisis subsided, the same union leaders remained dominant in those unions. Victor Gotbaum stayed at the helm of DC 37 and the Municipal Labor Committee; Barry Feinstein still headed Local 237; Albert Shanker maintained his position as president of the UFT and the AFT; John DeLury continued his more than quarter century of control of the USA; and Matthew Guinan remained president of the TWU's Local 100. Only in the UFA and PBA were there leadership changes because, as one might expect, the tradition of UFA and PBA rank-and-file participation caused a contentious internal debate about the best response to the fiscal crisis.

During the 1980s death and retirement changed union leadership. DeLury and Guinan retired and then died shortly afterward, although leaders loyal to them maintained control of the unions. In 1986 Shanker stepped down from presidency of the UFT (although he kept an office at local headquarters and his AFT presidency), and Victor Gotbaum announced his retirement as DC 37 executive director. Both men had dominated their unions for over twenty years; in retiring they handed control over to trusted assistants, Sandra Feldman as the new president of the UFT and Stanley Hill as the new DC 37 executive director. Whether the new leadership in the UFT, DC 37, TWU, and USA will pursue independent policies cannot yet be determined. All union history recounted here suggests that changed personnel does not affect union policy as much as the underlying structure of those unions.

From management's perspective, the conduct of labor relations also was little altered by the fiscal crisis. The mechanics of bargaining continued to be handled as in previous years: publicly, city officials and union leaders maintained antagonistic positions, while behind closed doors they were able to hammer out agreements, including several during the fiscal crisis that substantially reduced city employment and cut back on wages and benefits. Despite such clear management victories—or rather because of them—city officials were careful to allow union leaders to maintain their images as tough negotiators who held out for the best possible contract for their membership. Repeatedly the major stumbling block to these negotiations was not disagreement between union leaders and management representatives, but the inability of union officials to sell the settlement to their own members. Almost every protest that occurred during the fiscal crisis resulted from just such an impasse and was resolved when union leaders, with help from city officials, were able to regain control over the unions. This three-way conflict between management, unions, and rank-and-file workers is precisely the same scenario that typified labor relations in New York City prior to the fiscal crisis.

Paper Tigers?

Public statements by union leaders during the summer of 1975 suggest bitter opposition to the proposed cutbacks. John DeLury (USA): "I'm not going to stand still and let anybody cut the city in pieces." Victor Gotbaum (DC 37): "As for talk of a wage freeze, no labor leader can ask people . . . to give up an increase they have coming." Barry Feinstein (Local 237): "The banks are squeezing us to death. Let them take a piece of the action."[4] As an alternative policy, these labor leaders pointed out that state and federal aid could obviate the need for the city's proposed budget cuts.

Yet, later that summer, the same union leaders agreed to accept a pay freeze, postponement of a 6 percent raise negotiated the year before (inflation was running over 8 percent in 1975), and indefinite deferral of $8 million in city welfare fund contributions. In 1976 the unions further conceded $24 million in benefits and agreed to tie cost-of-living adjustments to productivity increases. The 1978 contract finally included a long-postponed wage increase of 5.5 percent that, combined with a cost-of-living adjustment, raised wages by about 10 percent, but far below the subsequent two-year, 25 percent inflation rate.[5] The 1975 pay deferral was put back into the wage structure the following year, but wages lost during 1975–76 did not begin to be repaid until 1985, and then only incrementally over the next seven-year period.

Obviously no union leader relished going to his membership to announce such agreements. Union newspapers tried to paint an optimistic picture, emphasizing whatever silver linings existed in the contracts, or simply the fact that more had not been conceded. Typical headlines of the period proclaimed: "Union Returns 200 Laid-off to Work"; "Union Draws Crisis Battle Line, No Mass Layoffs or Wage Freeze"; "Union Plan Saves Hospital Jobs."[6]

Even so, gaining membership approval for contracts negotiated during the fiscal crisis required particular aplomb on the part of labor leaders, and no one was more successful at this than DC 37's Victor Gotbaum. As chair of the Municipal Labor Committee and lead negotiator for the majority of city workers, he had dominated bargaining over so-called citywide issues such as time and leave rules since 1967. During the summer of 1975, early in his talks with bank representatives, Gotbaum agreed to go along with a wage freeze. He did not reveal his concession to the delegate assembly until July, when unrest over the layoffs of the previous months began to taper off. The following year Gotbaum adopted a similar strategy, agreeing in secret for the union to guarantee $14 million in savings. Once again Gotbaum delayed announcement of his concession until he had gained support from within his own union and from other union leaders whose members would be affected by the citywide pact.[7]

Much has been written about the changed role of Victor Gotbaum, who only four years before the fiscal crisis was vilified in the New York newspapers for his role in the drawbridge strike, but who now was extolled in a lengthy *New York Times* Sunday magazine feature. Gotbaum gained a favorable reputation outside the labor movement, including unprecedented praise from Citibank head Walter Wriston and Wall Street banker Felix Rohatyn. In 1977 Gotbaum and Rohatyn (whose personal friendship was now a matter of public record) joined Wriston to form the nucleus of an informal, off-the-record monthly discussion group that tried to reach points of agreement between the usually contentious banks and labor unions. Few union members were aware of these consultations until they were reported by the *Times* in December 1980.[8]

Victor Gotbaum's independent role in brokering a solution to the fiscal crisis was not simply a matter of his own evolving personal philosophy; the city's collective bargaining structure all but guaranteed that employees would be represented by a small group of union leaders minimally beholden to their rank and file. Thus, even though Gotbaum was personally convinced that the fiscal crisis called for unprecedented cooperation between union leaders and bank officials, anything else but a compliant response from him, or the other key union officials—Albert Shanker, John DeLury, Matthew Guinan, and Barry Feinstein—would have meant upsetting a relationship that had helped keep them in power for many years.

Years of accommodation to the city dulled rank-and-file fervor within the unions, so that when union leaders argued against a strike in response to the fiscal crisis, they were conceding the sad, but correct, point that the union could not rally its own members for a protracted strike, nor could they garner public support as they had for the strikes of the early 1960s. Four strikes did occur—by sanitation workers and teachers in 1975, hospital workers in 1976, and transit workers in 1980—but all except the hospital strike took place against union leadership counsel. These strikes, which did not win their stated goals, were resolved by reestablishing union leadership control over the dissident rank and file. And instead of rallying public support against retrenchment, the striking unions only alienated those dependent on city services.

Venting Discontent

The only two full-scale strikes in response to the summer 1975 layoffs came from sanitation workers and teachers. Both ended, however, not with a reduction in the planned layoffs, but when the authority of incumbent union leaders was reasserted within their respective unions.

On June 29, 1975, Mayor Abe Beame ordered 3,000 sanitation workers off the city payroll, about 30 percent of the total work force. Sanitation union president John DeLury publicly stated that he would be powerless to stop any protest; indeed, the entire sanitation force walked off the job for two consecutive days, allowing garbage to pile up, less than during the nine-day 1968 strike, but still creating a significant health and fire hazard on those hot summer days (the 1968 strike occurred in mid-winter).

Events subsequent to the strike indicate that despite its apparently spontaneous nature, both DeLury and city officials were more in control of the situation than their actions indicated. Although technically DeLury did not call the strike, most observers, including the courts, believed that DeLury's comment that "a strike is inevitable"[9] was a mandate for USA members to walk off their jobs. Immediately following the strike, DeLury's reputation among union members improved because he was now perceived as the only city union leader willing to act to prevent layoffs. Furthermore, the agreement settling the strike gave DeLury the appearance of having preserved jobs. The union set up a $1.6 million escrow account, which the union claimed was sufficient to rehire all laid-off workers through the end of the month. Such proved not to be the case; on July 18 Mayor Beame ordered the layoff of 1,434 sanitation workers for whom no pay was available in either the city budget or the union accounts.[10]

When these layoffs were announced, armed officers were placed on duty outside sanitation truck garages in order to prevent sabotage of trucks by disgruntled employees. Even so, some trucks were damaged; sick leaves were so numerous that sanitation service had to be curtailed in some neighborhoods. DeLury counseled restraint, asking that union members await the outcome of a court suit filed by the USA to prevent the layoffs. With union leadership now opposed to further protests, the city began to clamp down on picket lines by calling in police to keep them away from sanitation truck garages and by asking workers who called in sick to submit to a physician's examination.

By August labor relations were back to their prefiscal crisis stability: DeLury was still uncontested leader of the USA; union members were weary of protests and no longer called for a strike; and city officials had gained from sanitation workers the layoffs, the pay freeze, and wage deferral conceded by other unions, and they could count on DeLury to keep peace in the department. Meanwhile, with fewer sanitation workers, garbage pickups and street cleaning were cut back throughout the city so that by 1979 only 52 percent of New York City streets were rated "acceptably clean."[11]

New York City schools suffered the greatest number of layoffs of any single city service: 15,000 teachers and paraprofessionals lost their jobs in 1975. UFT president Albert Shanker urged restraint for the union, which was then in the process of negotiating a new contract. He later explained his position: "Since a strike represents a possibility of life and death for a union, you do not call a strike unless not calling it is also life and death. And I do not consider the questions we had a matter of life and death."[12] At first Shanker convinced the UFT negotiating committee to continue working under the old contract. But when school opened, the union's Executive Board reported to Shanker that they found "chaos," as teachers chafed under the increased workload brought about by the layoffs.[13] Shanker, admitting that "there wasn't any way of calling off the strike," backed down and agreed to a full-scale walkout.[14]

Leaflets distributed on the picket line stated, "This is a strike of the membership, not of the leadership."[15] But while the rank and file unquestionably caused the strike, its conduct was entirely in the hands of union leadership. Shanker explained: "There's no doubt that in the minds of many of the people the issue was bringing back the laid-off teachers. Some of the people on the negotiating committee felt that this was the main issue in the strike."[16] One week later teachers were already back on the job and Shanker admitted that rehiring of teachers had not been a serious union demand, neither in negotiations prior to September nor during the strike. Instead Shanker accepted a contract with settlement terms little different from those agreed upon before the strike: the board would not take away benefits won in previous contracts, and in return the union conceded extra preparation periods that had been allowed in "special service" schools where large numbers of students lagged behind their expected grade level.[17]

UFT leadership submitted the new contract terms to a membership vote on September 16, under circumstances that were less than democratic, even by UFT standards. In 1967 Shanker had told the Board of Education that he needed an agreement weeks in advance of a strike deadline so that members would have adequate time to study the contract terms. In 1975 such luxury of time was impossible in the middle of a strike, but union leaders did not even follow procedures adopted during other disputes—allowing a twenty-four-hour study period, with copies of the full agreement available for examination by members. Instead, teachers were told of a meeting to take place that afternoon at Madison Square Garden's Felt Forum, at which time a brief outline of the contract terms would be available. Shanker gave a rousing speech on how the contract was the best to be expected, only to be greeted by cries of "sellout," which were then muffled by "Solidarity Forever" sung by leadership supporters in the first row. Those members present voted 10,651 to 6,695 to accept the contract.[18]

The vote indicated considerable disenchantment with UFT leadership; it was not only a low turnout, but the lowest percentage of favorable votes for any contract ever recommended by UFT leadership. Nonetheless, for many years to come no sustained opposition challenged Shanker's dominance. Continually thwarted by undemocratic union rules and divided by their own factional disputes, dissidents found it difficult to mount an electoral challenge to Shanker's Unity Caucus. Teachers also report that frequent transfers brought about by chronic understaffing in some schools undermined camaraderie among teachers, making it difficult for them to maintain the informal networks that previously had challenged UFT policy in individual schools.[19]

Only in the high schools were dissidents able to mount a significant election opposition to the Unity Caucus, winning over 40 percent of the vote in 1981 and 1983 and finally defeating the Unity candidate George Altomare in 1985 for the high school's vice-presidency spot. Nonetheless, the result indicates possible weaknesses in Shanker's authority, although not without irony since Altomare was respected by many union dissidents for his independent stands, at least by the usual requirements of Unity Caucus discipline, on the 1968 strike and the Vietnam War.[20]

The powerlessness experienced by UFT members can be explained in part by the entrance of the Emergency Financial Control Board (EFCB) into teacher contract negotiations. As part of its oversight duties, the EFCB reviewed city contracts, including those signed with labor unions. The UFT contract provided a test case for EFCB powers: could they overturn an already-negotiated labor contract? In October the board did just that, ruling the UFT contract in violation of the financial plan worked out by bankers and politicians the previous summer. The board's already-enforced salary freeze and massive layoffs were not at issue; instead the board now wanted to extend its authority to include veto power over specific city policies, in this case cost increases incurred because of longevity promotions and the tradeoff of service reductions for pay increases. The EFCB finally approved the controversial contract terms with only minor alterations, but they did not do so until February 1977, seventeen months after the contract was first negotiated. By taking so long they served a warning to all city unions that contracts would come under similar EFCB scrutiny and only minor salary adjustments would be tolerated.[21]

Although the fiscal crisis seemingly presented the ideal opportunity for union-community coalitions, the 1975 UFT contract had just the opposite effect, exacerbating the union's alienation from parent organizations especially in minority group communities. A disproportionate number of those who lost their jobs during the cutbacks were members of minority groups. As a result, in 1975 the number of black and Hispanic teachers was only 11 percent and 3 percent respectively, for a student body 37 percent black and 28 percent Hispanic.[22] In addition, the 1975 contract agreement included a plan by the board to shorten the school day, thus saving on the number of teachers needed to cover during other teachers' preparation periods. The union's acceptance of the board's proposal put the union in opposition to community groups, which saw the school day cutback as yet another reduction in the quality of education. UFT officials maintained that some community school board leaders used the school-day issue to grandstand for their own political ambitions and Shanker insisted that pressure from parents would result in the reinstatement of the lost periods. But the net effect was that the UFT once again denied itself natural allies for improving the schools.[23]

Police and Firefighter Rebellion

Throughout the 1970s, police and firefighter unions were most vocal in their opposition to retrenchment in city services and also relatively successful in heading off management demands for changed
work rules and reduced benefit levels. Not surprisingly, then, the unprecedented cutbacks of June 1975 provoked from police and firefighters the most sustained protests from these groups and resulted
in somewhat fewer concessions being granted by them. As in past
years, rank-and-file demands were the catalyst for police and firefighter protests.

Firefighters first reacted to the threatened layoffs with a sickout
protest, supported by UFA president Richard Vizzini, who urged firefighters to "take care of their health." Members complied and checked
in sick after routine fires, causing the absence rate to climb. When the
city threatened to close twenty-six fire houses, firefighters joined
with community residents who had occupied buildings and in one
celebrated Bushwick, Brooklyn, case held the assistant fire commissioner captive as well.[24]

But the UFA's bargaining position was complicated: in addition to
fighting the layoffs, the union was still negotiating the previous year's
contract. Union leaders feared that in the climate of retrenchment
they might also lose wage increases retroactively for the 1974 contract. UFA members, frustrated by the delayed negotiations and continued layoffs, ousted their union leadership in July 1975. The new
UFA president, Michael Maye, another rank-and-filer elevated to the
union presidency, negotiated an 8 percent increase for the unsettled
contract, convincing members to go along with the July wage freeze,
layoffs totaling 10 percent of the work force, a loss of half an hour of
uninterrupted meal time, and greater leeway for the city in staffing
procedures.[25]

The PBA first responded to the layoffs threatened in mid-June by
distributing so-called "Fear City" pamphlets warning visitors that
"until things change, stay away from New York City if you possibly
can." Such lurid pronouncements brought quick condemnation from
the press, city officials, and other union leaders, all of whom argued
that the pamphlets added to the already irrational anxieties visitors
brought with them to New York. After a series of court suits, including a restraining order from the New York State Supreme Court ban-
ning distribution of the pamphlet, the PBA withdrew its threat. But
the proposal to lay off 5,000 police remained and disgruntlement
among police was undiminished. Those facing layoffs picketed first

their own precinct headquarters and then, despite opposition from the PBA delegate assembly, marched on City Hall and blocked Brooklyn Bridge rush hour traffic. At the end of June the state legislature voted sufficient funds to rehire about 2,000 police officers.[26]

In the following years, when extra state funds were not forthcoming, conflict between the police and city officials escalated to a level as intense as anything in New York City labor relations since the chaos of social service worker protests in 1967. In both situations there was not a single major strike, but almost continuous protests (sickouts, picket lines, and slowdowns), which had department officials worried about a general discipline breakdown among their employees. Also common to police and social worker struggles was an unwillingness by the employees involved to accept a contract until all outstanding issues were resolved. In both cases a settlement would appear close, only to have the pact rejected when a new topic of controversy erupted.

It took until November 1977 for the PBA and the city to reach agreement on a contract covering 1976–77, one that incorporated a partial victory for the union, although the PBA was forced to accept new workplace procedures, including such touchstone issues as one-person patrol cars and increased evening shifts. The city was forced to compromise somewhat on these changes (one-person patrol cars were limited to outer borough low-crime areas and the new duty chart included more time between sets of shifts), nonetheless both were bitter pills for the PBA, requiring a retreat on what had been hard-won principles. This outcome of better contract terms than those granted other city employees, combined with unprecedented work-rule changes, occurred only after extremely rancorous negotiations and a high level of dissension within the union.

Three different presidents headed the PBA during the tumultuous 1976–77 period. Ken McFeeley resigned in May 1976, despite having just won a court ruling that the ongoing wage freeze could not be imposed on police. McFeeley feared that he could neither sustain his own popularity nor maintain traditionally advantageous PBA contracts in the upcoming summer negotiations. His successor, Douglas Weaving, promoted from first vice-president, stayed in office for only nine months. Unable to win a contract acceptable to the PBA delegate assembly and subject to impending penalties for his participation in a PBA demonstration, he made way for Sam DeMilia, also promoted from a vice-presidency. DeMilia was later elected PBA president in his own right in June 1977, but with only 37 percent of the vote in a three-way election battle with McFeeley and PBA trustee Phillip Caruso. Rapid turnover of PBA leaders occurred in part because those out of power undercut negotiations by incumbents, spotlighting any failures and sabotaging successes. Such byzantine politicking notwithstanding, the intensity of protests indicated a deep and consistent discontent among rank-and-file police.[27]

The most bitter protests began in September 1976 after the PBA lost an impasse ruling on their work schedule. Off-duty picketing broke out, including noisy demonstrations around Gracie Mansion, leading to confrontations with neighborhood residents. Former PBA president Ken McFeeley, identified as a leader of the protest, was suspended from the police force and disciplinary action was taken against several hundred other police officers. On September 28, the same tactics of whistle blowing (in violation of a court antinoise ruling) were moved to Yankee Stadium, where a Muhammed Ali–Ken Norton fight was scheduled. Police protesters blocked traffic, allegedly encouraged gate-crashers, and uniformed police assigned to restrain their fellow officers were reported to have joined in the protest. City officials now talked openly about loss of control over the police force.[28]

After a two-day moratorium on protests, PBA president Weaving announced a compromise in which the city agreed to rehire some police in exchange for the PBA dropping its pending lawsuit about the 1975 6 percent wage deferral. Police would receive pay increases only for 1976 and 1977 and would be required to work a new duty chart, although the city promised to postpone implementation of the one-person patrol cars. The PBA delegate assembly unanimously rejected the proposal and street demonstrations resumed. Weaving then attempted to sidestep the delegate assembly with a rank-and-file referendum, this time on a slightly different settlement mediated by Columbia Law School dean Michael Sovern. But the rank and file proved just as obstinate, voting down the new proposal by a five-to-one margin.

It took all of 1977 to reach agreement on the now-mushrooming issues: pay increases for the old contract (1975) and the new contract (1976–77); changes in the duty chart; one-person patrol cars; and after the September demonstrations, amnesty for those facing penalties. Finally, in November, the EFCB put its imprimatur on a settlement, including payment of a previously negotiated 6 percent wage increase for 1975, which other unions had deferred. For the years 1976 and 1977, however, police wage increases were limited to 6 percent and deferred for the first year, just as they had been for other city employees. But the union hardly had time to take notice; almost immediately they opened negotiations for the 1978 contract.

Although, by comparison, bargaining went relatively smoothly in 1978, by 1980 PBA leadership once again was in flux. During June negotiations for that contract, Phillip Caruso (the third-place finisher in the 1977 elections) won the PBA presidency from Charles Peterson, the PBA vice-president who had served as union president for three months when DeMilia resigned citing health reasons. The PBA joined with firefighters, correction officers, and five smaller uniformed employee unions in what they termed "coalition bargaining." The UFA and the Correction Officer Benevolent Association (COBA) also had recently elected officers who, like Caruso, had little experience in bargaining for their respective unions. Speculation mounted in the *New York Times* about the ability of these neophyte leaders to "control" their membership; debate within the PBA focused not on the advisability of a strike, but whether it would be better to do so immediately after expiration of the contract, or later in August during the Democratic convention.[29]

PBA, UFA, and COBA union leaders later admitted that they feared a strike would have been a "kamikaze move"; instead they channeled unrest into a type of protest that had been used successfully in the 1960s and 1970s, the work slowdown, which caused traffic summonses to fall by 50 percent. Soon afterward, the city and union coalition reached agreement and obtained ratification from the delegate assemblies and members for a 21 percent pay raise, slightly less than that won by transit workers after their April strike, but more than the contract awarded other city employees.[30]

Austerity

The fiscal crisis initiated a long period of steadily declining living standards for New York City employees. Prior to 1975, civil service pay, like most other unionized sectors of the economy, generally kept pace with inflation through a combination of negotiated pay increases and cost-of-living adjustments. But according to a 1980 U.S. Department of Labor study encompassing pay for 100,000 New York City employees, none kept up with inflation between May 1975 and May 1979.[31] During the particularly high inflation period of 1978 through 1980, office workers, custodians, and motor vehicle operators lost over 15 percent in buying power. Even for police and firefighters, who had won somewhat better contracts, base pay corrected for inflation fell by more than 20 percent between 1975 and 1982.[32]

Both the layoffs and wage freeze meant savings for the city, although the latter effect was mitigated by a higher layoff rate for lower-paid employees. During the first year of the fiscal crisis, a 12 percent reduction in the city work force translated into a 5 percent reduction in the overall dollar payroll or, taking into account inflation, a more than 10 percent reduction in real outlay.[33] Additional long-term effects resulted from abandonment of automatic cost-of-living adjustments and decreased city funding of pension plans, both structural modifications sought by the EFCB.

Chastened by loss of membership, New York City unions entered the 1980s with a demonstrably tentative attitude. Transit negotiations exemplify union weakness. In 1985 the TWU departed dramatically from tradition when union president John Lawe proclaimed two weeks before the expiration of the contract, "I wouldn't call a strike, no way. The point is I can keep control of my people."[34] Lawe wanted to repeat the experience of 1982 when, still smarting from the 1980 strike, the union gained their contract through arbitration. Most likely the contract terms had been agreed to in advance, but the outside "authority" of an arbitrator (a panel chaired by OCB head Arvid Anderson) distanced union leadership from the contract's terms, including increased management latitude in assigning work. In 1982 the TWU faced loss of dues checkoff as a penalty for the 1980 strike. An eighteen-month penalty was imposed, but the New York State Public Employees Relations Board lifted it after only four months, officially on the grounds that the TWU could no longer process grievances (with reduced staff, the backlog reached 2,000), although TWU willingness to negotiate peacefully contributed to the board's leniency.[35]

In addition to ending the TWU "no contract, no work" policy, transit management gained a second victory over transit supervisors and their union. In 1977 an advisory committee, the Shinn Commission (see the "Conservative Policy" section later in this chapter) recommended that supervisory personnel be removed from civil service and union protection; out of 40,000 Transit Authority employees, only several hundred could be fired at the will of top management. Negotiations with the Subway Service Supervisory Union resulted in several hundred jobs being removed from union protection, an agreement reached in mid-January 1985, but not announced until after union elections were held. In addition, civil service competitive examination rules were eliminated for over a thousand transit jobs.[36]

In 1980 Victor Gotbaum conceded that his DC 37 members received less in their contract than the transit workers, but claimed that because of fines owed by the TWU for their strike, "in terms of cash received our [DC 37] members will be ahead in the long run."[37] Gotbaum's statement, while correct in the narrow sense since TWU members did come out behind in terms of total remuneration, nonetheless is remarkable for its shift in tone from the early days of DC 37 organizing, when gains by one union were viewed as targets for other unions. At that time strikes were not measured by the dollar cost of penalties versus immediate contract gains, but were defined instead as foundations for future contracts. In other words, a strike might be costly today, but was nonetheless beneficial because it established a tradition of union militancy that would benefit union members in future negotiations. Moreover, during the 1960s unions celebrated other unions' strikes because they typically established minimum contract terms for the nonstrikers. By 1980 not only had DC 37 clearly rejected the strike as a bargaining weapon, but its leader, Victor Gotbaum, had committed the union to accommodation with the city and, through private meetings, also cooperation with bank and corporate leaders.[38]

Productivity Deals

A key element of union-city cooperation instituted by DC 37 was the productivity deal. Long advocated by institutionalists, yet never achieved in New York City, productivity deals could make it possible to devise new work rules that would result in improved services for the public and greater efficiency for management. Because such changes would be brought about through collective bargaining, employees would be less likely to react negatively to management recommendations and, because the changes would be incorporated into union contracts, management would be assured that the unions would assist in their enforcement.

Productivity deals prior to the fiscal crisis only occasionally benefited the public, as they did with, for example, the high-technology fixes of the early 1970s, including "fast water" for firefighting and computer-assisted placement of public safety units. But such new technologies served primarily to promote public relations, giving the impression of a city management concerned about the quality of city services. More typically, productivity deals simply reduced benefits for city employees without increasing service levels, as in the case of sick leave reductions for transit workers of the 1950s. In these cases the major effect of productivity deals was stormy labor relations.

Productivity deals of the post-1975 period came full of promise and, for the first time, were applied across the board to all groups of city employees. Based on a congressional mandate in the New York City Loan Guarantee Act, the 1976 citywide contract and 1978 transit contract required pay increases to be covered by productivity. The burden of initiative now lay with union leaders, who had to negotiate productivity deals in order for members to receive pay and benefits as announced in the contract settlement.

Initially, union leaders emphasized the fact that cost-of-living increases were included in the 1976 contract, downplaying the need to fund them through productivity. Later, the DC 37 union newspaper, *Public Employee Press*, gave double-page spreads to show examples of productivity programs being used to gain the cost-of-living adjustment. Editorials and reports from a union-management productivity committee further exhorted members to come up with ideas that would save money. For such efforts, DC 37 received praise from an unlikely source, EFCB executive director Stephen Berger, who noted that the union acted "very responsibly, . . . making more sense than management."[39]

In actual practice, the productivity program involved little more than cuts in staffing or service. Over 20 percent of the 1976 productivity improvements (on a dollar basis) were accomplished by reducing staff levels in various agencies. A further 20 percent involved promises by city departments to do work "in house" that previously had been contracted out to private businesses. And the majority of the remaining programs required increased workload quotas from an unchanging work force. In several agencies, service suffered dramatically: the Addiction Services Agency, for example, lost 40 percent of its staff between June 1976 and March 1977—chalked up to productivity—and explained casually in the city productivity report, "Maintenance of its operation . . . has perforce required increased productivity from remaining employees." Attrition in the Department of Health and Family Court Services was supposed to be met with an increased work effort by those remaining; here, too, the city gave no explanation for how this was to be accomplished without reducing the quality of service. The Consumer Affairs office met productivity goals by reorienting staff toward revenue-producing inspections, taking staff away from other inspections, again without documenting how this could be accomplished without cutting back on needed services for city residents.[40]

Such productivity programs were simply cost-reduction efforts, which should be distinguished from actual productivity. Examples somewhat closer to a traditional definition of productivity were promises in the 1976 productivity negotiations to increase work hours by requiring Finance Department employees to give up coffee breaks, or for Personnel Department employees to sacrifice overtime pay usually given for conducting Saturday civil service examinations. These programs resembled the productivity deals required in the 1978 transit contract when workers lost time for cleanup and break time between train runs. Such changes can be counted as productivity because output per total person-hour is increased. But still, they are inherently limited productivity improvements, restricted to whatever extra hours can be shaved off workers' free time. Moreover, they undercut the institutionalist contention that productivity deals serve both labor and management interests. From the point of view of workers, cutting back break times or weekend pay is simply a concession.[41]

The only arrangement entirely consonant with institutionalists' ideal productivity arrangement was the 1980 sanitation contract, which accepted two-man trucks and extended routes. Although both required increased work effort by sanitation employees, a gain-sharing program partially compensated workers for increased productivity, passing along half the projected dollar savings. Such changes could have led to increased service levels, thus also benefiting city residents. But the two-man trucks replaced 300 laid-off sanitation workers, simply requiring two men to pick up as much garbage as three had formerly. Overall, the fiscal crisis cutbacks, even when introduced as productivity programs, meant less service, as evidenced by fewer garbage pickups in many neighborhoods and an 80 percent reduction in street cleaning operations.[42]

In summary, the productivity campaign of 1976–80 achieved more than early 1970s public relations–oriented productivity deals. Work effort was increased and money was saved. But if measured in terms of the promises made by institutionalists about productivity deals— that they would increase service delivery and improve relations between employees and management—then the productivity drive was not a success. As documented in this chapter, the major result of new work arrangements was to decrease public employment, while making only token efforts to sustain previous service levels. Furthermore, rather than engaging city employees in an effort to improve the quality of city services, the productivity deals consistently threatened them with loss of their jobs and, in the case of transit workers, exacerbated already bitter antagonism between rank-and-file workers and what they perceived as the combined conspiracy of management and union leaders.

Conservative Policy

For conservatives, the reversal in union success is perplexing.[43] If
New York City unions were so powerful, as conservatives argued, how
was it possible to impose austerity so quickly on precisely those
unions identified as such potent forces before the fiscal crisis? We are
left wondering why these unions neither raised significant protest at
the usurpation of their power by the EFCB nor engaged in major protests after the cutbacks were enforced.

Such questions resemble the conservatives' confusion about events
before 1975 when they exaggerated the bargaining power of unions
with dominant leaders. These unions won initially favorable contracts at the price of future suppression of wildcat strikes, enforcement of contract terms, and accedence to city demands for service
cutbacks. Having been tamed, these unions could not resist concessions demanded by management during the fiscal crisis and also
were unable to mobilize resistance to service cutbacks by showing
common cause with city service recipients.

Because conservatives did not recognize the collaborative role
played by union leaders during the fiscal crisis, they continued to call
for curtailment of collective bargaining, even as it was effecting the
very cutbacks in pay, benefits, and employment that the conservative
perspective had long endorsed. In spring 1977, for example, the Management Advisory Board, or Shinn Commission, after its chair, Metropolitan Life Insurance Company executive Richard Shinn, recommended that OCB be replaced by a five-member board with four city
appointees. The plan would have reinstituted pre-1968-style labor
relations in which the mayor's office unilaterally set rules for contract
negotiations.[44]

OCB officials successfully defended themselves from Shinn Commission proposals by pointing out that severe restrictions on union
activity had already been achieved through the tripartite structure.
On the scope of bargaining, for example, OCB officials argued that
management decisions could now be challenged only with demon-
strable "practical impact" on the employees involved.[45] Furthermore,
OCB chair Arvid Anderson pointed out that arbitrated settlements differed little from those reached through head-to-head bargaining. In
New York State, arbitrated police and firefighter contracts granted pay
increases lower than the national average.[46] Anderson summed up
OCB's new tough stance: "The principle issue at the bargaining table
today is what is to be given up or taken away."[47]

Overall, during the fiscal crisis union leaders acquiesced to cutbacks, the wage freeze, and subsequent minimal contract terms, and they agreed to put their pension funds in state bonds. Clearly, OCB was not a patsy for the unions. According to institutionalists, the EFCB's watchdog role only made negotiations more problematic, since neither the unions, the city, nor OCB could be certain that agreements would be approved. In view of retrenchment required by the fiscal crisis, protest was to be expected. But because of OCB's ability to work with union leaders, the 1975 sanitation strike and the 1976 hospital workers strike ended after only a few days of disruption. When the EFCB delayed its approval of the police settlement, discontent only smoldered and protests continued.

Even though the Shinn Commission did not succeed in dismantling OCB, the commission once again raised the issue of alleged extravagance in municipal labor contracts. Beginning with Wellington and Winter's 1971 Brookings Institution report, and reaffirmed in studies by the Committee for Economic Development and the Institute for Contemporary Studies, conservatives hammered away at the idea that public sector pay was too high.[48] During the fiscal crisis, the popular media picked up the theme, as in a *Time* news article (not an editorial) stating, "If there is a silver lining somewhere in the clouds over New York, it may be that the city's financial problem has become so serious that civil servants and other New Yorkers are willing to accept sacrifices that should have been made years ago."[49] The medicine recommended by conservatives—private oversight of public expenditures—was endorsed by *Time* as a "humiliating but well deserved intrusion on mismanaged home rule."[50]

Were New York City employees in fact overpaid? For all the generalizations made about the city's allegedly high pay, when we compare New York City pay rates with those of other large cities, one must conclude, as did Charles Morris, author of *The Cost of Good Intentions* and critic of Lindsay-era financial policies, "In short, for all the rancor that engulfed municipal labor relations, and despite Lindsay's apparent ineptitude in dealing with unions, overall changes in employee compensation appear to be not much different from those found anywhere else."[51] William Tabb examined the facts behind typical assertions about New York City's "overpaid" employees, including President Ford's statement that the "record shows" New York City wages are the highest in the United States; a Temporary Commission on City Finances report that the average city employee received $26,707 in wages and benefits; and a *New York Times* story about city employees receiving 60 percent more than their private sector counterparts. In each case, Tabb's analysis reveals distortion of the evidence by those eager to show high pay for New York City employees.[52]

Careful studies show that, on average, New York City does *not* have the highest municipal salaries and, when the cost of living is factored in, New York lags considerably behind the other highest-paid metropolitan areas. In terms of benefits, New York City is above the national average for uniformed employees, although not for nonuniformed employees, and it is not the highest paying for any single category of workers.[53] The absolute levels of New York City pay show little evidence of lavish salaries. Sanitation workers, for example, had a *top* base pay in 1982 of only $20,570. Although often supplemented with extra pay for weekend and overtime work, the base pay alone was 30 percent below the level set by the U.S. Department of Labor as "intermediate for a family of four."[54] Top base pay for other city jobs, in particular those likely to be held by women, was much lower— $13,058 for hospital aides and $14,980 for office aides.[55] Within DC 37, covering most nonuniformed city employees, in 1976 half of all members earned less than the federal minimum for an "adequate" standard of living ($10,487).[56] Does it make sense, as the EFCB recommends, not to permit salaries of $10,487 to keep up with inflation?

Unlike most comparable private sector jobs, these public sector jobs included health care benefits and pensions. But again, are health care benefits for secretaries and cleaning personnel the kind of sacrifices that "should have been made years ago," as *Time* argues? Such examples of adequate living standards should be applauded, not condemned as excessive.

Legacy of the Fiscal Crisis

Some union leaders see the preservation of collective bargaining after the fiscal crisis as a major victory, even with lower pay rates and fewer city employees. Supported by OCB officials and institutionalist policy advisers, unions were able to protect the principles of tripartitism from the most severe Shinn Commission recommendations. At a time when pressure from federal loan guarantors and bank and corporate leaders joined the traditional conservative appeal for less consultation with unions, certainly unions could have fared much worse. Under such conditions, it is difficult to determine whether the concessions advised by union leaders preserved union rights in the long run, or whether a different response might have made the cut-backs unnecessary.

The case of the PBA, which won relatively higher pay in their 1977 settlement, suggests an alternative, more militant approach. As the PBA director of labor relations, Nicholas Chorkas explained, "I can't be the DeLury or the Gotbaum. That's my problem. I can't sell out my guys. [Mayor] Beame and [Deputy Mayor] Cavanagh would meet with Vic Gotbaum or John DeLury and privately write scripts." [57] Had other unions followed the wishes of their membership and engaged in pro-tests, as did the PBA, they might have been able to resist the severe retrenchment of the fiscal crisis.

One alternative strategy was to opt out of collective bargaining alto-gether. In November 1976, after the most severe fiscal crisis cutbacks were already in place, Albert Shanker argued, "When there's nothing to be bargained for, it is a form of torture to send people in to bar-gain." As his aide William Scott explained, "He was really saying: 'Don't give me the option of telling my members I'm going to take $10 away from them or ten days away from them. You impose it on me. Don't let me bargain for that.'" [58] But Shanker's call for a World War II–type labor board did not interest other union leaders. Instead, they continued to follow the lead of Victor Gotbaum, who urged con-tinued union participation in fiscal crisis negotiations, even if that meant assisting in the design of a retrenchment program.

Because of veto power exerted by the Emergency Financial Control Board on teacher and other union contracts, one might argue that, whatever the charade of consultation with unions, Shanker's plan had been imposed all along. But as DC 37 research and negotiations director Alan Viani explained, "We would cooperate, because that was the only way that we could get some measure of control as to what was really going to happen. Had we taken a very hard line, bankruptcy would have given control to somebody else." [59] William Scott agrees, pointing out that "some banks thought of bankruptcy as a guaranteed payoff to their customers. . . . The *Wall Street Journal* looks for it as a way to break unions." [60] Given the high level of anti-union, anti–New York City media propaganda, it was likely that labor contracts would have been subject to unilateral readjustment down-ward by a bankruptcy court.

According to Gotbaum, the only alternative to the risky and likely losing cause of bankruptcy was consultative retrenchment, including the so-called productivity deals and, at several points early in the fiscal crisis, purchase of city debt by city unions. Here again Shanker disagreed with Gotbaum, but eventually capitulated, agreeing to pressure Teacher Retirement System trustees to invest in Municipal

Assistance Corporation bonds. City union investment totaled over 20 percent of city and MAC debt by the end of 1977, an investment of over $2 billion, about 38 percent of municipal union total assets.[61] Ironically, the bonds paid handsome returns, although subsequent refinancing of these bonds was possible precisely because the financial markets perceived municipal unions to be quiescent in their demands.

Bargaining during the 1980s demonstrates that city unions preserved some measure of bargaining ability, at least the structural sense of negotiated, signed, and enforceable contracts, clearly a better outcome for them than the *Wall Street Journal's* solution of breaking up the unions. If a resurgent union movement ever emerges, it will be on the basis of union structures preserved during the fiscal crisis. But as presently organized, those unions remain unable to reverse the continuing erosion of the well-being of both city employees and city residents.

Public sector unions acting alone could not redress the decline in city services during the fiscal crisis, nor could they have reversed the increased authority over city finances granted to bank and corporate powers. But by looking to the past we can find strategies that might turn this period of continued decline in the quality of New York City life into one of improvement for city residents and employees alike. As a start, two sets of changes would need to occur, both with historical precedents.

First, city employees would have to regain control over their own unions. The history of the fiscal crisis shows that even in the context of contract reversal, the city was still concerned with using the negotiations as a means to reassert dominance by favored union leaders. Union democracy is a necessary first step if union strategy is to come from the membership and not be filtered through the needs of city management. The early history of every union organizing drive shows that all groups of city employees have at one time participated actively in the functioning of their union; no organizing drive was successful without major support on the part of rank-and-filers.

A major theme of the previous chapter was that the diminution of this kind of participation resulted not from the maturing of unions as an organization, but rather from active attempts by city management to mold unions into more passive bodies that would accept the limits set down in collective bargaining law. Police and firefighters avoided management incursion into their internal union structures. But the democratic structures that emerged in the PBA and UFA consist primarily of rank-and-file veto power over settlements negotiated by union leaders. Thus, while rank-and-file police and firefighters ultimately control the policies adopted by their respective unions, they are not involved in devising alternative strategies to those they routinely reject. The history of the Social Service Employees Union provides a useful model of participatory democracy, in which union members had a meaningful consultative role. sseu's structure encouraged such involvement through newsletters, position papers, a "hotline," and mandatory rotation of union officers.

Active rank-and-file contribution to fiscal crisis negotiations would have prevented the scenarios in which union leaders used strikes to vent membership unrest, while privately negotiating a contract with little membership input. Yet, by itself, democratic participation would not likely have brought about different negotiated settlements. That would have required a second change in the structure of labor relations: a healing of the rift between service providers and service recipients.

As detailed in previous chapters, the structure of collective bargaining works against just such coalitions, and city management has squelched coalitions on the occasions when they did occur. The fiscal crisis provided a situation in which commonality of interests might have been easily recognized. At the same time that wages were frozen and massive layoffs enacted, city residents suffered significant decline in police, sanitation, firefighting, and education services, and complete dissolution of some day-care and welfare programs. Transit fares more than doubled, and for the first time tuition was introduced in the city university system. Although city unions supported some community protests, such as efforts to reopen fire houses, the dominant response by union leadership was to embrace service reductions disguised as productivity programs. Had union leaders instead encouraged community support for restitution of services along with employment, the outcome of the fiscal crisis might have been less harsh for city employees and residents alike.

Second-guessing union strategy is, of course, all too easy. Yet the concerns of city employees and residents remain, even as New York City regains access to the bond market. Negotiations for every contract in the 1980s show precisely the same conflicts that befuddled both institutionalist and conservative labor relations in the past. Whatever the roots of New York City's fiscal problems—and undoubtedly they run deep within our economic system—the problem cannot be resolved without overcoming the apathy and divisions now found in city life. If we want to resolve this crisis, then we can begin by reversing labor relations policies that alienate New York employees from their jobs, from their unions, and from the community as a whole.

Notes

1. Introduction

1. Charles R. Morris, *The Cost of Good Intentions* (New York: W. W. Norton, 1980); Ken Auletta, *The Streets Were Paved with Gold* (New York: Vintage, 1980); Raymond Horton, *Municipal Labor Relations in New York City: Lessons of the Lindsay-Wagner Years* (New York: Praeger, 1973).

2. Arvid Anderson, "The U.S. Experience in Collective Bargaining," in *Public Management at the Bargaining Table*, Kenneth O. Warner and Mary Hennessy, eds. (Chicago: Public Personnel Association, 1967), 21–52; George Hildebrand, "The Public Sector," in *Frontiers of Collective Bargaining*, John Dunlop and Neil Chamberlain, eds. (New York: Harper and Row, 1967), 125–154; Jack Newfield and Paul DuBrul, *The Abuse of Power* (New York: Viking Press, 1977); Roger E. Alcaly and David Mermelstein, *The Fiscal Crisis of American Cities* (New York: Vintage Books, 1977); William K. Tabb, *The Long Default* (New York: Monthly Review Press, 1982); Eric Lichten, *Class, Power and Austerity* (South Hadley, Mass.: Bergin and Garvey, 1986).

3. Clark Kerr, John Dunlop, Charles Myers, Frederick Harbison, *Industrialism and Industrial Man* (New York: McGraw-Hill, 1960).

4. Sterling Spero, *Government as Employer* (Carbondale, Ill.: Southern Illinois University Press, 1972). For a survey of the most recent traditional literature, see Richard B. Freeman, "Unionism Comes to the Public Sector," *Journal of Economic Literature* 25, no. 1 (March 1986): 41–86.

5. C. Wright Mills, *The New Men of Power: America's Labor Leaders* (New York: Harcourt, Brace, 1948), 9. For discussion of "managers of discontent," see Richard Hyman, *Industrial Relations: A Marxist Introduction* (London: Macmillan, 1975).

6. H. H. Wellington and R. K. Winter, *The Unions and the Cities* (Washington, D.C.: The Brookings Institution, 1971).

7. Marxist analyses of Depression-era U.S. labor relations include: James Green "Working Class Militancy in the Depression," *Radical America* 6, no. 6 (Nov. 1972): 1–35; Staughton Lynd, ed., "Part Two: CIO," in *American Labor Radicalism: Testimonies and Interpretations* (New York: John Wiley, 1973), 49–115; David Brody, "Radical Labor History and Rank and File Militancy," *Labor History* 16, no. 1 (Winter 1975): 117–126; Richard Hurd, "New Deal Labor Policy and the Containment of Radical Union Activity," *Review of Radical Political Economics* 8, no. 3 (Fall 1976): 32–43; F. F. Piven and R. Cloward, *Poor People's Movements* (New York: Pantheon, 1977), 96–180; Karl E. Klare, "Judicial Deradicalization of the Wagner Act and the Origins of

Modern Legal Consciousness," *Minnesota Law Review* 162, no. 3 (1978); Karl E. Klare, "Labor Law as Ideology: Toward a New Historiography of Collective Bargaining Law," *Industrial Relations Law Journal* 4, no. 3 (1981); Melvyn Dubofsky, "Legal Theory and Workers' Rights: A Historian's Critique," *Industrial Relations Law Journal* 4, no. 3 (1981); Christopher L. Tomlins, "The New Deal, Collective Bargaining and the Triumph of Industrial Pluralism," *Industrial Labor Relations Review* 39, no. 1 (Oct. 1985): 19–34.

8.   Marxist analysis of labor relations is summarized in Hyman, *Industrial Relations;* David M. Gordon, "The Best Defense Is a Good Defense— Toward a Marxian Theory of Labor Union Structure and Behavior," in *New Directions in Labor Economics,* M. Carter and W. Leahy, eds. (South Bend, Ind.: University of Notre Dame Press, 1980), 167–214; and Harry Braverman, *Labor and Monopoly Capital* (New York: Monthly Review Press, 1974).

9.   Samuel Bowles, David M. Gordon, and Thomas E. Weisskopf, *Beyond the Waste Land: A Democratic Alternative to Economic Decline* (New York: Anchor Press, 1983), 395–398.

10.   Mark Maier, "Management Strategies in Public Sector Labor Law: A Case Study of New York City," in *Marxism and the Metropolis: New Perspectives in Urban Political Economy,* William K. Tabb and Larry Sawers, eds. (New York: Oxford University Press, 1984), 346–363; Mark H. Maier, "The City and the Unions: Collective Bargaining in New York City 1954–1973" (Ph.D. diss., New School for Social Research, 1980); Mark H. Maier, "Public Sector Labor Relations," in *Crisis in the Public Sector,* Economics Education Project, ed. (New York: Monthly Review Press, n.d.), 261–272.

11.   Benjamin Aaron, Joseph B. Grodin, and James Stern, *Public Sector Bargaining* (Washington, D.C.: Bureau of National Affairs, 1979), 3.

2.   Prelude to Collective Bargaining

1.   J. J. McGinley, *Labor Relations to the New York Rapid Transit System* (New York: King's Crown Press, 1949), 360.

2.   John R. Commons, *Labor and Administration* (New York: Macmillan, 1913), 115.

3.   Reform Club of New York, *Municipal Affairs* (June 1898): 226–234; and Commons, *Labor,* 108–115.

4.   David Ziskind, *One Thousand Strikes of Government Employees* (New York: Columbia University Press, 1940), 85.

5.   Ibid., 84–86.

6.   David M. Gordon, Richard Edwards, and Michael Reich, *Segmented Work, Divided Workers: The Historical Transformation of Labor in the United States* (New York: Cambridge University Press), 110–111; and Joseph G. Rayback, *A History of American Labor* (New York: Free Press, 1966), 211.

7. Gordon, Edwards, and Reich, *Segmented Work,* 177.

8. Donald T. Barnum, *From Private to Public: Labor Relations in Urban Mass Transit* (Lubbock, Tex.: Texas Tech University, 1977), 14–15.

9. *New York Times,* 5 Sept. 1916, p. 6.

10. McGinley, *Labor Relations,* 211.

11. Ibid., 220–227, 260–265; Peter Freund, "Labor Relations in the New York City Rapid Transit Industry" (Ph.D. diss., New York University, 1964), 37–39.

12. McGinley, *Labor Relations,* 261–263; Freund, "Labor Relations," 39–42; Theodore W. Kheel and J. K. Turcott, *Transit and Arbitration: A Decade of Decisions and the Path to Transit Peace* (Englewood Cliffs, N.J.: Prentice-Hall, 1960), 22–24.

13. TWU *Express,* September 1969, p. 5; Shirley Quill, *Mike Quill—Himself: A Memoir* (Greenwich, Conn.: Devin-Adair, 1985), 57–102; L. H. Whittemore, *The Man Who Ran the Subways* (New York: Holt, Rinehart and Winston, 1968), 6–51; McGinley, *Labor Relations,* 257–327; August Meier and Elliot Rudnick, "Communists, Unions and the Black Community: The Case of the Transport Workers Union, 1934–1944," *Labor History* 23, no. 2 (Spring 1982): 165–197.

14. Joshua B. Freeman, "Catholics, Communists, and Republicans: Irish Workers and the Organization of the Transport Workers Union," in *Working Class America,* Michael H. Frisch and Daniel J. Walkowitz, eds. (Urbana, Ill.: University of Illinois Press, 1983), 256–283; Quill, *Mike Quill,* 62–63.

15. Amalgamated Association, "The Motormen, Conductor and Motor Coach Operator," August 1937. On display in "Moving Ahead: the TWU at 50," Automation House, New York City, 25 Apr.–25 May 1984.

16. Quill, *Mike Quill,* 39–55, 67; McGinley, *Labor Relations,* 319; Whittemore, *The Man Who Ran,* 16; Freund, "Labor Relations," 42–61.

17. McGinley, *Labor Relations,* 150–199, 502.

18. Quill, *Mike Quill,* 74.

19. McGinley, *Labor Relations,* 294–296; Quill, *Mike Quill,* 86–92.

20. McGinley, *Labor Relations,* 292–294.

21. Edward Sussna, "Collective Bargaining in the New York City Transit System," *Industrial and Labor Relations Review* 11, no. 4 (July 1958): 518–520; McGinley, *Labor Relations,* 296–327.

22. McGinley, *Labor Relations,* 299–327.

23. Sussna, "Collective Bargaining," 520.

24. McGinley, *Labor Relations,* 282–283.

25. For early history of the PBA and UFA, see Emma Schweppe, *The Firemen's and Patrolmen's Unions in the City of New York* (New York: Columbia University Press, 1948); J. P. Gifford, "The Political Relations of the Patrolmen's Benevolent Association in the City of New York (1946–1969)" (Ph.D. diss., Columbia University, 1970), 7–24; Sterling Spero, *Government as Employer* (Carbondale, Ill.: Southern Illinois University Press, 1972), 228–231, 281–282; James F. Richardson, *The New York Police: Colonial Times to 1901* (New York: Oxford University Press, 1970), 268–289.

26. Schweppe, *The Fireman's,* 102.

27. Ibid., 103–104.
28. Gifford, "The Political Relations," 22–24; Schweppe, The Fireman's, 92–163.
29. Schweppe, The Fireman's, 107–163.
30. Ibid., 148.
31. Ibid., 213–219.
32. Richard N. Billings and John Greenya, Power to the Public Worker (Washington, D.C.: Robert B. Luce, 1974), 13–24; interviews.
33. A. Flaxner, "Public Employee Unions," Public Management 21 (Sept. 1937): 262–266; Ralph T. Jones, "City Employee Unions in New York and Chicago" (Ph.D. diss., Harvard University, 1972), 86–87; New York Times, February–October 1941; interviews.
34. New York Times, 18 July 1941, p. 36.
35. Ibid., 17 Feb. 1941, p. 7; 26 May 1941, p. 8; 28 June 1941, p. 8; 29 June 1941, p. 31; 3 July 1941, p. 20; 31 Aug. 1941, p. 1; 26 Oct. 1941, p. 37.
36. Jones, "City Employee Unions," 107.
37. Jewel Bellush and Bernard Bellush, Union Power and New York: Victor Gotbaum and District Council 37 (New York: Praeger, 1984), 7–8, 13–16.
38. Ibid., 10–14.
39. Teamster 237, 30 Mar. 1960; Robert Friedman, "Pirates and Politicians: Sinking on the Same Ship," Working Papers for a New Society 4, no. 1 (Spring 1976): 45–56; Jones, "City Employee Unions," 103–104; Bellush and Bellush, Union Power, 7–8, 13–26.
40. "1952 Organizational Report," Social Service Employees Union Collection, Robert F. Wagner Archives, Tamiment Library, New York University.
41. Stephen Cole, The Unionization of Teachers: A Case Study of the UFT (New York: Praeger, 1969), 23, 40; Celilia Lewis Zitron, The New York City Teachers Union, 1916–1964: Story of Educational and Social Commitment (New York: Humanities Press, 1968), 123; William Edward Eaton, The American Federation of Teachers, 1916–1961 (Carbondale, Ill.: Southern Illinois University Press, 1975), 2–3, 40.
42. Philip Taft, United They Teach: The Story of the United Federation of Teachers (Los Angeles: Nash, 1974), 12–13; Wayne J. Urban, Why Teachers Organized (Detroit: Wayne State University Press, 1982), 91–99.
43. Eaton, The American Federation, 5–12; Robert J. Braun, Teachers and Power: The Story of the American Federation of Teachers (New York: Simon and Schuster, 1972), 19–39.
44. Taft, United They Teach, 7–8; Cole, The Unionization, 11, 15; Urban, Why Teachers, 99–110.
45. Eaton, The American Federation, 20; Braun, Teachers and Power, 33–34.
46. American Federation of Teachers, Commission on Educational Reconstruction, Organizing the Teaching Profession (New York: Free Press, 1955), 234–241, 296–297; Urban, Why Teachers, 99–108; Taft, United They Teach, 28–34, 89, 95; Cole, The Unionization, 26; Eaton, The American

Federation, 12, 90; Zitron, The New York City, 18; Braun, Teachers and Power, 49.
47. Eaton, The American Federation, 103.
48. Cole, The Unionization, 13.
49. Eaton, The American Federation, 103.
50. Zitron, The New York City, 213.
51. Ibid., 152, 174, 212–213.

3. Transit Labor Relations

1. New York Times, 7 May 1980, p. 1.
2. Ibid., sec. B, p. 6.
3. Steven Burghart, "The New York Transit Strike of 1980: The Story of a Rank and File Disaster," Against the Current 1, no. 1 (Fall 1980); Metropolitan Transportation Authority, "Highlights of Transit in New York" (n.d.); interviews.
4. Rick Hurd, "New Deal Labor Policy and the Containment of Radical Union Activity," Review of Radical Political Economics 8, no. 3 (Fall 1976): 36–38.
5. New York Times, 21 May 1948, p. 1.
6. Theodore W. Kheel and J. K. Turcott, Transit and Arbitration: A Decade of Decisions and the Path to Transit Peace (Englewood Cliffs, N.J.: Prentice-Hall, 1960), 31–32; New York Times, Apr.–Dec. 1948; interviews.
7. Joshua B. Freeman, "Catholics, Communists, and Republicans: Irish Workers and the Organization of the Transport Workers Union," in Working Class America, Michael H. Frisch and Daniel J. Walkowitz, eds. (Urbana, Ill.: University of Illinois Press, 1983), 256–283; Shirley Quill, Mike Quill—Himself: A Memoir (Greenwich, Conn.: Devin-Adair, 1985), 62–63; interviews.
8. New York Times, 7 Jan. 1955, p. 11.
9. Peter Freund, "Labor Relations in the New York City Rapid Transit Industry" (Ph.D. diss., New York University, 1964), 71–74.
10. Board of Transportation, "Memorandum of Understanding," 27 June 1950.
11. New York Times, 1950–1954 and 28 Dec. 1957, p. 16.
12. New York Times, 9 July 1955, p. 1.
13. New York Times, 27 June 1954, p. 1.
14. Freund, "Labor Relations," 157; New York Times, 9 Jan. 1954, p. 1; 21 July 1955, p. 25; Sept.–Oct. 1955; 23 Jan. 1959, p. 15.
15. New York Times, 13 Aug. 1955, p. 1.
16. New York Times, 4 Oct. 1955, p. 1.
17. New York Times, July 1956.
18. New York Times, June–Sept. 1956.
19. New York Times, Nov.–Dec. 1956.

20. *New York Times,* 24 June 1956, p. 1.

21. *New York Times,* 28 June 1956, p. 1.

22. *New York Times,* 22 Dec. 1957, sec. iv, p. 8.

23. *New York Times,* Dec. 1957–Jan. 1958.

24. *New York Times,* 27 Dec. 1957, p. 8.

25. From video recording of 1961 NBC show "The Nation's Future" on display at Transport Workers Union of America exhibition "Moving Ahead: The TWU at 50," Automation House, New York City, 25 Apr.–25 May 1984.

26. *New York Times,* Jan.–Aug. 1958.

27. *New York Times,* 17 Feb. 1968, p. 14; interviews.

28. TWU *Express,* Sept. 1969, p. 14A; Quill, *Mike Quill,* 282–299; interviews.

29. Transport Workers Union of Greater New York, "You and TWU" (n.d.), 2–3.

30. A. H. Raskin, "Politics Up-ends the Bargaining Table," in *Public Workers and Public Unions,* Sam Zagoria, ed. (Englewood Cliffs, N.J.: Prentice-Hall, 1972), 129. On inexperience of Lindsay, see Raymond D. Horton, *Municipal Labor Relations in New York City* (New York: Praeger, 1973), 80–81.

31. *New York Times,* 27 Dec. 1965, p. 1.

32. Transport Workers Union of Greater New York, "You and TWU," 9.

33. *New York Times,* Nov. 1969, Oct. 1971, Nov. 1972.

34. *New York Times,* Jan.–Feb. 1972.

35. *New York Times,* Jan.–July 1978; interviews.

36. "TWU Reformers Split Again," *Village Voice,* 2 Dec. 1981, p. 7; Burghart, "The New York Transit Strike," 18–23; interviews.

4. The Wagner Years

1. City of New York, Office of the Mayor, "Interim Order in the Conduct of Relations Between the City of New York and Its Employees," 21 July 1954.

2. Raymond Horton, *Municipal Labor Relations in New York City* (New York: Praeger, 1973), 24–28; Charles R. Morris, *The Cost of Good Intentions* (New York: W. W. Norton, 1980), 87–88; Sterling D. Spero and John M. Capozzola, *The Urban Community and Its Unionized Bureaucracies* (New York: Dunellen, 1973), 63–64.

3. Interview with Ida Klaus, Oral History Project, Robert F. Wagner Labor Archives, Tamiment Library, New York University.

4. Irving Bernstein, *The Turbulent Years: A History of the American Worker* (New York: Houghton Mifflin, 1970), 41.

5. See Chapter 1, n. 7.

6. Interviews; Ralph T. Jones, "City Employee Unions in New York and Chicago" (Ph.D. diss., Harvard University 1972), 116–117; Jewel Bellush and

Bernard Bellush, *Union Power and New York: Victor Gotbaum and District Council 37* (New York: Praeger, 1984), 33–38; *New York Times*, 1954–56.

7. Robert Caro, *The Power Broker* (New York: Vintage, 1974), 70–82.

8. Bellush and Bellush, *Union Power*, 47–61.

9. Jones, "City Employee Unions," 127–128.

10. Ibid., 135; Bellush and Bellush, *Union Power*, 14, 40; interviews.

11. Margaret Levi, *Conflict and Collusion: Police Collective Bargaining* (Cambridge, Mass.: MIT Operations Research Center, 1974), 18; *New York Times*, Jan. 1956; "1952 Organization Report," in SSEU–Local 371 Collection, Robert F. Wagner Labor Archives, Tamiment Library, New York University (hereafter SSEU Collection).

12. Klaus interview, Robert F. Wagner Archives; City of New York, Office of the Mayor, "Executive Order No. 49."

13. Daniel H. Kruger and Charles T. Schmitt, *Collective Bargaining in the Public Sector* (New York: Random House, 1969), 12.

14. City of New York, Office of the Mayor, "Executive Order No. 49."

15. Horton, *Municipal Labor*, 36.

16. Klaus interview, Robert F. Wagner Archives.

17. Alice Cook, "Public Employee Bargaining in New York City," *Industrial Relations* 9 (1970): 250–251.

18. *New York Times*, Nov. 1958.

19. *New York Times*, 29 July 1960, p. 1.

20. *New York Times*, July 1960.

21. Jones, "City Employee Unions," 135–135a; *New York Times*, 8 Sept. 1960, p. 28.

22. Jones, "City Employee Unions," 134–135; Bellush and Bellush, *Union Power*, 41.

23. Bellush and Bellush, *Union Power*, 71; *Public Employee Press*, 14 Apr. 1961, pp. 1, 3; *New York Times*, Mar.–Apr. 1959.

24. *New York Times*, 1961. Twenty-two craftsmen of Local 374 at the Brooklyn Botanic Garden struck for eighty days in the summer of 1959, but they failed to win union recognition. See *Public Employee Press*, 12 June 1959, p. 7; 8 July 1959, p. 2.

25. *New York Times*, 1962; Jones, "City Employee Unions," 147.

26. *Public Employee Press*, 7 Dec. 1962, p. 1; Cook, "Public Employee," 253.

27. James F. Farmer, *Lay Bare the Heart* (New York: Arbor House, 1985), 178.

28. Campaign leaflets in SSEU Collection.

29. District Council 37, "22 Years" (n.d.); Sumner M. Rosen and Nancy L. Rappaport, *City Personnel: Forces for Change*, Institute of Public Administration (Beverly Hills, Calif.: Sage Publications, 1970), 25–45; DC 37 organizing leaflets in SSEU files; *New York Times*, 1961–65; *Public Employee Press*, April 1978; interviews.

30. Bellush and Bellush, *Union Power*, 305; on Lillian Roberts, see Susan Reverby, "From Aide to Organizer: The Oral History of Lillian Roberts," in

Women of America: A History, Carol Berkin and Mary Beth Norton (Boston: Houghton Mifflin, 1979); Susan Reverby, "Hospital Organizing in the 1950s: An Interview with Lillian Roberts," *Signs* (1976): 1053–1063; *New York Times*, 12 Jan. 1981, sec. ii, p. 4; and Bayard Rustin, "Lillian Roberts' Cause," in *Sorry . . . No Government Today*, Robert E. Walsh, ed. (Boston: Beacon Press, 1969), 94–95.

31. Bellush and Bellush, *Union Power*, 148–156; Horton, *Municipal Labor*, 37–38; District Council 37, "Local 420, 22 Years" (n.d.), 5.

32. Bellush and Bellush, *Union Power*, 56; *Public Employee Press*, 12 Nov. 1965, p. 1, 29 Nov. 1965, p. 1; 10 Dec. 1965, p. 1; Aug. 1966, pp. 2, 3.

33. Bellush and Bellush, *Union Power*, 81–102; *Public Employee Press*, 15 Feb. 1963, p. 1.

5. Social Service Workers

1. Raymond Horton, *Municipal Labor Relations in New York City* (New York: Praeger, 1973), 67–68; Joyce L. Miller, "Constraints on Collective Bargaining: A Case Study," *Urban Analysis* 1 (1978): 87–110.

2. Labor Research Association, *Labor Fact Book* (1946) (New York: International Publishers, 1947), 76.

3. Al Lee, "Hilliard Versus Local 1: Welfare History 1948–1951" (n.d.), SSEU–Local 371 Collection, Robert F. Wagner Archives, Tamiment Library, New York University (hereafter SSEU Collection).

4. Ibid., 1.

5. Hilliard to president of Local 371, 21 Nov. 1950, SSEU Collection.

6. Lee, "Hilliard," 6.

7. Hilliard to president of Local 371, 21 Nov. 1950, SSEU Collection.

8. Lee, "Hilliard," 3.

9. *SSEU News*, 10 Mar. 1967, p. 3.

10. *SSEU News*, 25 Oct. 1965, p. 2; Richard Mendes, "The Professional Union: A Study of the Social Service Employees Union of the New York City Department of Social Services" (Ph.D. diss., Columbia University, 1975), 30.

11. "Committee for a More Militant and Responsive Union" (n.d.), SSEU Collection; interviews.

12. Telegrams from A. Zander to A. Coury, May 6, May 7, 1963, in SSEU Collection.

13. Ballot results 1955–64 in SSEU Collection.

14. Mendes, "The Professional Union."

15. "Committee for a More Responsive Union" (n.d.), SSEU Collection.

16. *New York Times*, Sept.–Oct. 1962; SSEU leaflets in SSEU Collection.

17. Mendes, "The Professional Union," 48; *SSEU News*, 28 Feb. 1963, p. 1; 10 Mar. 1967, p. 3.

18. SSEU survey (1965) in SSEU Collection; interviews.

19. *New York Times*, 11 Aug. 1963, p. 1; 11 Oct. 1963, p. 30.
20. Mendes, "The Professional Union," 57, 60.
21. This is the thesis of Mendes, "The Professional Union."
22. Leaflet to Wyckoff Center newcomers, SSEU Collection.
23. "SSEU Organizing Manual" (n.d.); "To the New Caseworker" (n.d.); "Introducing the Social Service Employees Union," SSEU Collection; Klipes, "SSEU–Local 371: The First Decade" (Nov. 1973); Mendes, "The Professional Union," ii, 14, 63; interviews.
24. *New York Times*, Sept.–Dec. 1964; "Introducing the Social Service Employees Union."
25. *New York Times*, Dec. 1964–June 1965; Mendes, "The Professional Union," 81–91; Jewel Bellush and Bernard Bellush, *Union Power and New York: Victor Gotbaum and District Council 37* (New York: Praeger, 1984), 123–127; interviews.
26. Mendes, "The Professional Union," 41, 81.
27. Ibid., 111–113; *New York Times*, 20 Jan. 1965, p. 38; *New York Post*, 13 Jan. 1965, p. 1.
28. Letters between SSEU and Local 371; SSEU Collection.
29. Bellush and Bellush, *Union Power*, 122; letter from A. Viani to J. Wurf, 8 Aug. 1966, SSEU Collection.
30. *Public Employee Press*, Jan. 1967; Mendes, "The Professional Union," 105–113; Miller, "Constraints," 91; Bellush and Bellush, *Union Power*, 110.
31. Mendes, "The Professional Union," 92.
32. Miller, "Constraints," 92.
33. *New York Times*, Feb.–Apr. 1965; Miller, "Constraints," 92–94; Tripartite Panel, "Statement of Public Members of Tripartite Panel to Improve Municipal Collective Bargaining Procedures."
34. Tripartite Panel, "Statement," 1.
35. *New York Times*, 27 July 1965, p. 67; 29 July 1965, p. 28.
36. Mendes, "The Professional Union," 226; *SSEU News*, 13 May 1966, p. 2.
37. Miller, "Constraints," 94–95; interviews.
38. Ibid., 95–97; Mendes, "The Professional Union," 173–194.
39. "We Are Organizing to Change the Department of Welfare"; "What Is Community Action"; "How to Fight the Slum Landlord" (all leaflets in SSEU Collection); Mendes, "The Professional Union," 194, 532; interviews.
40. Miller, "Constraints," 95–96; Mendes, "The Professional Union," 297; *New York Times*, 14 Dec. 1966, p. 27; 16 Dec. 1966, p. 48.
41. Miller, "Constraints," 97; Mendes, "The Professional Union," *SSEU News*, 6 Jan. 1967, p. 1.
42. *New York Times*, Jan. 1967; Bellush and Bellush, *Union Power*, 130–136.
43. *New York Times*, 8 Feb. 1967, p. 16; 9 Feb. 1967, p. 77; 10 Feb. 1967, p. 40; 15 Feb. 1967, p. 31.
44. Ibid., 20 June 1967, p. 1; *SSEU News*, 16 June 1967, p. 1; 18 Aug. 1967, p. 1.

45. *New York Times,* 20 June 1967, p. 1; 24 June 1967, p. 1.

46. *New York Times,* July–Sept. 1967.

47. Mendes, "The Professional Union," 226.

48. Memorandum from SSEU leadership to membership, 5 June 1969, SSEU Collection.

49. "Reorganization and Workload Committee Reports" (1969–1973), delegate assembly minutes, 31 Aug. 1970, SSEU Collection; Miller, "Constraints," 104–105; *New York Times,* 4 Dec. 1970, p. 26; 8 Dec. 1970, p. 55.

50. Miller, "Constraints," 100; interviews.

51. M. Rosenblatt, A. Viani, S. Gorelick, "Committee for Effective Leadership" (n.d.), SSEU Collection; interviews.

52. "Report of the Affiliations Committee," Jan. 1968, SSEU Collection.

53. Ibid.; "Down Memory Lane" (n.d.), SSEU Collection.

54. SSEU Executive Board minutes, 9 Oct. 1967; 16 Oct. 1967; 23 Oct. 1967, SSEU Collection; *SSEU News,* 7 Nov. 1966, p. 1.

55. *New York Times,* 11 Jan. 1969, p. 38.

6. District Council 37 and OCB

1. City of New York, Office of the Mayor, "Interim Order on the Conduct of Relations Between the City of New York and Its Employees," 21 July 1954; City of New York, Office of the Mayor, "Executive Order No. 49," 31 Mar. 1958; City of New York, Office of Collective Bargaining, "New York City Collective Bargaining Law" (as amended 1972).

2. Irving Bernstein, *The Turbulent Years* (Boston: Houghton Mifflin, 1970), 316.

3. Labor Management Institute of the American Arbitration Association, "Statement of Public Members of the Tripartite Panel to Improve Municipal Collective Bargaining Procedures," 31 Mar. 1966.

4. Ibid., preamble, pp. 1–3.

5. *SSEU News,* 9 Mar. 1966, p. 1; 4 Apr. 1966, p. 1; 27 May 1966, p. 1; 9 Dec. 1966, p. 1; "Summary of the Cost of the Tripartite Report" (1966) and "Tripartite Report" (1966), both in SSEU–Local 371 Collection, Robert F. Wagner Labor Archives, Tamiment Library, New York University (hereafter SSEU Collection); *New York Times,* 31 Mar. 1966, p. 1; 1 Apr. 1966, p. 23.

6. *Public Employee Press,* 15 Apr. 1966, p. 8.

7. *New York Times,* June 1966; interviews.

8. For summary of the Taylor Law see New York State Public Employee Relations Board, "What Is the Taylor Law? . . . and How Does It Work?" New York State Public Employee Relations Board (1974); Gerald A. Schillan, "The Taylor Law, the OCB and the Public Employee," *Brooklyn Law Review* 35 (1969): 214–237.

9. On differences between the OCB and PERB see Schillan, "The Taylor Law," 236–237.

10. *New York Times,* 10 Apr. 1966, p. 61; 20 June 1966, p. 32; 27 June 1966, p. 34; 29 Nov. 1966, p. 46.

11. City of New York, Office of the Mayor, "Executive Order 52," 19 Sept. 1967; City of New York, "New York City Collective Bargaining Law"; Schillan, "The Taylor Law," 236.

12. City of New York, "New York City Collective Bargaining Law," 5.

13. City of New York, Office of Collective Bargaining, "Impasse Procedures in New York City," 17 Nov. 1971.

14. City of New York, Office of Collective Bargaining, "Revised Consolidated Rules of the Office of Collective Bargaining," 21.

15. City of New York, Office of Collective Bargaining, "Annual Report" (1975), 5.

16. Ibid., "Introduction."

17. City of New York, "New York City Collective Bargaining Law," 7; Schillan, "The Taylor Law," 236.

18. *New York Times,* 11 Jan. 1969, p. 38; Alice Cook, "Public Employee Bargaining in New York City," *Industrial Relations* 9 (1970): 262. ocb rulings on "practical impact" have been erratic, sometimes interpreting the phrase narrowly, other times permitting the union to bargain over issues such as use of civilians in the Fire Department.

19. *Public Employee Press,* 8 May 1968, p. 7.

20. Raymond Palombo, "Collective Bargaining and the Merit System in the City of New York" (Ph.D. diss., New York University, 1970), 180–185.

21. *Public Employee Press,* 1966–68; *New York Times,* 1966–68.

22. On the sanitation strike, see *New York Times,* Jan.–Mar. 1968; Raskin, "Politics Up-ends the Bargaining Table," in *Public Workers and Public Unions,* Sam Zagoria, ed. (Englewood Cliffs, N.J.: Prentice-Hall, 1972), 133; Charles R. Morris, *The Cost of Good Intentions* (New York: W. W. Norton, 1980), 103–106.

23. Jewel Bellush and Bernard Bellush, *Union Power and New York: Victor Gotbaum and District Council 37* (New York: Praeger, 1984), 192–193, 239–275.

24. On concern over public sector productivity see, for example, Committee for Economic Development, "Improving Productivity in State and Local Government" (Mar. 1976).

25. *New York Times,* 4 May 1971, p. 51.

26. *Public Employee Press,* July 1971.

27. *New York Times,* 20 Nov. 1971, p. 35.

28. *New York Times,* Apr.–July 1971; Raskin, "Politics Up-ends," 141–142; Morris, *The Cost,* p. 156; interviews.

29. *Public Employee Press,* 2 May 1969, p. 3.

30. *Public Employee Press,* 19 June 1970, p. 2

31. *New York Times,* 5 June 1972, p. 22.

32. *New York Times,* May 1973.

33. *New York Times,* Aug. 1972–Oct. 1973.

34. *New York Times,* 10 Aug. 1972, p. 39.

35. *Public Employee Press,* 5 Jan. 1972, p. 2.

36. *Public Employee Press*, 29 Mar. 1967, p. 2; 20 Sept. 1967, p. 7; 31 May 1967, p. 1A.

7. Police and Firefighters

1. J. P. Gifford, "The Political Relations of the Patrolmen's Benevolent Association in the City of New York (1946–1969)" (Ph.D. diss., Columbia University, 1970), 31–37.
2. Margaret Levi, *Bureaucratic Insurgency: The Case of Police Unions* (Lexington, Mass.: D. C. Heath, 1977), 29.
3. Gifford, "The Political Relations," 38.
4. Ibid., 93–94.
5. Levi, *Bureaucratic Insurgency*, 29.
6. Stephen P. Kennedy, "No Union for New York City Police," *American City* 73 (Oct. 1958), 179–181.
7. Levi, *Bureaucratic Insurgency*, 45.
8. *New York Times*, 7 Jan. 1959, p. 21.
9. Levi, *Bureaucratic Insurgency*, 48–49.
10. Gifford, "The Political Relations," 177.
11. *New York Times*, 9 Jan. 1959, p. 18.
12. Gifford, "The Political Relations," 172.
13. Ibid., 180; *New York Times*, 28 Oct. 1960, p. 64.
14. Raymond D. Horton, *Municipal Labor Relations in New York City* (New York: Praeger, 1973), 95; Levi, *Bureaucratic Insurgency*, 50–52.
15. Gifford, "The Political Relations," 106; Levi, *Bureaucratic Insurgency*, 54.
16. *New York Times*, 12 Apr. 1956, p. 1.
17. Ibid.
18. *New York Times*, 7 Oct. 1960, p. 1.
19. *New York Times*, 21 June 1962, p. 27; 25 Oct. 1962, p. 20.
20. *New York Times*, Dec. 1966, Jan.–Mar. 1967.
21. *New York Times*, Mar.–Apr. 1967.
22. *New York Times*, Oct. 1968.
23. Ibid.
24. *New York Times*, Oct.–Nov. 1968.
25. Levi, *Bureaucratic Insurgency*, 71.
26. On the parity debate, see Horton, *Municipal Labor*, 87–90; Charles R. Morris, *The Cost of Good Intentions* (New York: W. W. Norton, 1980), 120–124; A. H. Raskin, "Politics Up-ends the Bargaining Table," in *Public Workers and Public Unions*, Sam Zagoria, ed. (Englewood Cliffs, N.J.: Prentice-Hall, 1972), 135–139.
27. *New York Times*, 26 Jan. 1971, p. 42.
28. *New York Times*, 18 Jan. 1971, p. 1.
29. *New York Times*, 21 Jan. 1971, p. 1; Levi, *Bureaucratic Insurgency*, 78.

30. *New York Times*, Jan. 1971.
31. Levi, *Bureaucratic Insurgency*, 68–77.
32. Ibid., 71.
33. Ibid., 68–77.
34. *New York Times*, 1970–71.
35. *New York Times*, 7 June 1971, p. 66.
36. *New York Times*, Nov. 1971.
37. Ibid.
38. Levi, *Bureaucratic Insurgency*, 81–84; *New York Times*, July 1972.
39. *New York Times*, Apr. 1973.
40. *New York Times*, 7 Nov. 1973, p. 1.
41. *New York Times*, Apr. 1973–June 1974.
42. *New York Times*, Nov. 1973–June 1974.
43. *New York Times*, 19 Nov. 1973, p. 1.
44. *New York Times*, 30 Nov. 1973, p. 41.
45. *New York Times*, 26 Nov. 1973, p. 33.
46. *New York Times*, 30 Jan. 1974, p. 40; 26 Feb. 1974, p. 33; 3 Mar. 1974, p. 50; 29 May 1974, p. 1; 22 June 1974, p. 28; 5 Sept. 1974, p. 1.
47. See, for example, Horton, *Municipal Labor*, 87–90.

8.   United Federation of Teachers

1. David Selden, *The Teacher Rebellion* (Washington, D.C.: Howard University Press), 15.
2. Stephen Cole, *The Unionization of Teachers: A Case Study of the UFT* (New York: Praeger, 1969), 23; U.S. Department of Commerce, Bureau of the Census, "Average Annual Earnings of Employees," in *Historical Statistics of the United States* (Sept. 1975), 164.
3. *New York Times*, 5 Apr. 1950, p. 25; 26 Jan. 1951, p. 25; 16 Apr. 1951, p. 1; Cole, *The Unionization*, 18, 54; Selden, *The Teacher*, 30–39.
4. *New York Times*, 29 Mar. 1956, p. 1; 2 Apr. 1956, p. 1; 6 May 1956, p. 50; 9 June 1957, p. 48; Cole, *The Unionization*, 18, 54; Selden, *The Teacher*, 30–39.
5. Selden, *The Teacher*, 25.
6. *New York Times*, 30 Jan. 1954, p. 17; 22 Mar. 1956, p. 1; 23 Mar. 1956, p. 52; interviews.
7. Cole, *The Unionization*, 54–59, 182; *New York Times*, 1 Jan. 1959, p. 18; Feb. 1959.
8. Robert J. Braun, *Teachers and Power: The Story of the American Federation of Teachers* (New York: Simon and Schuster, 1972), 135; Selden, *The Teacher*, 3–31.
9. Selden, *The Teacher*, 17.
10. Ibid., 31, 33; personal correspondence from David Selden, 18 May 1986.

11. Cole, The Unionization, 59–62.

12. Ibid., 19, 36; "Executive Board Minutes," Sept. and Oct. 1952, in UFT Collection, Robert F. Wagner Archives, Tamiment Library, New York University (hereafter UFT Collection).

13. Cole, The Unionization, 79–108, 131.

14. Ibid. See also Alan Rosenthal, "The Strength of Teacher Organizations," Sociology of Education 39 (1966): 359–380; and William T. Lowe, "Who Joins Which Teacher's Group?" in Collective Negotiations in Public Education, S. M. Elam, M. Lieberman, M. H. Moskow, eds. (Chicago: Rand McNally, 1970).

15. Selden, The Teacher, 25; interviews.

16. Cole, The Unionization, 36; interviews.

17. Interview with Rebecca Simonson, Oral History Project, Robert F. Wagner Labor Archives, Tamiment Library, New York University.

18. Cole, The Unionization, 17; Braun, Teachers and Power, 132–145; interviews.

19. Selden, The Teacher, 38.

20. Cole, The Unionization, 47, 170–177; interviews.

21. "Executive Board Minutes," 1960, UFT Collection.

22. New York Times, Oct. 1960; A. H. Raskin, "He Leads His Teachers Up the Down Staircase," New York Times Magazine, 3 Sept. 1967, p. 30.

23. New York Times, Nov. 1960; Selden, The Teacher, 47.

24. Interview with Charles Cogen, Oral History Project, Robert F. Wagner Labor Archives, Tamiment Library, New York University; Philip Taft, United They Teach: The Story of the United Federation of Teachers (Los Angeles: Nash, 1974), 111–113.

25. Cogen to Van Arsdale, 29 May 1961, UFT Collection.

26. Cole, The Unionization, 167; New York Times, 10 Nov. 1960, p. 51.

27. Selden, The Teacher, 47.

28. Ibid., 50.

29. "AFT Executive Committee Minutes," 17 Dec. 1960, UFT Collection.

30. New York Times, 16 Feb. 1961, p. 28; 8 Nov. 1976, p. 1.

31. New York Times, June–Sept. 1961.

32. Ida Klaus, "The Evolution of a Collective Bargaining Relationship in Public Education: New York City's Changing Seven Year History," Michigan Law Review 67 (1969): 1037; Hochberg and Cogen to UFT membership, 29 May 1961, UFT Collection.

33. "Collective Bargaining Committee Minutes," 2 Dec. 1960, UFT Collection.

34. Taft, United They Teach, 116; Teachers Union election material in UFT Collection.

35. John C. Cort, "'U' is for Unions," The Commonweal (26 May 1961): 226–229; Eric Rhodes, "The New York City Teacher Election," NEA Journal (Feb. 1962): 21–22; "The Professional Teacher," New Republic (1 Jan. 1962): 146; Myron Lieberman, "The Battle for New York City's Teachers," Phi Delta Kappan (October 1961): 2–8; Robbins Barstow, "Which Way New York City—Which Way the Profession?" Phi Delta Kappan (December 1961): 118–124.

36. Michael Moskow, "Teacher Organizations," in *Collective Negotiations,* Elam et al., 243; UFT election leaflets in UFT Collection.

37. Barstow, "Which Way New York City."

38. TBO leaflets in UFT Collection; telegrams of Cogen to labor leaders, UFT Collection; Michael Moskow, "Teacher Organizations," 321, in *Collective Negotiations for Public and Professional Employees,* Robert T. Woodsworth and Richard E. Peterson, eds. (Glenview, Ill.: Scott, Foresman, 1969), 315–329; Rhodes, "The New York City Teacher."

39. Anonymous notes on meeting with Mayor Wagner, 24 Feb. 1962, UFT Collection.

40. Cole, *The Unionization,* 67–68.

41. *New York Times,* 12 Apr. 1962, p. 32.

42. "Summary of Negotiations Since the Strike" (23 May 1962), UFT Collection; Fred M. Hechinger, "The Story Behind the Strike," *Saturday Review* (19 May 1962): 54–78; *New York Times,* Apr.–May 1962; Selden, *The Teacher,* 71–77; personal correspondence from David Selden, 18 May 1986; interviews.

43. Interview.

44. *New York Times,* 18 Apr. 1962, p. 19; Cole, *The Unionization,* 64–65.

45. *New York Times,* 20 June 1962, p. 26.

46. *New York Times,* 14 Sept. 1962, p. 38; Selden, *The Teacher,* 78.

47. Cole, *The Unionization,* 179; *New York Times,* 1 May 1962, p. 26; 11 June 1962, p. 33; interviews.

48. Interviews.

49. Michael Moskow, *Teachers and Unions* (Philadelphia: Industrial Research Unit, Warton School, University of Pennsylvania, 1965), 152–157.

50. Taft, *United They Teach,* 113.

51. *New York Times,* 26 May 1961, p. 22; 15 June 1961, p. 27; 29 Sept. 1961, p. 27; 4 Nov. 1961, p. 21.

52. Klaus, "The Evolution," 1039–1043; interviews.

53. *New York Times,* 9 Sept. 1963, p. 1.

54. Letter to the editor from Charles Cogen, *Newsweek* (30 Sept. 1963): 4.

55. Moskow, "Teacher Organizations."

56. Klaus, "The Evolution," 1041–1047.

57. David Selden, "Class Size and the New York Contract," *Phi Delta Kappan* (Mar. 1964): 283–286; "The Professional Teacher," *New Republic* (21 Sept. 1963): 4.

58. *New York Times,* 16 Apr. 1964, p. 75.

59. *New York Times,* 27 Nov. 1963, p. 25; 5 Dec. 1963, p. 61.

60. *New York Times,* 11 Sept. 1965, p. 1.

61. Cole, *The Unionization,* 79–108, 131.

62. *New York Times,* 7 Sept. 1967, p. 1; 8 Apr. 1967, p. 29; 7 Jan. 1969, p. 43.

63. Steve Zeluck, "The UFT Strike: A Blow Against Teacher Unionism," reprinted from *New Politics* 7, no. 1 (Winter 1968): 6.

64. *New York Times,* 15 Mar. 1967, p. 1; 21 Mar. 1967, p. 33; 18 May 1967, p. 41.

65. Deborah Meier, "The New York Teachers Strike," *Midstream* 13, no. 10 (December 1967): 37; *New York Times*, Sept. 1967.

66. Taft, *United They Teach*, 150.

67. *New York Times*, 13 Jan. 1974, p. 64.

68. Cogen interview, Oral History Project, Robert F. Wagner Labor Archives, Tamiment Library, New York University.

69. Maurice R. Berube and Marilyn Gittell, eds., *Confrontation at Ocean Hill–Brownsville: The New York School Strike of 1968* (New York: Praeger, 1969); Barbara Carter, *Pickets, Parents and Power: The Story Behind the New York City Teachers Strike* (New York: Citation Press, 1971); Martin Mayer, *The Teachers Strike: New York 1968* (New York: Harper and Row, 1969); Melvin Urofsky, *Why Teachers Strike: Teacher Rights and Community Control* (New York: Doubleday, 1970); Miriam Wasserman, *The School Fix, NYC, USA* (New York: Simon and Schuster, 1971).

70. *New York Times*, 26 Oct. 1968, p. 25; interviews.

71. Taft, *United They Teach*, 169; Meier, "The New York," 36–47; Selden, *The Teacher*, 146, 150; *New York Times*, 16 Sept. 1967, p. 12.

72. Wasserman, *The School Fix*, 200–202, 316–318; interviews.

73. Albert Shanker interview in Urofsky, *Why Teachers Strike*, 173.

74. "Letter of Transfer," in *Confrontation*, Berube and Gittell, eds., 33.

75. UFT leaflets (1968), UFT Collection; *New York Times*, 15 Oct. 1968, p. 51; 23 Oct. 1968, p. 1.

76. Selden, *The Teacher*, 153; Berube and Gittell, *Confrontation*, 165–170.

77. Diane Ravitch, *The Great School Wars, New York City 1805–1973: A History of the Public Schools as Battlefield for Social Change* (New York: Basic Books, 1974), 358. For a more complete statement of McCoy's beliefs, see Rhody McCoy, "A Black Educator Assails the White System," *Phi Delta Kappan* (Apr. 1968): 448–449.

78. *New York Times*, 5 Jan. 1969, p. 43.

79. Steve Zeluck "The UFT Strike," 8; interviews.

80. Carter, *Pickets, Parents and Power*, 68.

81. *New York Times*, 21 Oct. 1968, p. 1.

82. Ravitch, "The Great School Wars," 389; *New York Times*, 13 May 1975, p. 23; interviews.

83. Urofsky, *Why Teachers Strike*.

84. *New York Times*, 19 Nov. 1968, p. 38.

85. Urofsky, *Why Teachers Strike*, 183.

86. Internal politics of the UFT from: *New York Times*, 24 Feb. 1971, p. 43; Coalition of New York City School Workers, "Democracy and Politics in the UFT" (n.d.); Selden, *The Teacher*, 157–161; Zeluck, "Democracy and Politics in the UFT"; Taft, *United They Teach*, 229–230; Neil G. Ellman, "The Role of the United Federation of Teacher Chapters in the Union and Their Respective Schools" (Ph.D. diss., Teachers College, Columbia University, 1973); Roy Pellicano, "Analytical Essay—the Policies and Politics of the UFT," *Educational Studies* 10 (1979): 357–373; Roy R. Pellicano, "New York City Public School Reform: A Line Teacher's View," *Phi Delta Kappan* (Nov. 1980): 174–177; Roy R. Pellicano, "Teacher Unionism in New York City: A

Process that Reinforces Bureaucracy," *Urban Education* 71, no. 1 (Apr. 1982): 97–115; Lois Weiner, "Cracks in Shanker's Empire," *New Politics* 11:4 (Fall 1976): 51–57. Lois Weiner, "Shanker Embraces Reagan-Style Education Reforms at AFT Convention," *Labor Notes* (27 July 1983): 16; Richard Stutman, "Teachers Convention: Least Open in Years, Shanker Machine Maintains Control," *Labor Notes* (29 Sept. 1981): 10.

87. Selden, *The Teacher*, 84.

88. *New York Times*, 24 Feb. 1971, p. 43.

89. *New York Times*, 7 Apr. 1974, p. D-9.

90. Coalition of New York City School Workers, "Democracy and Politics," 7.

91. Letter from Shanker to Parente, 1 Feb. 1965, UFT Collection.

92. Selden, *The Teacher*, 114, 171; interviews.

93. Cole, *The Unionization*, 23; *New York Times*, 8 Sept. 1975, p. 38; corrected for inflation by the author.

9. Managing Discontent

1. See, for example, Raymond D. Horton, *Municipal Labor Relations in New York City* (New York: Praeger, 1973); and Jack D. Douglas, "Urban Politics and Public Employee Unions," in *Public Employee Unions*, A. Lawrence Chickering, ed. (San Francisco: Institute for Contemporary Studies, 1976), 91–107.

2. See Office of Collective Bargaining, *Annual Report* (1973), 6.

3. *New York Times*, 5 June 1960, p. 58; 6 June 1960, p. 22; 9 June 1960, p. 34.

4. Commerce Clearing House, *1976 Guidebook to Labor Relations* (Chicago: Commerce Clearing House, 1976), 69–112.

5. J. J. McGinley, *Labor Relations in the New York Rapid Transit System* (New York: King's Crown Press, 1949), 104.

6. Horton, *Municipal Labor*, 37.

7. Peter Freund, "Labor Relations in the New York City Rapid Transit Industry" (Ph.D. diss., New York University, 1964), 109.

8. *New York Times*, 9 July 1955, p. 1.

9. Irwin Beller, "Collective Bargaining and the City of Philadelphia," in *Unions and Union Leadership*, Jack Barbash (New York: Harper and Row, 1959), 159; Sterling D. Spero and John M. Capozzola, *The Urban Community and Its Unionized Bureaucracies* (New York: Dunellen, 1973), 41–44; *New York Times*, 14 Feb. 1957, p. 1; July–Feb. 1969; July 1978.

10. W. D. Heisel, "Anatomy of a Strike," *Public Personnel Review* (Oct. 1969), 226–233; W. D. Heisel and J. P. Santa Emma, "Unions in City Government: The Cincinnati Story," *Public Personnel Review* (Jan. 1971), 35–39.

11. Commerce Clearing House, *1976 Guidebook*, 260–262, 281–310.

12. Commerce Clearing House, *Labor Law Reporter* 1981.

13. Office of Collective Bargaining, *Annual Report* (1968, 1969, 1970, 1971, 1972, 1973, 1974).

14. Michael Moskow, "Teacher Organizations," in *Collective Negotiations in Public Education*, S. M. Elam, M. Lieberman, M. H. Moskow, eds. (Chicago: Rand McNally, 1970).

15. Richard A. Lester, *As Unions Mature* (Princeton, N.J.: Princeton University Press, 1958).

16. Office of Collective Bargaining, *Annual Report* (1969–1975).

10. Union Response

1. On New York City, see, for example, Raymond Horton, *Municipal Labor Relations in New York City: Lessons of the Lindsay-Wagner years* (New York: Praeger, 1973). For conservative approach in general, see, H. H. Wellington and R. K. Winter, *The Unions and the Cities* (Washington, D.C.: The Brookings Institution, 1971); Melvin W. Reder, "The Theory of Employment and Wages in the Public Sector," in *Labor in the Public and Nonprofit Sectors*, Daniel Hamermesh, ed. (Princeton, N.J.: Princeton University Press, 1975); Robert A. Nisbet, "Public Unions and the Decline of Social Trust," and Jack D. Douglas, "Urban Politics and Public Employee Unions," both in *Public Employee Unions*, A. Lawrence Chickering, ed. (San Francisco: Institute for Contemporary Studies, 1976), 13–33, 91–107.

2. See, for example, Jack Stieber, "Collective Bargaining in the Public Sector," in *Challenges to Collective Bargaining*, Lloyd Ulman, ed. (Englewood Cliffs, N.J.: Prentice-Hall, 1967), 65–88; Michael H. Moskow, J. Joseph Loewenberg, and Edward C. Koziara, *Collective Bargaining in Public Employment* (New York: Random House, 1970); Sam Zagoria, ed., *Public Workers and Public Unions* (Englewood Cliffs, N.J.: Prentice-Hall, 1972); David T. Stanley, *Managing Local Government Under Union Pressure* (Washington D.C.: The Brookings Institution, 1972); Sterling D. Spero and John M. Capozzola, *The Urban Community and Its Unionized Bureaucracies* (New York: Dunellen, 1973); and David Lewin, Peter Feuille, and Thomas Kochan, *Public Sector Labor Relations: Analysis and Readings* (Glen Ridge, N.J.: Thomas Horton, 1977).

3. See, for example, Arnold S. Tannebaum, *Participation in Union Locals* (Evanston, Ill.: Row, Peterson, 1958); and Richard A. Lester, *As Unions Mature* (Princeton, N.J.: Princeton University Press, 1958), 66–70. Labor journalist William Serrin provides a fascinating account of the United Auto Workers and General Motors in *The Company and the Union* (New York: Random House, 1974).

4. For a survey of union democracy issues, see H. W. Benson, *Democratic Rights for Unions Members* (New York: Association for Union Democracy, 1979).

5. Victor Gotbaum, "Collective Bargaining and the Union Leader," in *Public Workers and Public Unions*, ed. Sam Zagoria (Englewood, Cliffs, N.J.: Prentice-Hall, 1972), 79.

6. Raymond Palombo, "Collective Bargaining and the Merit System in the City of New York" (Ph.D. diss., New York University, 1970), 76; Barbara Wertheimer and Ann Nelson, *Trade Union Women: A Study of Their Participation in New York City Locals* (New York: Praeger, 1975), 50; DC 37 average wages from DC 37 Research Department.

7. Quoted in Steve Zeluck, "Toward Workers Power" (Highland Park, Mich.: Sun Press, n.d.).

8. Quoted in Roy R. Pellicano, "Teacher Unionism in New York City: A Process that Reinforces School Bureaucracy," *Urban Education* 17, no. 1 (Apr. 1982): 101.

11. The Fiscal Crisis and Beyond

1. Eric Lichten, *Class, Power and Authority: The New York City Fiscal Crisis* (South Hadley, Mass.: Bergin and Garvey, 1986), 95–126; William K. Tabb, *The Long Default: New York City and the Urban Fiscal Crisis* (New York: Monthly Review Press, 1982), 22–25; Jack Newfield and Paul Du Brul, *The Abuse of Power: The Permanent Government and the Fall of New York* (New York: Viking, 1977); Roger E. Alcaly and David Mermelstein, eds., *The Fiscal Crisis of American Cities* (New York: Vintage, 1977).

2. Joan Weitzman, *City Workers and Fiscal Crisis: Cutbacks, Givebacks and Survival* (New Brunswick, N.J.: Rutgers University Press, 1979), 15; Arvid Anderon and Marjorie A. London, "Collective Bargaining and the Fiscal Crisis in New York City: Cooperation for Survival," *Fordham Law Journal* 10 (1983): 392.

3. Raymond D. Horton, *Municipal Labor Relations in New York City* (New York, Praeger, 1973), 8; Weitzman, *City Workers*, 26, 98.

4. *New York Times*, 15 May 1975, p. 39.

5. The contract called for two cost-of-living payments of $750 each. Assuming average pay of less than $15,000 per year as the median income (see *New York Times Index*, 1978, p. 718), the adjustment was at most 10 percent.

6. *Public Employee Press*, 30 Jan. 1976, p. 4; 24 Oct. 1975, p. 3; 7 Nov. 1975, p. 3.

7. *New York Times*, 3 Aug. 1975, p. 1; 3 July 1976, p. 24.

8. *New York Times*, 2 Dec. 1980, p. B-1; 4 June 1978, sec. vi, p. 27; Lichten, *Class, Power*, 149–184; Martin Shefter, *Political Crisis/Fiscal Crisis: The Collapse and Revival of New York City* (New York: Basic Books, 1985), 163–166.

9. *New York Times*, 3 July 1975, p. 1.

10. *New York Times*, June–Aug. 1975.

11. Tabb, *The Long Default*, 30.
12. *New York Times*, 30 Sept. 1975, p. 30.
13. Ibid.
14. Ibid.
15. *New York Times*, 17 Sept. 1975, p. 1.
16. *New York Times*, 30 Sept. 1975, p. 30.
17. Ibid.
18. *New York Times*, Sept. 1975; interviews.
19. Interviews.
20. Interviews.
21. Robert W. Bailey, *The Crisis Regime: The* MAC, *the* EFCB, *and the Political Impact of the New York City Financial Crisis* (Albany, N.Y.: State University of New York Press, 1984), 84–90; *New York Times*, Sept. 1975–Feb. 1977.
22. Tabb, *The Long Default*, 30; *New York Times*, 24 June 1976, p. 30.
23. Diane Ravitch, *The Great School Wars: New York City 1805–1973* (New York: Basic Books, 1974), 389; interviews.
24. *New York Times*, 2 July 1975, p. 1; 3 July 1975, p. 11; 4 July 1975, p. 6.
25. *New York Times*, 18 July 1975, p. 35; 21 July 1975, p. 1; 3 Sept. 1975, p. 48; 6 Sept. 1975, p. 9.
26. *New York Times*, 2 July 1975, p. 1; Weitzman, *City Workers*, 71–92, 118–121.
27. *New York Times*, 15 Feb. 1977, p. 35; 16 Feb. 1977, sec. ii, p. 5; 12 July 1977, p. 32.
28. *New York Times*, 30 Sept. 1976, p. 1; 17 Oct. 1976, p. 1.
29. *New York Times*, 6 June 1980, sec. 2, p. 3; 7 June 1980, p. 23; 14 July 1980, sec. ii, p. 1.
30. *New York Times*, 27 June 1980, p. 1; 1 July 1980, p. 1; 3 July 1980, p. 1; 14 July 1980, sec. ii, p. 1.
31. U.S. Department of Labor, Bureau of Labor Statistics, "Wages and Benefits of New York City Municipal Government Workers," Regional Report Number 68 (Sept. 1980), 3.
32. *New York Times*, 5 Apr. 1982, sec. ii, p. 1; and Charles R. Morris, *The Cost of Good Intentions* (New York: W. W. Norton, 1980), 179. On decline in standard of living, see also Tabb, *The Long Default*, 61–62; Municipal Labor Committee, "New York Revisited" (n.d.); Schefter, *Politics Crisis/Fiscal Crisis*, 141; and *New York Times*, 9 Nov. 1980, p. 54.
33. *New York Times*, 23 July 1976, p. 52.
34. *New York Times*, 18 Mar. 1985, p. 1.
35. *New York Times*, 30 Apr. 1982, p. 1; 12 Feb. 1983, sec. i, p. 25.
36. *New York Times*, 15 Feb. 1984, sec. i, p. 1; 17 May 1984, sec. ii, p. 9; 31 Jan. 1985, sec. ii, p. 1; 8 Apr. 1985, sec. ii, p. 1.
37. *New York Times*, 20 June 1976, p. 1.
38. The 1976 four-day hospital strike, sponsored by Local 420 of DC 37, is an exception to DC 37's unwillingness to strike. It was prompted by a number of factors, including a perceived double-cross on the part of city admin-

istrators and an emerging conflict between Local 420 leaders, DC executive director Victor Gotbaum, and AFSCME president Jerry Wurf. See New York Times, Aug. 1976.

39. "A Broke City Searches for Higher Productivity," Business Week, 14 June 1976, p. 88.

40. City of New York, Office of the Mayor, "The Joint Labor Management Productivity Committee to Fund the COLA for the Period October 1, 1976 to March 31, 1977" (6 Dec. 1976); Public Employee Press, 5 Nov. 1976, p. 7; Mark Maier, "Management Strategies in Public Sector Labor Law: A Case Study of New York City," in Marxism and the Metropolis: New Perspectives in Urban Political Economy, William K. Tabb and Larry Sawers, eds. (New York: Oxford University Press, 1984), 346–363; Mark H. Maier, "Public Sector Labor Relations," in Crisis in the Public Sector, Economics Education Project of the Union for Radical Political Economics, ed. (New York: Monthly Review Press, n.d.), 261–272.

41. City of New York, "The Joint Labor Management."

42. New York Times, 12 Nov. 1980, sec. ii, p. 3; Anderson and London, "Collective Bargaining," 383.

43. Horton, Municipal Labor, chap. 8; Ken Auletta, The Streets Were Paved with Gold (New York: Vintage, 1980), 45–49.

44. New York Times, 19 Mar. 1977, p. 1; 4 May 1977, sec. iv, p. 15; 15 May 1977, p. 50; Weitzman, City Workers, 109–110. The report called for one union representative, one management representative, and three so-called "public members" appointed by the mayor, but not on a collaborative basis as for current OCB "public" members. The report also recommended removal of supervisory personnel from collective bargaining; tying wage and benefit increases to demonstrated cost savings; fewer bargaining units; elimination of union ability to bargain on "practical impact" of managerial decisions; and broader powers for management in laying off employees.

45. New York Times, 15 May 1977, p. 50.

46. New York Times, 24 Sept. 1981, p. 26.

47. Lecture by Arvid Anderson, New School for Social Research, 16 Nov. 1976.

48. H. H. Wellington and R. K. Winter, The Unions and the Cities (Washington, D.C.: The Brookings Institution, 1971); Committee for Economic Development, Improving Productivity in State and Local Government (New York: Committee for Economic Development, 1976); A. Lawrence Chickering, ed., Public Employee Unions (San Francisco: Institute for Contemporary Studies, 1976).

49. "The Big Apple on the Brink," Time, 7 Apr. 1975, pp. 50–51.

50. "How New York Lurched to the Brink," Time, 16 May 1975, p. 16.

51. Morris, The Cost, 184–185.

52. Tabb, The Long Default, 61–62.

53. Morris, The Cost, 172–185; Tabb, The Long Default, 61–62; Municipal Labor Committee, "New York Revisited"; and Daniel J. P. Mitchell, "Collective Bargaining and Wage Determination in the Public Sector: Is Armaged-

don Really at Hand?" *Public Personnel Management* (Mar.–Apr. 1978): 90–91.

54. *New York Times*, 5 Apr. 1982, sec. ii, p. 4.
55. Ibid.
56. *New York Times*, 26 May 1976, p. 51.
57. Weitzman, *City Workers*, 89.
58. Lichten, *Class, Power*, 162–163.
59. Ibid., 170.
60. Ibid., 171.
61. Ibid., 178.

Index

Afro-American Teachers Association, 130
Altomare, George, 113, 124, 176–177
Amalgamated Association. *See* Amalgamated Transit Union
Amalgamated Transit Union, 14–16, 34, 42
American Federation of Labor–Congress of Industrial Organizations (AFL-CIO): anticommunism of, 28–29; TWU and, 39–40; UFT and, 118
American Federation of State, County, and Municipal Employees (AFSCME): early organizing in NYC, 24–26; formation of, 22–23; organizing in Chicago, 56. *See also* District Council 37
American Federation of Teachers (AFT): formation of, 27; TU-TG split in, 28–29; UFT and, 113, 135. *See also* United Federation of Teachers
American Transit Union, 37–38, 157
Anderson, Arvid, 182, 186
anticommunism, 28–29, 32–33, 47, 58, 140
anti-semitism, 118, 130
Auletta, Ken (*The Streets Were Paved With Gold*), 4

bargaining, scope of: city policy on, 80, 83–84, 144–145, 186; teach-

ers and, 122–123; welfare workers and, 64, 68, 70
bargaining units: city policy on, 49–50, 78, 80, 83–84, 141–144; subway workers and, 34; teachers and, 121–122
Beame, Abraham, 174–175
benefits. *See* pay levels; pensions
Berger, Stephen, 184
black workers: DC 37 and, 54–55, 85, 167; in hospitals, 54; and police, 164; on subways, 40; in teaching, 177; TWU and, 40, 41, 42; in welfare department, 62. *See also* civil rights movement
BMT. *See* subways, New York City
Board of Education, 116–117, 120–121, 122, 123, 176
Board of Higher Education, 82
Board of Transportation. *See* transit management
BRT. *See* subways, New York City

Career and Salary Plan, 50, 55, 84–85, 143, 153
Carton, John, 93–94
Caruso, Phillip, 179, 181
Cassese, John, 94–95, 101
Cavanagh, Edward F., 96
Central Labor Council, 52, 66, 114, 115–116
certification, 48, 49–50, 60
checkoff. *See* dues checkoff
Chokas, Nicholas, 189
Cincinnati, 143–144

civil rights movement, 53–54, 55, 63, 65, 66, 74, 85, 118, 125–126, 127–131, 153, 167. *See also* black workers

Civil Service Forum, 19

class size. *See* work load, teachers

clerical workers, 55

closed shop. *See* union shop

Cogen, Charles, 112, 113, 118, 122, 123–124, 127, 168

Cole, David, 33, 142–143

Committee for Action Through Unity (CATU), 112, 114

Committee for Economic Development, 187

Committee of 41, 12–13

Commons, John R., 12

Communications Workers of America (CWA), 143

Communist Party: AFT and, 28–29; role in 1930s, 7, 32; SCMWA and, 24; TWU and, 17, 32; UFT and, 113; UPW and, 58

community alliances, 58, 65, 125, 177, 191

company unions: police, 20, 139; sanitation, 12–13, 139; subway, 15–16, 138–139

Congress of Industrial Organizations (CIO): formation of, 7; organizing in NYC, 23, 24, 93. *See also entries for individual unions*

Congress of Racial Equality (CORE), 53, 127

conservative labor relations policy, 5–6, 137–138, 149, 186–188

contract enforcement, 33–34, 35–36, 145–148

Correction Officers Benevolent Association (COBA), 181

Coury, Albert, 59

Delury, John: and certification of USA, 50–51, 165; fiscal crisis and, 171, 172, 174–175; split with AFSCME, 25

Demilia, Sam, 179, 181

depression-era labor relations, 6, 16, 32, 45, 77–78, 111, 153

Dillworth, Richardson, 143–144

District Council 37 (DC 37): civil rights movement and, 74, 85, 167; contract negotiations by, 70, 85, 182–184, 189; decline in militancy of, 89–91; dues checkoff and, 48; fiscal crisis and, 171, 172, 173–174, 182–184, 188; internal organization of, 166–168; membership in, 85, 167; organizing drives by, 45–46, 51–56, 84–85, 143; pensions and, 85, 87–88; strikes by, 52, 87–88, 152–153; welfare Local 371 of, 58–61, 63–67, 71–76, 141

Donovan, Raymond, 93

drawbridge workers, 87–88

Dubinsky, David, 66, 115

dues checkoff: city rules on, 47–48; police and, 94–95; suspension of, 82, 146–147; TWU and, 19; UFT and, 147

Dumpson, James, 60–62, 69

elections, union: PBA, 21, 92–93, 106, 179–180; TWU, 34, 38–39; UFA, 92–93, 104–105, 106, 178; UFT, 124, 176–177; welfare workers, 59–60, 69–70

Emergency Financial Control Board (EFCB), 170, 177, 180, 184, 187, 188, 189

employment, public, 72–73, 170

evening teachers, 110–112

exclusive representation: city policy on, 47–48, 142–144; police and, 95; subway workers and, 34, 35–36; teachers and, 121

Executive Order 49 (EO 49), 48, 64, 77, 83, 95

Executive Order 52 (EO 52), 82, 84

fact finding, 97, 115

Farmer, James, 53, 65

favoritism, management: police

unions and, 93, 94, 95, 106, 140;
sanitation unions and, 23–24;
strategy of, 160–162, 172–173;
Teamsters and, 25; TWU and,
30–31, 32–34, 139–142, 166;
Wagner policy on, 49, 60–61,
63–64, 66, 78, 79, 139
federal legislation: FDR and, 6–7,
NLRA, 6–7, 141, 144, 161; Norris-La Guardia Act, 16
Feinstein, Barry: background of,
54–55, 165; fiscal crisis and, 171,
172
Feinstein, Henry, 25, 165
Feldman, Sandra, 171
firefighting. See Uniformed Firefighters Association
Firemen's Mutual Benevolent Association (FMBA), 19
fiscal crisis, New York City: banks
role in, 170, 177, 189; blame for,
4, 187–188; cutbacks during,
170–171, 172, 174, 175, 176, 178,
180, 181, 184–185, 191; media response to, 187–188, 189, 190;
protests during, 174–176,
178–181; union response to,
172–191
Foner, Henry, 75
Frank, Norman, 101
free speech: as civil liberty issue,
27–28
Fur, Leather and Machine Workers
(FLM), 74–75

Ginsberg, Mitchell, 69, 72
Gotbaum, Victor: background of, 53,
56, 166; cooperation with city, 89,
164; fiscal crisis and, 171, 172,
173, 182–183, 189; OCB and, 80;
and relations with SSEU, 71, 74,
80; strikes and, 88; UFA and, 105
Grass Roots Movement, 109–110
Gross, Calvin, 122
Guinan, Matthew, 38, 41, 42, 166,
171

Haber, Herbert, 71, 97, 99
Hall, Paul, 67
Health and Hospitals Corporation,
82
Heitner, Lou, 114
High School Teachers Association
(HSTA), 109–112, 121
Hill, Stanley, 171
Hilliard, Raymond, 58
Hispanic workers, 177
Hochberg, Samuel, 110–112, 120
Hoffa, James, 94, 141
Hogan, Austin, 32–33
Horton, Raymond (Municipal Labor
Relations in New York City), 4
hospital workers, 53–55, 140, 152
Housing Authority, 82

impasse proceedings, 83
Industrialism and Industrial Man,
5, 81
injunctions, court: against strikes,
37, 98
Institute for Contemporary Studies,
187
institutionalism: early development
of, 12; theory of, 4–5, 49, 79, 81,
82, 137–138, 142–143, 149–150,
161, 183, 188
Interim Order of 1954, 45–46, 77
IRT. See subways, New York City
ISS. See subways, New York City
Iushewitz, Morris, 116, 119

Kane, Vincent, 22, 96
Kennedy, Stephen, 94–95, 163
Kheel, Theodore, 99
Kiernan, Ed, 103
Klaus, Ida, 45, 48

labor-management committees: san-
itation, 12–13
Labor Management Institute–
American Arbitration Associa-
tion, 73, 79
La Guardia, Fiorello (Mayor):
SCWMA and, 23–24; TWU and, 19

Lawe, John, 30–31, 42, 182
Leary, Howard, 101
Lester, Richard (*As Unions Mature*), 149
Lewis, Bill, 54–55
Lindsay, John V. (Mayor): citywide contract and, 55; labor relations policy of, 137–138, 187; police and, 98, 101; productivity program of, 90, 148; TWU and, 41; USA and, 86–87; welfare workers and, 69, 72–73
Linville, Henry, 27–28
Local 237: democracy of, 165–166; dues checkoff and, 48; OCB and, 80–81; organizing drives by, 53, 54–55, 165–166
Local 371. *See* District Council 37, welfare Local 371 of

McCoy, Rhody, 130
McFeeley, Ken, 179
Mage, Judy, 61, 69, 70, 71, 72, 80
Management Advisory Board. *See* Shinn Commission
marxism, 7
Maye, Michael, 102–103, 178
Mazen, Ben, 114, 120, 124
Meany, George, 54, 67, 74, 116, 119
Metropolitan Transportation Authority (MTA). *See* transit management
Mills, C. Wright, 5
moonlighting, 95
Moran, Joseph, 21
More Effective Schools (MES), 126, 129
Morgenstern, Marty, 73
Morris, Charles (*The Cost of Good Intentions*), 4, 187
Moses, Robert, 46
Motormens Benevolent Association (MBA), 36–40, 141, 146, 157
motor vehicle operators, 52, 90, 152
Municipal Assistance Corporation (MAC), 189–190
municipal bonds, 189–190

Municipal Labor Committee (MLC), 80–81, 173
Murphy, Michael, 95

National Civic Federation, 13
National Education Association (NEA), 27, 115, 117–118
neoclassical economics. *See* conservative labor relations policy
New York Times, 36, 48, 51, 173, 181, 187
New York City Collective Bargaining Law, 77, 82, 161
New York Civil Liberties Unions, 127
New York State United Teachers (NYSUT), 135
no-strike clause, 87, 146

Ocean Hill–Brownsville, 127–131
O'Dwyer, William (Mayor), 32–33, 109
Office of Collective Bargaining (OCB): decisions by, 84, 85, 87, 102, 137–138, 149, 163; defense of, 186–187, 188; formation of, 73, 79–82; functioning of, 82–84, 90–91; SSEU relations with, 74, 84
Off Track Betting Corporation, 82
O'Hagan, John T., 105
one-person patrol cars, 179–180
organizing drives, union: AFSMCE, 23; cycles in, 152–157; DC 37, 45–47, 51–56; PBA, 19–22; SCMWA, 23–24; SSEU, 59–64; TU, 27–29; TWU, 16–19; UFA, 19–22; UFT, 112–114

Parente, Michael, 110, 120, 135
parity, 97, 98–100, 103, 106
Parks Department, 46–47, 90, 152
Parrish, Richard, 128
Patrolmen's Benevolent Association (PBA): contracts negotiated by, 95, 96–103, 106, 178–181; democracy in, 163–165; dues checkoff

and, 48; early history of, 19–22;
elections in, 21, 92–93; fiscal crisis and, 178–181, 189, 190–191;
formation of, 19–20; protests by,
93, 95, 97, 98, 100–102, 178–181;
rival organizations and, 93, 94,
140, 141; compared with UFT, 135
pay levels, New York City public
sector, 181–182, 187–188
penalties, antistrike: DC 37, 88; MBA,
36, 38, 146–147; TWU, 31, 147,
182; UFA, 105, 147; UFT, 147
pensions: DC 37 and, 85, 87–88;
level of in NYC, 188
Peterson, Charles, 181
Philadelphia, 143–144
platoon system: firefighter, 20,
21–22; police, 20, 101–102
Podell, Sam, 59
police. See Patrolmen's Benevolent
Association
productivity: DC 37 and, 89–91,
148, 184; fiscal crisis and,
183–185; police and, 101, 179,
180; subway workers and, 31, 33,
34–35, 148; versus relations of
exchange, 7
Public Employee Press, 55, 90, 184
Public Employee Relations Board
(PERB), 81

Quill, Michael: anticommunism of,
32–33, 140; background of, 17;
contracts negotiated by, 35, 146;
control over TWU by, 40–41,
139–140, 142–143, 166; death of,
41; police and, 93; teachers and,
120

Roberts, Lillian, 53–54
Rockefeller, Nelson, 81, 86–87, 119
Rohatyn, Felix, 173
Russo, Anthony, 59, 142

sabotage, union, 39
Sanitation Department: CIO organizing in, 23; Committee of 41,

12–13; fiscal crisis and, 174–175,
185; labor policy of, 142
sanitation workers. See Uniformed
Sanitationmen's Association
Schottland, Charles, 67–68
Schottland Commission, 67–68, 73
Secondary School Teachers Association (SSTA). See High School
Teachers Association
Selden, David, 111, 113, 114, 119
service levels: fiscal crisis and,
170–171, 175, 178, 184–185,
191; of subways, 33, 37, 148; of
welfare department, 58, 61,
69–70
sewage treatment workers, 87–88
Shanker, Albert: background of,
113, 123–124; control over UFT,
132–135, 168, 171; fiscal crisis
and, 189; strikes and, 125–126,
131, 175–176
Shinn Commission, 182, 186–187,
188
Simonson, Rebecca, 113
single-salary dispute, 109
sit-down strikes, 18, 71
socialists: AFSCME, 25; AFT, 27; DC
37, 168; SSEU, 62; UFT, 113, 132
Social Services, Department of. See
Welfare Department
Social Service Employees Union
(SSEU): contracts negotiated by,
67–68, 71, 72, 143; democracy of,
63, 75, 162–163, 191; formation
of, 59–60; Local 371 and, 59–64,
65–66, 67, 74–76, 141; members
of, 62–63; OCB and, 79–81, 84;
and reaffiliation debate, 72–76;
and relations with welfare recipients, 62, 69–70, 73; strikes by,
64–66, 68, 70–72, 152; work load
and, 61–62, 67, 68, 70–71, 72–73
Sovern, Michael, 180
Spero, Sterling (*The Public Worker*),
5
spying, management: BRT, 16; TA,
38–39

State, County, and Municipal Workers of America (SCMWA), 23–24, 57
state legislation: Condon-Wadlin Act, 52, 67, 118, 147; public unions and, 5, 11, 81–82, 145–146; Taylor Law, 31, 81–82, 88, 146, 147, 182
street cleaning. See Sanitation Department
strikebreakers: and Sanitation Department, 13; and subways, 15
strikes, slowdowns, and sickouts: cycles in, 152–157; DC 37, 52, 87–88; firefighters, 98, 103–105, 178; Lindsay administration and, 137–138, 149; police, 95, 98, 100–101, 178–181; sanitation, 86–87, 165–166, 174–175; subway, 14–16, 17–18, 30–32, 33–34, 35, 36–40, 41, 42, 146–147; teachers, 109–111, 114–116, 119, 125–126, 127–131, 175–176; welfare, 61, 65–67, 68, 70–72
subways, New York City: building of, 13–14; city buyout of, 18–19; strikes on, 15, 16, 30–32, 33–34, 35, 36–40, 41, 42; union organizing in, 14–18

Tabb, William, 187–188
Taibi, Calogero, 56, 74, 166
Taylor, George, 81, 116
Taylor Law. See state legislation
teachers, U.S., 26–29
Teachers Bargaining Organization. See National Education Association
Teachers Guild (TG): formation of, 28–29; relations with other groups, 109–114
Teachers Union (TU): end of, 115, 117–118, 140; formation of, 27; relations with other groups, 109–110; split from TG, 28–29
Teamsters: Local 658, 13, 139; organizing in New York City, 47, 52, 94, 139, 141, 165. See also Local 237; Uniformed Sanitationmen's Association
Tepedino, Joe, 61, 67, 69, 70
Transit Authority. See transit management
Transit management: compared with Board of Education, 116, 121; contracts signed by, 31, 34–35, 39–40, 41–42, 146, 148, 183, 185; fiscal crisis and, 182, 185; safety and, 15, 36; service levels and, 33, 37, 148; spying by, 16, 38–39; strikes and, 14–16, 17–18, 30–32, 33–34, 35, 36–40, 41, 42, 146–147; union recognition by, 14–16, 19, 33–34, 139, 141
Transport Workers Union of America (TWU): anticommunism of, 32–33; compared with UFT, 135; contracts signed by, 31, 34–36, 39–40, 41–42, 146, 148, 183, 185; fiscal crisis and, 182, 185; formation of, 16–18; internal conflict in, 36–42, 166; Irish heritage of, 17, 40; minority groups in, 40–42; police and, 93; protests by, 17–18, 30–32, 39, 41, 152; recognition of, 18, 34, 41, 139–140; service levels and, 33, 148
tripartism, 67, 68, 73, 78–81, 82–83, 149
Tron, Emil, 111

Uniformed Firefighters Association (UFA): certification of, 50; contracts negotiated for, 96–106; democracy in, 163–165; early history of, 19–22; fiscal crisis and, 178, 181, 190–191; protests by, 96, 97, 98, 102–103, 104–105, 147, 178, 181; strike vote misrepresentation by, 104–105; UFT compared with, 135

Uniformed Sanitationmen's Association (USA): certification of, 50, 165; democracy in, 50–51, 165; dues checkoff and, 48; fiscal crisis and, 171, 173, 174–175, 185; OCB and, 80; strikes by, 50–51, 86–87, 174–175

union coalitions, 80–81, 106–107, 164–165, 181

union democracy: DC 37, 166–168; management strategy and, 161–162; PBA, 163–165, 190–191; private sector, 161; proportional representation and, 120, 134; SSEU, 63, 75, 162–163, 190; UFA, 163–165, 190–191; UFT, 114, 119, 120–121, 126, 131–135, 176

union leaders versus rank and file: DC 37, 59–60, 74, 89, 173, 182–183; general, 8; Local 237, 165; PBA, 94, 96–97, 98, 163–165, 179–181, 189, 190–191; TWU, 30–32, 35, 36, 37, 40–42, 157; UFA, 96, 97, 102, 163–165, 181, 190–191; UFT, 116, 119–120, 124, 128, 132, 145, 175–176; USA, 50–51, 86, 174–175

union shop, 16, 18, 19, 38

United Federation of Teachers (UFT): class size and, 123; control over, 120–121, 123–124, 126, 131–135; and cooperation with community, 125–126, 128; democracy in, 119, 132–135; fiscal crisis and, 171, 173, 175–177, 189–190; formation of, 111–112; membership characteristics of, 112–113, 124–125; negotiations by 114–117, 119–120, 121–123, 124, 125–126, 131, 143, 145, 146; organizing drives by, 112–118, 143; race relations and, 125–126, 127–131; strikes by, 114–116, 119, 125–126, 127–131, 141, 147, 153, 175–177

United Mine Workers of America, 144

United Patrolmen's Association (UPA), 93

United Public Workers (UPW), 29, 47, 57–58, 140–141, 142

Unity Caucus, 123–124, 128, 132, 176–177

Van Arsdale, Harry, 52, 66, 115–116, 119

Vann, Albert, 130

Viani, Alan, 189

Vietnam War, 74, 75, 133

Vizzini, Richard, 103–105, 178

Wagner, Jr., Robert (Mayor): labor relations policy of, 45–50, 51, 52, 77–79, 94, 142–144, 147, 165; teachers and, 110, 119; TWU and, 39; welfare workers and, 60, 64, 66–68

Waring, G. E., 12

Weaving, Douglas, 179

Welfare, Department of, 57–76, 100

welfare recipients, 58, 69–70, 72, 73

welfare rights movement, 73

Wellington, H. H. (*The Unions and the Cities*), 5, 187

women in unions: hospital workers, 53–54; pay of, 188; police and, 164; teachers, 27, 113

work load: teachers, 123; welfare workers, 61–62, 64, 70, 71

workplace democracy, 126, 152

Wurf, Jerry: as AFSCME president, 66, 67; background of, 25; early organizing of DC 37, 45–47, 51–53; and labor relations philosophy, 167

yellow dog contract, 15, 16

Zander, Arnold, 23

zookeepers, 52